Thoughts On An Advanced Generalist Education

Models, Readings and Essays

Edited by

Ann W. Roy

and

Francine J. Vecchiolla

Springfield College

eddie bowers publishing co., inc.

ii

COVER DESIGN
Cover artwork © Julio Mateo
Diamond XVIII, 1988. (Oil on canvas, 52" square)
Contact the artist: jmateo@mateo.net
Visit artist's web site: http://www.mateo.net/

Exclusive marketing and distributor rights for
U.K., Eire, and Continental Europe held by:

Gazelle Book Services Limited
Falcon House
Queen Square
Lancaster
LA1 1RN
U.K.

---

eddie bowers publishing co., inc.
P. O. Box 130
Peosta, Iowa 52068 USA

www.eddiebowerspublishing.com

ISBN 1-57879-052-2

Copyright © 2004, by *eddie bowers publishing co., inc.*

TABLE OF CONTENTS

Section 2: A Theoretical Perspective

Section 3: The Challenge of Field Education

Section 4: Essays and Readings

PREFACE

A small social work program with large ideas was awarded its first CSWE accreditation in 1993. The MSW program at Springfield College became the School of Social Work in 1997. We called ourselves Advanced Generalists. Now, 10 years later, with 250 MSW students, state-of-the-art facilities, a full-time weekday and part-time weekend program, an MSW/JD degree program, and a Child and Adolescent Certificate Program, we still proudly call ourselves Advanced Generalists. And yet, we still find ourselves explaining to others, and attempting to capture for ourselves, the full extent of what it means to offer an Advanced Generalist Curriculum...hence, the origin of our book!

We were interested in learning about and sharing in the evolution and ongoing development of graduate Advanced Generalist curriculum models. By examining current models of Advanced Generalist Practice (AGP) and exploring applications to areas of practice, we believe this text fills a gap in the literature. We would like to acknowledge that there are more than a dozen graduate social work programs that consider themselves Advanced Generalists. We wish that each and every program could have been included. Limitations of time, alas, precluded such a comprehensive exploration. In the end, the choice of "Advanced Generalist Models" was based on individual faculty members who kindly agreed to contribute a chapter reflecting the development of their respective Advanced Generalist curriculums. We hope one day to have an opportunity to capture the breadth of the Advanced Generalist offerings.

The key feature is the fact that this is the only text, of which we are aware, to present Advanced Generalist models in use today at six schools of social work. Additional contributions include a chapter devoted to the application and integration of the Advanced Generalist philosophy to Field Practicum, and a chapter providing an analytical exploration of an important Advanced Generalist challenge, Defining Complexity: The Theoretical Basis of Advanced Generalist Practice.

The text is timely in its inclusion of four essays on practice environments that represent societal shifts (mental health and managed health care, school social work, and human rights) as well as a more traditional practice arena (social work practice with children) with implications and applications of an Advanced Generalist perspective. Also new to an Advanced Generalist text is the inclusion of a graduate scholar illustrating the effectiveness of an Advanced Generalist approach with an interesting HMO case. In a future edition we hope to showcase a broad array of graduate scholars who will contribute their practice wisdom by illustrating the reality of Advanced Generalist practice in the 21st century.

We wish to thank our contributors who so generously shared their models and stories with us, adroitly tracing the development of Advanced Generalist curriculums at schools of social work around the country. We are, as well, indebted to contributors for their thoughtful essays on Advanced Generalist practice perspectives. This was an ambitious project with a short time frame, and were it not for the outstanding work ethic of each and every contributor we would never have met our deadline. We wish to acknowledge the support, guidance, and excellent advice provided by our publisher, Eddie Bowers of eddie bowers publishing co., inc. and by our copy editor, Eddy Goldberg of Amherst, Massachusetts. Finally, we would like to express our gratitude to Julio Mateo, an artist residing in New Mexico, for his gracious consent to use his *Diamond: XVIII, 1988* as our cover design. If you are interested in seeing more of Julio's work, he may be found at: www.mateo.net.

SECTION 1: SIX MODELS

Chapter 1

Model One: Springfield College

ADVANCED GENERALIST SOCIAL WORK EDUCATION AND THE CHALLENGE OF THE NEW MILLENNIUM

Ann W. Roy and Francine J. Vecchiolla
Springfield College

Social work educators are faced with enormous challenges as we enter the twenty-first century. Our capacity to respond to contemporary events, most notably the shift in cultural and ethnic demographics, managed health care, and welfare reform, may well determine the success or failure of schools of social work to remain relevant. Schools must develop a well-constructed response to ensure that the social work professionals of tomorrow are prepared for a broad range of roles, both to shape the direction of the changing world of social services and to function competently in emerging practice environments.

Social work educators continue to deliberate about how best to prepare graduate students for multilevel practice. We believe that a fully integrated advanced generalist curriculum giving equal weight to micro, mezzo, and macro level knowledge and practice, underscored by the themes of human rights, social justice, and social change fills a gap in the evolving conceptualization of advanced generalist practice models.

Landon (1995), in the *Encyclopedia of Social Work*, notes agreement on elements central to generalist practice:

> There appears to be definitional agreement on the centrality of the multimethod and multilevel approaches, based on an eclectic choice of theory base and the necessity for incorporating the dual vision of the profession on private issues and social justice concerns. (p. 1101)

Nevertheless, while the literature consistently views generalist practice as forming the conceptual underpinning of social work (Gibbs, Locke, & Lohmann, 1990; Minahan & Pincus, 1977), social work educators struggle with the generalist and advanced generalist concepts. On the one hand, a generalist curriculum is viewed as appropriate at the BSW and first-year MSW foundation level with an advanced generalist curriculum conceptualized as a second-year specialization. On the other, Gibbs, Locke, and Lohmann state: "Rather than conceptualizing advanced generalist as an area of specialization—which in and of itself seems a contradiction in terms—the proposed paradigm conceptualizes advanced generalist as framework for the entire graduate curriculum" (p. 242).

Furthermore, although by 1974 the Council on Social Work Education (CSWE) required BSW programs to be generalist in nature and by 1988 granted schools permission to offer a graduate level advanced generalist curriculum (Thompson, Menefee, & Marley, 1999) there has yet to be a single model to guide generalist social work practice (Carroll, 1977; Minahan & Pincus, 1977). In their summary of the generalist perspective, Sheafor and Landon (1987) state that the "knowledge base for generalist practice reflects a combination of several theoretical frameworks" (p. 666). They note that the most widely used theoretical approaches are the systems perspective and ecological theory, and conclude that the next step should be refinement of the generalist practice model into a solid conceptual framework. Carroll (1977), Evans (1976), and Parsons, Hernandez, and Jorgensen (1988) present one such framework, that of integrated practice. Carroll's contribution is her call to transcend the tendency to define practice unidimensionally, as in, for example, a problem locus, methods, or fields of practice orientation. Her conclusion, similar to that of Sheafor and Landon, is that: "one of the profession's greatest needs at present is an organizing framework for its knowledge base. The three-dimensional model of professional social work practice helps to meet the need" (p. 432). Carroll urges the profession to focus on a problem-oriented conceptualization, offering a model that includes social problem, unit of concern, and technology.

Parsons, Hernandez, and Jorgensen (1988) offer a slight variation on the theme of integrated practice. They propose a similar focus on social problem with the addition of differential role taking in the intervention. This framework assumes that the origin of the problem is in the larger environmental context and that collective action by "victims" and "non-victims" is required to ameliorate the situation. The authors draw upon the life model of Germain and Gitterman (1980) and Maluccio's (1981) competency-oriented practice to present their perspective on integrated practice.

RELEVANT STUDIES

Several studies appear to support the efficacy of a generalist and/or an advanced generalist curriculum. Bakalinsky (1982) studied graduate teaching curricula in the United States. He concluded that generalist practice is beneficial because methodology can be matched to client need or problem rather than a priori, and students are prepared to participate in a wide array of professional social work activities and roles. This study revealed a high level of consensus on the definition of generalist practice that included both micro and macro perspectives. In a study assessing curriculum needs (Biggerstaff, Baskind, & Jensen, 1994), respondents from a variety of practice settings were asked to identify knowledge and skills necessary to practice in a wide range of social work settings. Three themes emerged: (a) curriculum must reflect a commitment to values and ethics, (b) curriculum must incorporate a variety of theoretical models, and (c) curriculum must encourage multiple-level intervention. The results indicated the need for a practice model that "integrates essential direct and indirect practice roles of the social worker to adequately prepare them for agency practice" (p. 222)—all themes consistent with an advanced generalist perspective.

A third study, by Thompson, Menefee, and Marley (1999), compared administrative and supervisory competencies in a purposeful sample of managers and direct practitioners. They found no significant differences in the patterns of job behavior and the extent to which each group performed administrative tasks. It was apparent that all social work practitioners, managers and direct practitioners alike, engaged in managerial functions. The authors suggest that an advanced generalist framework with its emphasis on integration of "macro competencies in supervision, administration, policy development and program evaluation" (p. 116) may be the most appropriate educational approach for all social work practitioners, regardless of field of practice.

RATIONALE FOR ADVANCED GENERALIST PRACTICE

Springfield College is located in Massachusetts, minutes from Springfield, a multicultural city 90 miles west of Boston and 147 miles northeast of New York City. The college was founded in 1885 to train YMCA professionals and is one of country's earliest preprofessional, group-work training institutions. It draws students from a highly urbanized local area, as well as from rural regions of upstate New York, New Hampshire, and Maine. The advanced generalist practice model at the Springfield College School of Social Work takes advantage of this diverse geographic locale in that it is consistent with "an opportunity to train practitioners to address a variety of social problems with diverse client groups in [sic] variety of geographic locations" (Program Review, 2001, p. 6).

As is apparent in the following statement, the advanced generalist practice model is highly compatible with the Springfield College mission: "The mission of Springfield College is to educate students in spirit, mind and body for leadership in service to humanity by building upon its foundation of Humanics [sic] and academic excellence" (Status Report, 2002).

The college is dedicated to the preparation of future leaders in both the private and public sectors who will improve the quality of life worldwide. This service-oriented, internationalist perspective in a small liberal arts institution is unusual and, as it happens, a close fit with an advanced generalist practice model. In particular, the themes of human rights, social justice, and social change with an international perspective at the School of Social Work are compatible with the mission of the college. More interesting yet is the historical role of Springfield College in the late 1800s and early 1900s. During this epoch the college prepared students for work in settlement houses and charitable agencies, resonating with the history of the social work profession itself.

Also important in the decision to adopt an advanced generalist practice model at Springfield College was the changing social and political climate in which the social work profession found itself in the 1990s. Specifically, throughout the 1990s there was a movement toward accountability, cost containment, privatization, and a political climate of intolerance toward the poor. In response to these political and economic developments, we felt it incumbent upon educators to promote practice interventions, actions, and policies that provide social workers not only with the expertise to understand the nature of injustice and oppression, but also with the skills to challenge such phenomena.

Another rationale for the implementation of an advanced generalist curriculum is related to the progressive Western expansion of the conceptualization of oppression. We feel strongly that social work educators must provide its graduates with an understanding of the antecedents of today's social problems, highlighting historical, political, and social actions of the Progressive Era that ultimately led to legislation addressing the rights of women, children, and laborers, and more recently, civil rights. The integrative (macro, mezzo and micro) unitary curriculum of advanced generalist practice provides an appropriate framework to explore the significance of the unprecedented expansion of human rights, gay rights, rights of the disabled, and others.

Consistent with the above discussion, Jarman-Rhode, McFall, Kolar, and Strom (1997) note that the changing context of social work practice calls for the implementation of specific curriculum content across all concentrations:

> Students in all concentrations should receive training in outcome measurements, collaboration, management, administration, advocacy and system reform; learn the effects of policy on the availability and delivery of services, and develop skills in multicultural practice and in goal-focused forms of intervention with specific objectives. (p. 39)

McMahon (1994) has nicely captured the idea that advanced generalist practice may hold promise for the future: "Advanced Generalist Practice is an emerging model of global awareness and integrated methodology that promotes commitment, confidence and competence for social workers to face emerging issues and problems as we move into the year 2000 and beyond" (p. 238).

Finally, to paraphrase Debra Stone, it should be noted that there is no "One Best Way" (Stone, 1997, p. xii) to develop students' intellectual talents to meet the demands of an increasingly complex social environment. Schools of social work with programs organized around specialized areas of study have, historically, produced graduates who have made invaluable contributions to the social work profession, all the while committed to social justice. Nonetheless, we are suggesting that advanced generalist practice is a particularly promising approach to curriculum integration; one that is intended to meet the dilemmas posed by conflicting social policy initiatives and, we might sadly note, an uncharted national and international order brought about by the events of September 11, 2001 and the resolution of the U.S. Congress in October 2002 to support an attack on Iraq by ceding its power to declare war to the president.

ADVANCED GENERALIST FRAMEWORK

Advanced Generalist Practice Model and Our Three Programmatic Themes

Advanced generalist practice is taught as a model of assessment, theoretical perspectives, and intervention underscored by three major themes: human rights, social justice, and social change. These themes are derived from the mission statement, put forward in the self-study MSW Program Objectives, and infused throughout the curriculum:

> Human rights is a major commitment of the School of Social Work....Campus faculty students, and administration are invited to participate in vigils, exposed to internationally renown [sic] figures in human rights, and participate in satellite conferencing and similar actions that illustrate a vital commitment to the alleviation of human suffering in all its forms. (Program Review, 2001, p. 4)

Advanced Generalist Practice Curriculum Objectives

The advanced generalist practice model at Springfield College has eight MSW program objectives, with objectives one, five, and two especially relevant to human rights, social justice, and social change. Objective 1 is explicit in its concern for the major programmatic themes:

> To provide experiences and content that will prepare social work practitioners responsive to the needs of diverse racial, ethnic and cultural groups with the ultimate goal to eliminate oppression and discrimination, and to promote social justice, human rights and social change. (Program Review, 2001, p. 9)

Objective 5 is relevant in that it alludes to knowledge building and policy skill development for the purpose of affecting society in socially just ways:

> To critically examine the history of [sic] social work profession and its relationship to the development of programs and policies with particular attention to the impact of these policies on oppressed populations, integrating the art and skill of policy analysis, development and implementation for the purposes of impacting both private and public policy sectors. (Program Review, 2001, p. 9)

Objective 2, a key objective underscoring all others, is the development of critical thinking skills: "To cultivate a professional use of self that prepares students to apply critical thinking skills via the integration of both theoretical and practical content in application to systems of all sizes including practice with individuals, families, groups and communities" (Program Review, 2001, p. 9).

It is the ability to analyze and evaluate complex societal issues that prepares students for an advocacy role, later enabling them to seek change in larger social systems. As such, it is an important element in the development of student competencies necessary to undertake real-life advocacy for human rights, social justice, and social change. Critical thinking can be considered among the "skill sets" of our advanced generalist practice model that promote socially just, large systems intervention, not only in the policy sequence (where one might expect such content), but also, just as importantly, throughout all sequences:

> Policy 2 seeks to promote human rights culture with emphasis on how to create a socially just world. HSBE 1 addresses the impact of social problems on the family, as in for example, how economic ideologies impact the family. This content is readily applied to issues of social justice. In HBSE 3 (Biopsychosocial Theories of Psychopathology), where the DSM-IV is incorporated, students are challenged to think critically about the impact of the use of a classification system, as well as the medical model with client groups. For example, what is the impact of labeling and stigmatization? And how might this be related to oppression and/or promoting a socially just world? (Program Review, 2001, p. 4)

It must be said, too, that an element that comes into play (no doubt relevant to all MSW programs) is the role of faculty in authenticating and legitimizing the range of rich social work identities. Our faculty, as dedicated advanced generalists, model potential roles graduates might someday assume. Thus, as we are human rights advocates, socially conscious and politically aware clinicians, scholar-practitioners, and community activists, so we hope our students will become.

ADVANCED GENERALIST CURRICULUM

At Springfield College the program is designed around a first-year foundation curriculum and a second-year advanced generalist concentration. The foundation curriculum provides students with theoretical perspectives across four sequences as well as grounding in fundamental skills in individual, family, group, and community intervention. As noted above, the advanced generalist concentration curriculum provides students with the opportunity to develop a series of skill sets across curriculum components including administrative skills (e.g., supervisory techniques, leadership styles), more comprehensive practice models of psychosocial assessment and multilevel intervention, a set of complex social action skills in policy (e.g., legislative actions), and an integrated set of research skills (e.g., quantitative and qualitative). The focus on skill sets occurs within the context of three programmatic themes: human rights, social justice, and social change (see Figures 1.1 and 1.2).

The second-year advanced generalist concentration consists of six credit hours of advanced Social Work Practice, three credit hours of advanced Social Welfare Policy, three credit hours of Human Behavior in the Social Environment (HBSE), three credit hours of Social Work Research, eight credit hours of Field Practicum, and six credit hours of Electives. In the first semester of the second year, students take HBSE 3, Social Work Practice 3, Social Work Research 3, one Elective, and Field Practicum. In the second semester of the second year, students take Social Welfare Policy 3, Social Work Practice 4, two Electives, and Field Practicum.

An innovative aspect of our advanced generalist practice model is that it is conceived from both a multilevel practice (micro, mezzo, and macro) and a multilevel integration (sequence, cross-sequence, and comprehensive) orientation. This approach is used to teach increasingly complex, advanced levels of knowledge, practice, and critical thinking skills. Sequence integration is created by insuring that subsequent courses in the curriculum build on the content of prior courses. Cross-sequence integration is created by purposefully connecting course content across all sequences, and comprehensive integration is created by incorporating the school's themes of human rights, social justice, and social change in each course, including the Field Practicum.

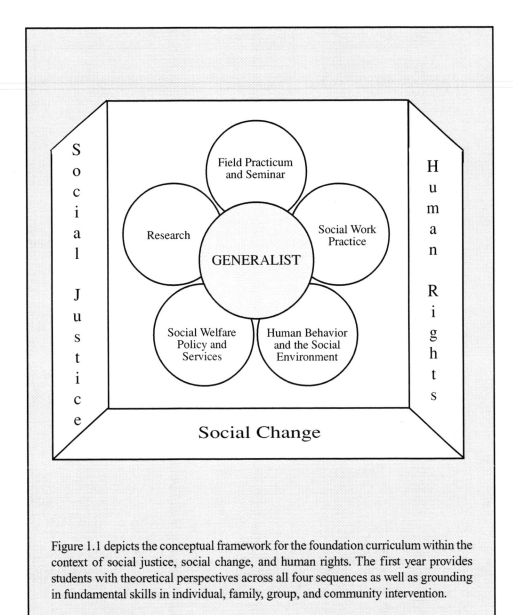

Figure 1.1 depicts the conceptual framework for the foundation curriculum within the context of social justice, social change, and human rights. The first year provides students with theoretical perspectives across all four sequences as well as grounding in fundamental skills in individual, family, group, and community intervention.

Figure 1.1 Foundation Curriculum

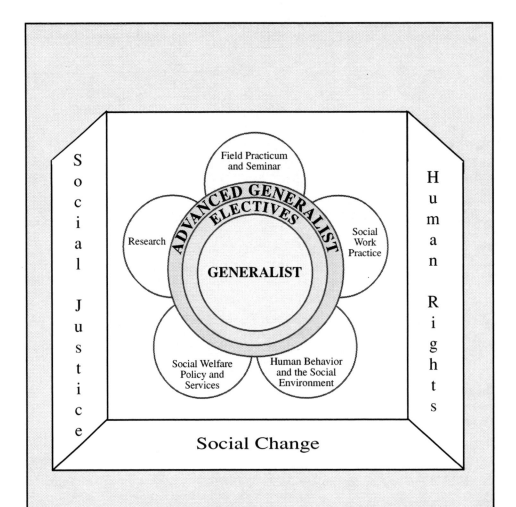

Figure 1.2 depicts the conceptual framework for the concentration curriculum within the context of social justice, social change, and human rights. The advanced generalist concentration is designed around "skill sets" that build on the foundation year and draw upon each sequence to build an interactive model.

Figure 1.2 Concentration Curriculum

The following is an illustration of multilevel practice with the social work practice concentration course, Social Work Practice 3: Advanced Generalist Practice with Vulnerable Populations. This course utilizes the knowledge and skills gained in the foundation courses and advances them using more comprehensive models of psychosocial assessment and multilevel intervention. A wide range of contemporary practice models and skills are explicated and applied to work with vulnerable and/or at-risk populations with complex presenting problems. Attention is given to the importance of diversity, policy, and research as the context for practice assessment and intervention.

The first major assignment in Social Work Practice 3 is a case conference presentation of advanced generalist practice. Working in small groups, class members prepare a case from a vulnerable population (e.g., children and families in urban settings, clients facing serious medical illness and grief, clients with serious and persistent mental disorders, or clients with trauma related disorders) to "conference" in a class presentation. Students are expected to describe the following: the presenting concerns and history of the client; issues related to engagement/relationship building with the client; theoretical formulations used to guide intervention with the client; an assessment of the client's strengths, resources, and possibilities; and an appropriate intervention strategy for the client. The assignment is designed to demonstrate the knowledge and skills of advanced generalist social work practice. It is, therefore, an opportunity to draw upon and integrate knowledge gained throughout the advanced generalist curriculum.

Multilevel integration can be illustrated through our Research 2 foundation course. In this course students apply their clinical skills from Practice 1 and Practice 2 (an example of cross-sequence integration) to the assessment and intervention phases of a single system design study. Furthermore, knowledge acquired in Research 1 (an example of sequence integration) is used in the design, implementation, and analysis of their study. Thus, faculty, with some discretion, focus on both the clinical aspects of the study intervention and the development of systematic observational and analytical research skills. Finally, what we term comprehensive integration is achieved through emphasis on socially just and ethical research practices.

In summary, similar to each core course in the advanced generalist practice curriculum, Practice 3 and Research 2 have evolved within a multilevel practice (micro, mezzo, and macro) and multilevel integration (sequence, cross-sequence, and comprehensive) framework.

FIELD APPLICATION AND INTEGRATION

The second-year Field Practicum is a critical ingredient of the advanced generalist curriculum. Each student is matched with a social work practice environment that provides an opportunity to apply theory-based, multilevel practice: advanced direct practice, advanced group practice, and advanced mezzo/macro practice. The following is a general description of the Field Practicum and Field Seminar, excerpted from Program Review (2001):

> Concentration courses in advanced generalist practice are taken concurrently with Field Practicum and Field Seminar. The agency-based practicum emphasizes direct service organizations, diverse multi-problem clients requiring complex multi-level interventions and advocacy. The administration experience requires an active contribution to the ongoing management activities of the practicum agency. (p. 9)

The companion Field Seminar is described as follows: "Field Seminar emphasizes preparation for advanced generalist practice. Practice with diverse client populations, multilevel intervention, complex skills, complex legal and ethical issues are reviewed" (p. 9).

Field Practicum placements include a range of social work agencies commonly associated with graduate social work programs. There are no uniquely designed "advanced direct practice" or "macro practice placements." Rather, it is the school's advanced generalist curriculum expectations (i.e., for students to gain advanced experience in both direct and indirect practice) and the agency's contractual agreement to meet these expectations that enable students to develop more complex micro, mezzo, and macro practice skills.

Advanced direct practice with individuals and advanced practice with groups build on the first-year foundation experience. We digress briefly to describe the first-year field experience. First-year field is conceived of as an integrated approach requiring students to develop beginning direct practice skills with individuals, families, and groups (micro-level practice), to work with agency groups/administrative groups (mezzo-level practice), and to work with communities (macro-level practice). The following macro level projects were undertaken by first-year field students: (a) collaborating with agency staff, consumers, and the media, a student developed an anti-stigma campaign to educate the community regarding problems faced by residents with psychiatric disorders; (b) a student led an advocacy campaign on early childhood education/intervention to educate the public and legislators; and (c) a student developed a map of county services for women being released from the local correctional center. It is expected that many of the beginning skills in practice with individuals and groups will be useful to a student's work within the context of the larger community. The essential idea is that although first- and second-year expectations in the advanced generalist field practice require that students engage in multilevel practice, the distinction between first-year and second-year advanced generalist field practice is in terms of the complexity level expected in second-year field practicum.

Students in the second-year field practicum are required to have the following: (a) experience with more diverse, vulnerable, and/or at-risk client populations with complex presenting problems requiring multilevel interventions including counseling and advocacy; (b) more challenging relationship building; (c) at least one solo leadership group experience; (d) a more sophisticated use of self in the helping process with advanced skill in relating to clients different from the student in race, personality, sexual orientation, and/or socioeconomic status; and (e) flexibility in moving from large community system interventions to agency level interventions to direct service interventions as needed. Practice 3 provides course support for the advanced direct practice Field Practicum. It emphasizes depth of knowledge as students integrate practice models that demand a high level of critical thinking skills. Attention is given to the importance of diversity, policy, and research as the context for practice assessment and intervention.

Advanced macro practice requirements focus on administration, with students expected to participate in a management activity. Specific agency administrative opportunities vary, but in general students participate in one or more of the following: (a) agency committees, (b) agency board meetings, (c) program development or evaluation projects, (d) networking with the administration of other agencies, and (e) identifying agency problems and proposals to change administrative protocol. Practice 4 provides course support for the advanced macro practice Field Practicum. It emphasizes supervision, management, and administration with particular attention to leadership, committee and board development, and issues of diversity relative to contemporary social work administration.

Student administrative projects in second-year Field Practicum must meet the advanced generalist requirement to demonstrate a more sophisticated understanding of complex, multilevel systems. Typically, these projects are developed by the student in collaboration with the agency supervisor and faculty supervisor. Second year field students developed the following macro-level projects: (a) a new agency policy that addressed the solicitation of funds from the community and their dispersal among various agency programs, (b) review and revision of agency intake procedures to decrease waiting time for new clients, and (c) development of a grant proposal for an after-school group services program in collaboration with agency and community representatives. In a fourth instance, while developing a proposal to honor a male World War II veteran at a local nursing home, a student recognized that a female resident also was a veteran of that war. After obtaining official recognition for the female veteran, the student invited the local congressional representative, media, and staff to honor both veterans, thereby orchestrating a ceremony free of gender bias.

For any single agency to satisfy the demands of an advanced generalist practice model, a close working relationship must exist among school and agency administrators, field supervisors, and faculty advisors. This goal is met, in part, by the requirement that supervisors attend a series of "supervisory training classes" throughout the year that provide a thorough orientation to the advanced generalist curriculum. Faculty advisers provide further linkage among school, agency, field supervisor, and student through agency visitation and phone contacts. In addition, periodic, half-day conferences composed of agency field supervisors, field director, assistant director, field staff, and faculty support relationship building and problem solving over time. This arrangement has fostered strong and mutually respectful relationships between the agencies and the school while at the same time reinforcing the expectations of an advanced generalist practice model.

TRIALS AND TRIBULATIONS

The question to which we now address ourselves is: As a school of social work, what does it mean to offer an advanced generalist practice model? Indeed, the very meaning and definition of advanced generalist is a common concern to all advanced generalist faculty. At this stage not only is there no single definition to which we all adhere, there often are competing definitions among faculty members themselves. How have we, at Springfield College School of Social work, met this challenge?

Early in the development of our advanced generalist perspective, we identified the three themes that have continued to provide vision and continuity for the curriculum: human rights, social justice, and social change. These concepts were seen as essential to our conceptualization of an advanced generalist practice model. They were established to serve as the mission for our school and the underpinnings of the curriculum. Nonetheless, as the saying goes, "The devil is in the details." How these themes have played out over the years has been an evolutionary process, often revisited.

The School Curriculum Committee encourages periodic, intensive discussion of our advanced generalist conceptualization and accomplishes this with periodic curriculum retreats. Early in our development we brought in persons with more extensive experience with the advanced generalist practice model to share their struggles with us. Ongoing dialogue among sequence chairs, committee members, and other faculty helps address the many tensions inherent in social work education, particularly in terms of the advanced generalist model.

The assignment of co-chairs for the practice sequence was a deliberate strategy to more fully represent micro, mezzo, and macro strengths. With the practice sequence leadership incorporating these perspectives, we start the discussion from a place in which several levels of practice methodologies are equally valued. Further, we believe that the co-chair arrangement makes it easier to implement the three-tiered integrated curriculum (vertical, cross-sequence, and comprehensive), which is the hallmark of our advanced generalist practice model.

Another important and ongoing matter involves the need to provide depth in the curriculum by identifying theoretical frameworks fundamental to the entire curriculum. Currently the School Curriculum Committee is revisiting the broad array of theories now included in HBSE. Discussion is under way to narrow the HBSE focus by identifying major theories central to advanced generalist practice. The result, we hope, will be increased depth of knowledge, a major goal we continue to strive toward.

OUTCOME ASSESSMENT

Measuring success requires a clear operational definition of success. The important question to be answered is: Having completed an advanced generalist MSW program, what outcomes should graduates be expected to have achieved with respect to entry into the profession of social work? One means by which our advanced generalist program seeks to address this question is by conducting biannual alumni surveys. We have conducted alumni surveys every two years since 1993, our first accreditation as an advanced generalist MSW program. Over the years we have used the feedback to fine-tune the advanced generalist curriculum. When consistent themes were identified, we responded with substantial modifications of the curriculum content and structure.

Evidence of Success

The following is a report on the most recent alumni survey, conducted in the 2001 fall semester. Questionnaires were mailed to 128 graduates who completed the program between 1999 and 2001 (Roy, 2001). We had a response rate of 54% ($N = 69$) with 84% female and 16% male, and 81% Caucasian and 19% persons of color. In terms of employment, 89% were employed full-time with 77% of respondents reporting an income of $30,000 and above.

Alumni were asked to report their overall level of professional satisfaction, a global item indicating whether or not the advanced generalist curriculum prepared graduates to move into the social work profession with a sense of competence. Students reported both a consistently high level of professional satisfaction and, importantly, the acquisition and utilization of a wide array of social work knowledge and skills consistent with an advanced generalist practice model. For example, graduates reported skill in supervision, working with diverse populations, human rights, policy analysis, and research. Graduates also reported competencies in individual and family counseling, treatment planning, crisis intervention, intake and assessment, critical thinking, and ethical decision-making. These competencies are consistent with an integrated curriculum giving similar weight to micro, mezzo, and macro skills.

Graduates were asked to assess the effectiveness of the advanced generalist program by responding to a five-point satisfaction scale. In response to the question: "How satisfied were you with the way advanced generalist curriculum prepared you for the social work profession?" we found that 90% reported being satisfied to very satisfied.

Survey responses also underscored graduates' commitment to continued professional development. Among other post-graduate activities, alumni reported presenting at professional conferences. Five graduates reported that they had published a book, article, or similar work since graduation, and ten were either applying to a doctoral program or were seriously considering pursuing doctoral education. Finally, 67% of those surveyed reported that they were likely or very likely to enroll in a post-master's certificate program if it were offered by our school. The value of post-graduate educational pursuits is important for several reasons. First, it is a measure of success of our advanced generalist model in that it reflects the fulfill-ment of Objective 7 of our MSW program:

> To emphasize the importance of life-long learning and, specifically, to pro-mote the value of the social work practitioner to pursue continuing educa-tion in the social work profession and the continuation of professional growth through participation in local, state, national, [and] international confer-ences. (Program Review, 2001, p. 10)

Second, its value is supported by a study by Biggerstaff, Baskind, and Jensen (1994), who conclude that graduates must continue learning throughout their life-time. And third, it is consistent with Thompson, Menefee, and Marley (1999) who observe that continuing education is important for social workers who, although they may begin their career in direct practice, "will eventually make upwardly mo-bile job changes and thus need knowledge and skills in human services manage-ment. It is here that continuing education can play a vital role" (p. 122).

These survey findings suggest that the advanced generalist practice model at the Springfield College School of Social Work has contributed to the successful development of socially responsible, professional social workers competent to work in multilevel systems and assume a wide range of roles and responsibilities in the community.

THE FUTURE OF THE ADVANCED GENERALIST PERSPECTIVE

Research Implications

A more comprehensive alumni survey that includes a qualitative component would provide greater depth of meaning to our alumni findings. This might include the addition of open-ended questions that tap the perception of new graduates in terms of their sense of preparation and professional competence. An even larger outcome study might entail interviewing advanced generalist graduates and their employers to assess the match. It should be said, candidly, that most schools of social work do not have a budget to undertake such studies. Therefore, in the not-too-distant future it may be feasible to suggest collaboration among several advanced generalist schools of social work. A scientifically rigorous study would have the potential to establish a more definitive evaluation of the efficacy of the advanced generalist practice model.

Curriculum Implications

We are about to begin a self-study for our next reaccreditation in 2005. This creates opportunities to advance our thinking and adjust curriculum accordingly. We continue to streamline key theories and strengthen horizontal (across sequence) integration. We also are assuring that cross-cultural competence is reflected throughout the curriculum. We will be revisiting the extent to which we provide in-depth knowledge in the practice curriculum relative to emerging needs of vulnerable/at-risk groups, especially as expressed by the needs of children and adolescents, an aging society, substance abusers, and the chronically mentally ill.

Theoretical Development on the Horizon

We note with excitement the creative work of GlenMaye, Lewandowski, and Bolin linking chaos and complexity theory to advanced generalist practice (see Chapter 7). Their work furthers the task of theoretical unification, advancing both social work theory and advanced generalist thinking.

An article by Kondrat (2002) may also have the potential to further advanced generalist thinking. She elucidates the work of Anthony Giddens, a British sociologist and director of the London School of Economics and Political Science. Giddens' theory of structuration suggests the elimination of artificial distinctions between micro and macro structures so predominant in social work theorizing over the last 20 years. According to his theory of structuration, human agency has as important an impact in constructing societal systems as societal systems have on human agents. Person-in-environment and ecological theory, the current mainstays of advanced generalist thinking, emphasize the latter, not the former (Kondrat, 2002).

A fresh point of view would supplant our advanced generalist goal to thoroughly integrate micro and macro structures with a unified perspective that posits human agency as inherently operating simultaneously at the micro and macro levels. How so? Giddens suggests that the individual has the capacity for knowledge and reflexive action to do something different and to choose not to perpetuate societal structures; structures, after all, that are enacted in each and every daily, routine interaction. The exciting implication of Giddens' work is that in each of us is the capability to profoundly alter the implacable structures of racism, classism, and genderism (Kondrat, 2002). We look forward to further development of these ideas in the years ahead.

Based on "Advanced Generalist Practice: A Framework for Social Work Practice in the Twenty-First Century" by F. J. Vecchiolla, A. W. Roy, J. G. Lesser, J. Wronka, K. Walsh-Burke, J. R. Gianesin, D. Foster, and L. K. Negroni, published in the *Journal of Teaching in Social Work, August 2001. Adapted with permission.*

REFERENCES

Bakalinsky, R. (1982). Generic practice in graduate social work curricula: A study of educators' experiences and attitudes. *Journal of Education for Social Work, 18*(3), 46-54.

Biggerstaff, M., Baskind, F., & Jensen, C. (1994). The field of advanced generalist practice: Changing practice needs. In M. O. McMahon (Ed.), *Advanced generalist practice with an international perspective.* Englewood Cliffs, NJ: Prentice Hall.

Carroll, N. (1977). Three-dimensional model of social work practice. *Journal of Education for Social Work*, 428-432.

Evans, R. (1976). Some implications of an integrated model of social work for theory and practice. *British Journal of Social Work, 6*(2), 177-199.

Germain, C., & Gitterman, A. (1980). *The life model of social work practice.* New York: Columbia University Press.

Gibbs, P., Locke, B. L., & Lohmann, R. (1990). Paradigm for the generalist-advanced generalist continuum. *Journal of Social Work Education, 26*(3), 233-243.

Jarman-Rhode, L., McFall, J., Kolar, P., & Strom, G. (1997). The changing context of social work practice: Implications and recommendations for social work educators. *Journal of Social Work Education, 33*(1), 29-45.

Kondrat, M. E. (2002). Actor-centered social work: Re-visioning "person-in-environment" through a critical theory lens. *Social Work, 47*(4), 435-448.

Landon, P. S. (1995). Generalist and advanced generalist practice. In K. L. Edwards (Ed.), *Encyclopedia of social work*, (pp. 1101-1108). Silver Springs, MD: National Association of Social Workers.

Maluccio, A. (1981). *Promoting competence in clients: A new/old approach to social work practice.* New York: Free Press.

McMahon, M. O. (1994). *Advanced generalist practice with an international per-spective*. Englewood Cliffs, NJ: Prentice Hall.

Minahan, L. A., & Pincus, A. (1977). Conceptual framework for social work prac-tice. *Social Work*, *22*, 347-352.

Parsons, R. J., Hernandez, S. H., & Jorgensen, J. (1988). Integrated practice: A framework for problem solving. *Social Work*, *33*, 417-421.

Program Review (2001). Unpublished report, F. J. Vecchiolla & A. W. Roy, School of Social Work, Springfield College.

Roy, A. W. (2001). *Alumni Survey* (unpublished report), School of Social Work, Springfield College.

Sheafor, B. W., & Landon, P. S. (1987). Generalist perspective. In A. Minahan et al. (Eds.) *Encyclopedia of social work* (18th ed.). Silver Springs, MD: National Association of Social Workers, 660-669.

Springfield College (2002). *Status Report* (unpublished report)

Stone, D. (1997). *Policy paradox: The art of political decision making*. New York: W. W. Norton & Company.

Thompson, J., Menefee, D., & Marley, M. (1999). A comparative analysis of social workers' macro practice activities: Identifying functions common to direct prac-tice and administration. *Journal of Social Work Education*, *35*(1), 115-124.

Chapter 2

Model Two: Salem State College

ADVANCED GENERALIST PRACTICE WITH A PUBLIC SECTOR FOCUS

Christopher G. Hudson
Salem State College

Since Ada Sheffield (1937) introduced the term "total situation" in the 1930s, social workers have been attracted to the vision of a holistic practice. Despite some early progress in implementing this ideal through the work of the functionalists, and through the consolidation of professional social work organizations in the 1940s and 1950s, the goal of an integrated practice was eclipsed in the 1960s and 1970s by the rapid expansion of the mental health field and the concomitant need for workers with specialized clinical skills.

However, beginning in the 1980s, with the expansion of managed care and the slowdown in the growth of the mental health field, the human services faced an increasing demand for professionals prepared for diverse fields of practice and for a wide range of methods reaching beyond the set of clinical competencies traditionally taught. Thus, the final decades of the twentieth century saw a considerable expansion in the number of graduate social work programs, several of which have been designed specifically to fill the needs described above. These programs have often emphasized generalist or advanced generalist practice. The program at Salem State College, just north of Boston, exemplifies this emergent initiative. It also illustrates some of the unique solutions such programs have evolved to balance the needs for specialized and, at the same time, integrated, holistic, or generalist practice.

During the 1970s and early 1980s baccalaureate social work education was formally recognized by the Council of Social Work Education (CSWE) and underwent a dramatic expansion. These programs have routinely promoted the notion of generalist practice. This trend formed an important backdrop not only to national developments, but specifically to the development of the MSW program at Salem State College, which has been built on top of existing BSW programs. Not long after the creation and accreditation of the BSW program at Salem State in 1982, the president committed the college to the goal of developing a master's program. At that time Massachusetts had no publicly supported master's program of social work.

The same four private colleges and universities in Massachusetts that had been educating master's level social workers for many years, turning out mostly clinical social workers, won new opportunities in the early 1980s for third-party reimbursement and the possibilities of private practice. The introduction of third-party reimbursement, along with the attraction of private psychotherapeutic practice, contributed to the difficulties that public agencies experienced in attracting master's level social workers. This, in turn, contributed to their unhappiness with many of the private MSW programs that, at the time, focused mainly on preparing social workers for clinical practice.

For these reasons, administrators of the various public human service agencies had for some years advocated for a publicly supported MSW program, one that would be generalist in nature, committed to preparing students for work in public agencies in the child welfare, mental health, older adults, and other fields. These practitioners were conceived of not as primarily clinicians, but rather as professionals involved in a wide range of administrative, program development, advocacy, case management, and other roles (in addition to the traditional clinical responsibilities). Thus, the needs of the public human service agencies dovetailed remarkably well with a reemerging interest by social work educators in a vision of generalist practice, creating a synergistic movement supportive of Salem State's bid to create the first publicly supported MSW program in Massachusetts. In hearings before the state's Board of Higher Education in 1986, this initiative was able to withstand the vociferous opposition of representatives of the existing private schools of social work.

With the approval from the Board of Higher Education in hand, as well as CSWE's pre-accreditation status, Salem State proceeded to immediately hire six experienced Ph.D. social work faculty in 1986 and 1987 and admitted its first MSW students in the fall of 1987. The most pivotal themes of the curriculum (public-sector and advanced generalist orientation) and its overall structure have remained constant since its inception, although there have been continual refinements in the details of their delivery and organization. Other themes include the strengths perspective, empowerment, the ecosystems framework, ethical decision making, and practice with diverse and oppressed populations. With only minimal delay, the program was fully accredited by the CSWE in 1992 and, most recently, was renewed in 2002.

THE ADVANCED GENERALIST MODEL

Although each faculty member at Salem State has developed their own approach to advanced generalist practice, commonly recognized features of the advanced generalist model are routinely taught by Salem State faculty. The most emphasized is the problem-solving approach, which details the progression from engagement to assessment, contracting and goal setting, intervention planning, intervention, and evaluation. Many faculty emphasize that this is a multilevel problem-solving process. It involves either parallel or alternating problem-solving efforts occurring with systems on the micro or clinical level, on the mezzo or organizational and/or community level, and on the macro or policy level. For example, practitioners may be concerned with engaging organizations, assessing or analyzing them, working out a plan of intervention, and the like. Then, within the context of this established plan-perhaps a job description or social action strategy-they may shift gears to repeat this as a nested process with a group, family, or individual.

As is the case with social work practice in general, the advanced generalist model emphasizes the need to pay careful attention to what it is that the client (individual, organization, or community) is motivated to work on, starting where the client "is at." It is typically emphasized that it is no small task determining what the client is actually asking for, which can require considerable exploration. This exploration may be organized around the goal of understanding the client's motivation, opportunities, and capacities (Ripple & Alexander, 1956). In this manner, faculty challenge students to discover the links between a client's interests, strengths, and environmental resources, whether these involve psychological qualities, concrete resources, or general social supports. It is through such means that students are challenged to understand the relationship between problem solving and the strengths perspective, which are too often treated by many in the field as being at odds with each other.

The advanced generalist model as taught at Salem State is also grounded in the tenets of ecosystems theory, which argues that assessment should be concerned with examining and promoting the goodness-of-fit between individuals (persons, organizations, or other entities) and their relevant environments (Germain & Gitterman, 1980). This approach emphasizes helping clients to establish balance and equilibrium. While this is a valid goal in many situations, critiques of the older functionalist and general systems theories, from both the left and from the field of complex systems or nonequilibrium theory, have led some faculty to increasingly moderate their earlier indiscriminate emphasis on the goodness-of-fit ideal. Instead, there is a growing recognition that living systems, especially human beings, exist and often thrive at conditions far from equilibrium, popularly referred to as the "edge of chaos" (Hudson, 2000). Thus, helping people either to return to an idealized past level of adjustment or to adjust to inhumane current conditions thwarts problem solving, creativity, and growth. The faculty at Salem State do not necessarily regard generalist practice as only a method of encouraging individual adjustment and competence, but also as a means of social development, including community building, policy advocacy, and other similar methods.

The generalist model is also taught as a multimethod approach to practice. Faculty emphasize that this does not mean simply an eclectic or "smorgasbord" approach to selecting methods, but instead an approach based on a systematic assessment of relevant systems, drawing on professional theory and research and guided by defined values and ethical principles. For example, some conceptualize the multimethod approach using Eugene Jackson's quadrant model (1984). Jackson argues that two key dimensions define practice: (a) the *target system*, whether it involves small systems (individuals, groups, families) or large systems (communities); and (b) the type of *action system*, whether the practitioner is working directly with the target population (direct practice) or with others on behalf of the target population (indirect practice). These two dimensions define four major types of practice methodologies: (a) *interpersonal practice* (direct work with small systems); (b) *social treatment* (indirect work with small systems); (c) *community practice* (direct work with large systems); and (d) *policy practice* (indirect work with large systems). This framework exemplifies one of several approaches to systematically organizing practice and identifying explicit principles for using various methodologies. Other examples include the strengths perspective and, in policy advocacy, Roland Warren's principle of "least contest": the idea that one first tries collaboration; and, if that is not possible, then considers a campaign strategy; and, as a last resort, moves to conflict strategies (Warren, 1963; see also Goldberg, 1974).

The faculty at Salem State have met periodically to discuss alternative conceptions of the generalist model. There has been little felt need to agree on a single formulation of the model, as a recognition exists that there are sufficient common denominators in the various formulations to make such a task unnecessary. This is not to say that there have not been ongoing tensions between those who are committed to a macro policy focus and those whose expertise is specifically clinical. For example, some of the clinical faculty have been challenged regarding their interest in including self psychology in the practice curriculum, especially during the foundation year, as some have regarded this content as either too specialized or too intrapsychically oriented. Also, because the practice courses have been split between micro and macro content during each of the two years, a concern has been expressed that the program represents more of a multimethod model than a truly advanced generalist model. Despite this anxiety, the faculty have considered an adaptation of the generalist model during the advanced year that would permit greater focus within the clinical generalist and policy generalist areas. A minority of the faculty have expressed fears that this would be antithetical to the advanced generalist model. In addition, some have objected, arguing that if students were given a choice between a clinical generalist or policy generalist practice course in their advanced year, an insufficient number would elect the latter.

Thus, at Salem State advanced generalist practice can mean many things. It usually involves an understanding of problem-solving practice as differentially applied to systems that exist on many levels, usually entailing both "private troubles/ public issues." It is based on careful assessment, drawing generally on complex systems and ecological theories and, more specifically, on a wide range of theories and research. Such assessment is commonly organized around such rubrics as the motivation-opportunity-capacity (MOC) triad proposed by Ripple (Ripple & Alexander, 1956). Besides being a multilevel model, advanced generalist practice is also a multimethod approach, one that draws on empirically tested methods using a coherent framework of theory and principle. Whichever features of the model a faculty member or student finds most meaningful, what is considered by all to be especially important is supporting each student in achieving their own coherent, integrated understanding and competence in practice, whether or not they find all of the "advanced generalist" terms and concepts to be meaningful.

ORGANIZATION OF CURRICULUM

The program's curriculum is organized around the progression from foundation generalist to advanced generalist practice. For the students in the two-year full-time program, the aim is to master the competencies required for foundational generalist practice, similar to what undergraduate social work majors are expected to achieve. These include basic client engagement, assessment, and problem-solving skills, applicable in a wide range of settings. In contrast, during the second half of the program, students master advanced generalist skills. These involve the ability to apply the foundational skills to complex systems, often involving ambiguously defined problems with significant risk. It also involves the ability to apply the generic skills to a particular field of practice, such as child welfare or mental health, including specialized methods such as program development or psychotherapy.

A central principle underpinning the organization of the MSW curriculum at Salem State is that social work practice classes will not be taught on a specialized basis, as is done in many traditional social work programs. In the first year, the two-semester practice sequence begins with a review of direct practice methods, such as engagement and assessment, with both individuals and families. In the spring semester it shifts to an introduction to group work and community practice. Similarly, in the advanced year, the practice sequence moves from a focus on clinical work in the fall semester to administrative and program development practice in the spring. During both years, students from all three concentrations (child and family services, health/mental health, and older adults) share the same practice courses, given the commonalities of practice between these fields. Even in the concentration year, faculty have been committed to the notion that practice is essentially generalist in nature, and the task is not to learn methods unique to particular fields, but to apply the methods to the specific needs of these diverse fields of practice. Nonetheless, students within these generalist sequences are expected to selectively focus their assignments on problems involving their concentration.

Because not all methods are taught within the same semester, the problem of teaching these methods in a specialized, disjointed fashion is not altogether avoided. Thus, in recent years the program has introduced a required monthly field seminar concerned not only with bridging the class and field experiences, but also with helping students develop a better understanding of the integration of and transitions between the diverse micro and macro methods taught in the class.

Although students declare their intended concentration as part of the application process, their foundation year is not organized around these concentrations, but instead systematically reviews the foundations of social work practice in several of the standard curricular areas. The theoretical foundations of practice are reviewed with a two-course human behavior sequence and a two-course policy sequence. The human behavior and the social environment (HBSE) sequence begins in the fall with micro-level theories involving ecosystems theory, object relations, human development, and family dynamics. In the spring, the sequence focuses on communities, organizations, and the workplace. This progression is designed specifically to parallel and support the progression in the practice and field curricula from direct practice in the fall to indirect practice with community and organizations in the spring. While some macro-level theories are covered in the human behavior sequence, the policy sequence specifically addresses the need for students to understand the historical context of social work as well as to obtain skills in analyzing the performance of current social welfare policies and programs.

Critical components of the foundation curriculum also include a course on diversity and a course in basic research methods. The diversity course is designed to support the infusion of content on diverse populations and multicultural practice throughout the curriculum by means of a one-semester concerted introduction. As is the case with the other foundation requirements, the course on research methods reviews and builds on the student's undergraduate experience. It emphasizes an inclusive, multiperspective approach that combines the best features of qualitative and quantitative methodologies. It reviews the uses of several commonly used methodologies, such as surveys, program evaluations, and single-subject designs, with a focus on the underlying logic of causal inference that informs these methodologies.

The final year of the MSW program (the advanced curriculum) is organized around concentrations defined by fields of public sector practice: child and family services, health/mental health, and older adults. The curriculum retains the commitment to generalist practice through several cross-concentration, integrative components. The practice sequence includes students from each of the three concentrations in its various sections, permitting considerable cross-fertilization of ideas. This sequence moves from an introduction to basic clinical methods in the fall to such mezzo and macro methods as administration, supervision, and program development in the spring. As in the foundation year, students in the advanced year also participate in a monthly field seminar. In addition, students are asked to select two elective courses, most of which involve cross-cutting issues such as spirituality and social work, trauma, or AIDS/HIV.

Each of the advanced year concentrations includes several specialized components involving human behavior, policy, research, and field education. Each concentration requires the student to take a third human behavior course in the fall and a policy and services course in the spring (this order is reversed with the older adults concentration). These concentrations focus on the theoretical foundations of practice unique to the field the student expects to practice in. These courses are supplemented by a 600-hour internship that falls within the student's chosen concentration. In addition, the student participates in a two-course, year-long research laboratory experience. With a group of their fellow concentration students, each student conducts an applied research study, beginning with problem formulation and literature review and progressing through research design, data collection, analysis, and write-up. This experience culminates in a research symposium and permits each group to present their project to the MSW student body and faculty.

PROGRAM DEVELOPMENT

Since its inception in 1987, the MSW program has undergone regular changes while retaining its essential advanced generalist focus and structure. Initially the foundation practice and human behavior sequences moved from indirect practice concerns and large systems in the fall semester to direct practice and small systems in the spring. It was believed that by starting with a study of larger systems students would be able to more easily develop an integration of mezzo and micro practice skills. However, students, especially those new to the field, struggled with their internships in the fall as these assignments assumed familiarity with clinical practice. For this reason, the faculty decided in the early 1990s to reverse this sequence and to introduce some of the larger systems material in an initial, extended orientation to field education.

Another set of changes involved development of the research sequence. The initial plan consisted of an ambitious four-semester sequence, involving two courses in the foundation year: the research methods course and a computer applications course. This was followed by a fairly independent two-semester research project in the second year (for one credit a semester) and a course on program evaluation. After several adjustments, this plan was scaled back to the current three-semester sequence, which includes the two three-hour research laboratory courses in the fall. These extended laboratory courses include additional instruction in computer applications, such as the use of statistical analysis software (SPSS) in lieu of the first-year research course. It was felt that this more applied and scaled-down focus was more consistent with both student priorities and competing curricular demands. This scaling back permitted the addition of a course on practice with diverse populations during the first year.

A more recent development includes a restructuring of the school's advanced standing program. This is the option for graduates of accredited BSW programs to directly enter into the advanced year of the MSW program after taking a few bridge courses during the summer. The plan initially consisted of four summer courses: practice methods, human behavior, research, and professional issues. Improvements in BSW education have reduced the need for the research and professional issues courses. However, continuing deficits in the field preparation of these students have required additional internship assignments. Thus, the faculty have recently decided to discontinue the research and professional issues bridge requirements for these students and instead ask them to begin their internship during the summer, extending it from a 9-month to nearly a 12-month experience, as this is the only MSW internship these students will be asked to take.

FIELD EDUCATION

As is the case with many MSW programs, field education is viewed as a linchpin of advanced generalist education at Salem State. During both years, each field agency is expected to provide their students with a range of assignments, not only in direct work with clients, but also in community and administrative practice. During the foundation year internship, consisting of 450 hours of agency placement, students are expected to develop and implement a community practice project. This may consist of such tasks as forming and staffing an advisory committee, acting as liaison with community groups, or organizing some community action. During the advanced year, the indirect practice project involves administrative practice, or something more internal to the agency. This could involve developing an AIDS/HIV policy, developing a proposal for a new program, or providing support to a staff committee developing new intake criteria and procedures.

Unlike the more straightforward direct service assignments, these projects have posed an ongoing challenge to students, their field instructors, and their faculty liaison. Students often enter the field with little conception of indirect practice, and it is not unusual for their internship agencies to have limited interest or experience in these areas. In addition, students do not take their indirect practice courses until the spring of their foundation and advanced years. Thus, the field education and faculty liaison have had to provide substantial orientation to students and field instructors early in the year, many examples of past projects, and regular visits to agencies. It is not unusual that faculty liaisons need to arrange for a preceptor (a secondary field instructor who may be an administrator or someone specifically involved in macro practice) to work with the student on their project, supplementing the regular field instructor. Recently the initiation of regular seminars has provided an extra source of support to students struggling to define meaningful macro practice projects. However, even with these supports, along with others, faculty have not been entirely satisfied with the success of this component of the field curriculum.

Field instructors are asked to attend orientations and training, not only on the program's procedures, but also on its generalist model. Considerable attention is paid to the educational dimensions of the student-field instructor relationship. Students are expected to receive a minimum of three hours a week of supervision, at least one of which involves individual meetings. All students are expected to maintain a log of their activities and write at least two process recordings a week. In addition, the program requires students to turn in two psychosocial assessments to their field instructors plus written reports on their macro project. These are typically presented and discussed during field seminars. At Salem State (unlike in an increasing number of MSW programs), full-time classroom faculty have the option to act as liaison for field students; in practice, approximately one half of the liaisons consist of such faculty.

EVALUATION

Evaluating the success of any educational program is an ambitious endeavor. The problem of assessing the accomplishment of the wide range of process and outcome objectives inherent in any advanced generalist program is even more so. For this reason, the faculty have been progressively adding evaluative components, both qualitative and quantitative, involving a variety of data sources. While it would be inappropriate here to elaborate on the full spectrum of these efforts, this section instead will provide an overview of a few of the recent findings, involving surveys of students, employers, and objective national licensing tests.

Each year graduating MSW students are surveyed anonymously to determine their perceptions of the adequacy of their preparation for professional practice and the contribution of the curriculum to this end. They typically report that they are "well prepared," or at about 4 on a 1-to-5 scale (see Table 1). In the most recent year for which data are available, graduates were slightly less favorable about the HBSE (3.7) and Policy and Services (3.6) sequences, and more enthusiastic about Generalist Practice (4.2) and Research (4.3). The final rating is noteworthy given the historic aversion many MSW students have had toward research.

In more detailed questions, students have reported feeling least prepared with respect to group work, and only moderately well prepared in family treatment. Although they rate their research preparation highly, students report that they struggle with computer applications. Perhaps this is because the research lab projects usually involve the use of a statistical software package (SPSS) in the advanced year—yet most do not have any preparation in social statistics, and the use of the software is not covered until the time of these projects.

Student Perceptions of Quality of MSW Curriculum Components

How well have each of the following parts of the MSW curriculum prepared you for practice?	1999 Exit Survey	2000 Exit Survey
Human Behavior and the Social Environment	4.0	3.7
Practice	3.8	4.2
Policy and Services	4.1	3.6
Research	3.8	4.3

Note. The above are means, on the following scale: 1 (unprepared) to 5 (very well prepared).

Table 1

In the same survey of exiting MSW students, the respondents also were asked to rate the adequacy of some of the concerns of generalist social work education. These involve issues that the CSWE requires all schools of social work, generalist or not, to incorporate into their curricula. Table 2 provides an overview of these responses and indicates that the MSW graduates felt well prepared in each of these areas, especially in relation to values and ethics (4.2). They were somewhat less impressed with the coverage of diversity (3.7).

While it is important for students to have a sense of competence upon completion of their education, such feelings are known to be very imperfect indicators of actual competency. It is not unusual for some students to master the rhetoric of a field and go away with the illusion of competency, while others learn much more through critical self-examination but are so self-critical that they dramatically underestimate their level of competence. For this reason, faculty have sought to use multiple and independent sources of data for assessing the achievement of key outcomes. One such means has been to survey employers of our MSW alumni. Table 3 reveals that these employers rate their employees more highly than the employees rate themselves. On a 1-to-5 scale, the employers gave ratings typically in the 4.2 to 4.9 range on the consistency of application of key skills. Among the most highly regarded skills of Salem State graduates are their ability to practice within an ethi-

Student Perceptions of Integration of Key Generalist Themes into Curriculum

How well has the curriculum pertaining to each of the following areas prepared you for practice?	1999 Exit Survey	2000 Exit Survey
Values and ethics	3.9	4.2
Diversity	3.5	3.7
Social and economic justice	3.8	3.9
Populations-at-risk	3.9	4.0

Note. The above are means, on the following scale: 1 (unprepared) to 5 (very well prepared).

Table 2

Employer Assessments of Preparation of MSW Graduates (N=53)

Uses theory as a framework for practice	4.2
Applies skills of generalist social work practice at an advanced level	4.5
Is sensitive to issues of culture and diversity	4.7
Practices within a framework of values and ethics	4.9
Adheres to the vision of the agency	4.7
Compared with graduates from other schools, this SSC graduate performs at an equal or superior level of competence	4.7

Note. The above are means, on the following scale: 1 (never) to 5 (always).

Table 3

cal framework (4.9), their application of advanced generalist skills (4.5), and their general preparation compared with graduates of other programs (4.7). The employers were slightly less enthusiastic about graduates' ability to use theory in practice, but were still very positive (4.2).

Finally, the ongoing evaluation of the program has involved monitoring success of the graduates in passing both the Massachusetts licensing exam (taken upon graduation) and the advanced clinical exam (typically taken at least two years after graduation). Although this is a Massachusetts state exam, it is given by the same company that provides examinations for many of the states; thus national norms are available for assessing the success of an individual or cohort of test takers. Table 4 reveals that Salem State's MSW graduates have routinely performed above the national norm on both the intermediate and clinical exams, with pass rates ranging between 83% and 97%, compared with 69% to 83% for the national population taking these exams.

Comparison of Percentage of Students Passing Licensing Exams

Year of Exam	Intermediate Exam		Clinical Exam	
	Salem State	National	Salem State	National
1997	97%	83%	87%	83%
1998	92%	83%	85%	81%
1999	83%	79%	86%	69%

Table 4

DISCUSSION

Despite the fact that various models of integrated or generalist practice have been on the social work scene for several decades, they are still in the initial stages of development. While a remarkable consensus has evolved about many essential elements of the model, there are continuing struggles about how specifically the multiple levels and methods of practice are best integrated. How do practitioners make the transition between one method and another, or nest one level of practice within other levels? There is agreement that generalist practice is much more than eclectic practice, and one grounded in a rich biopsychosocial ecosystemic assessment, but what these extra elements actually mean is elusive. This is especially the case given the trend to shorter-term models that preclude collecting the extensive information needed for a holistic assessment of the multiple systems involved in any presenting problem.

All who seek to teach and learn generalist models face both conceptual and empirical challenges. A central need remains to define the approach in a sufficiently precise manner so that it can be a practical guide to professionals. This involves the need to define when and how one uses various underlying theories and models, whether ego psychology, decision making theory, or some family systems approach. No less important is the empirical challenge of grounding the approach in research, certainly an ethical responsibility of social work educators and practitioners.

Related to each of the above challenges is the need to clearly differentiate generalist from advanced generalist practice. One of the key defining features is the complexity of the target and action systems involved. When target systems are sufficiently stable such that practice can be broken down into easily definable procedures and protocols, then we speak of generalist or foundation practice. But when— in cases of conflict, ambiguity, risk, and, in general, complexity and unpredictability—recognized protocols no longer apply and professional judgment becomes paramount, advanced generalist practice is particularly needed. While it may be easy to argue that all practice involves complex systems, a considerably clearer understanding exists for some complex systems. With these, interventive tasks can be broken down to definable protocols that can be implemented by workers with less advanced levels of education.

Perhaps one of the most significant challenges of the MSW program, one that the advanced generalist model has helped to surmount, has been pressure on faculty to specialize. In many larger MSW programs it is not unusual for faculty to become balkanized into research, policy, practice, and HBSE camps, especially when the belief exists that faculty can be expert enough to teach in only one area. While a few faculty at Salem State have preferred to teach in only a single area, most have actively used the generalist model to argue for the right to teach in two or three different areas. In the author's experience, this has significantly supported exchange and cohesiveness among the faculty. It also has improved their teaching, given the cross-fertilization of ideas that inevitably occurs when faculty are forced to stay current in more than one area. Thus the advanced generalist model has not only supported integrative thinking among the students, but also has served as a basis for the formation of a cohesive academic atmosphere, characterized by a progressively improving quality of intellectual exchange among both faculty and students.

The program at Salem State is an ongoing experiment, but is one, like others, that has accumulated increasing empirical support. Both its alumni and their employers clearly value the approach, and its alumni have demonstrated success on traditional measures of career advancement. However, the ultimate test will be the efficacy of its practitioners in objectively resolving identifiable problems in personal and larger social system functioning. To conduct such tests, it is critical that the field be able to define clearly what it is that advanced generalist practitioners are taught to do and actually do, and it is toward this end that this chapter is directed.

REFERENCES

Germain, C., & Gitterman, A. (1980). *The life model of social work practice.* New York: Columbia University Press.

Goldberg, G. (1974). Structural approach to practice: A new model. *Social Work, 19*(2), 150-155.

Hudson, C. G. (2000). At the edge of chaos: A new paradigm for social work? *Journal of Social Work Education, 36*(2), 215-230.

Hudson, C. G. (2000). From social Darwinism to self-organization: Implications for social change theory. *Social Service Review, 74*(4), 533-559.

Jackson, E. (1984). A simultaneity model of social work education. *Journal of Social Work Education, 20*(2), 17.

Ripple, L., & Alexander, E. (1956). Motivation, capacity, opportunity as related to the use of casework service: Nature of client's problem. *Social Service Review, 30*, 38-59.

Sheffield, A. (1937). *Social insight in case situations*. New York: Appleton Century.

Warren, R. (1963*). The community in America*. Chicago: Rand McNally & Co.

Chapter 3

Model Three: Stephen F. Austin State University

ADVANCED GENERALIST SOCIAL WORK FOR RURAL PRACTICE

Michael R. Daley and Freddie L. Avant
Stephen F. Austin State University

RATIONALE FOR AN ADVANCED GENERALIST PERSPECTIVE

The advanced rural generalist model employed by Stephen F. Austin State University (SFASU) is designed to prepare students for advanced practice in rural contexts. The rationale for the development of this model flowed from the program's needs assessment, which identified both the characteristics of and service needs for the program's service region. This needs assessment clearly identified the program's context as rural and indicated a great need for advanced level social work practitioners.

Based on our needs assessment, we were able to determine that the region served by SFASU is predominantly rural, in that it is both large and has a low population density. It covers a geographic area of Texas roughly the size of West Virginia with only a slightly smaller population. Specifically, SFASU's service region consists of 36 counties in Northeast Texas and borders the neighboring states of Arkansas, Louisiana, and Oklahoma.

In comparison with the rest of the state, the population density of Northeast Texas is relatively low. While Texas averages 65.6 residents per square mile, the Northeast Texas region averages only 50.2 residents per square mile, with no major metropolitan areas. The economic system in the region is dependent on agriculture, timber, and related industries.

The region faces needs and challenges typical of many rural areas in that poverty is widespread. In several counties of the region, the poverty rate is above the state average. This makes our region a relatively poor region economically since Texas currently has the eighth highest poverty rate in the country. Furthermore, poverty is even higher for some groups, especially African Americans. In 28 of the 36 counties, more than 40% of African Americans live in poverty. In every county in the region, at least 35-49% of the households were low income, and 18-25% were of extremely low income.

Despite these numbers, inadequate resources to meet these needs constitutes a major challenge to the residents of the region. Area social service providers often must administer services to multiple counties simultaneously, rather than to just one county. This is a particular problem given the large size of many of these counties. The many problems addressed by service providers in the region include substandard and insufficient housing (especially emergency shelters), limited employment opportunities, inadequate health care (especially long-term care), few mental health services, and limited prevention resources for problems of school dropout, teen pregnancy, and substance abuse. Compounding factors in accessing resources for rural residents are physical isolation and the lack of public transportation in the region.

Also a limited number of professionally educated social workers are available for meeting the service needs of the region, and the scarcity of advanced level social workers presents an even greater problem (Daley & Avant, 1999). Given these characteristics of our service region, the program developed a mission statement that emphasized the rural context of practice. The mission statement of the School of Social Work and the Advanced Generalist Method is as follows:

> The School of Social Work assists the university in fulfilling its mission by providing leadership for the region in identifying and addressing community needs and issues, including those related to social and economic justice, oppression, and cultural diversity. The mission of the School of Social Work at Stephen F. Austin State University is the provision of quality education and training for the preparation of professional social workers, able to respond to the needs of rural communities and to the challenges faced by people with rural lifestyles. The School is dedicated to excellence in teaching, research, scholarship and professional and voluntary service in support of its educational endeavors.

Once this mission was defined with a clear focus on our rural region, we were able to consider the question of an appropriate social work model for advanced practice. Given the rural context of our program, the decision to pursue an advanced generalist approach was a relatively easy choice.

It has generally been accepted in the rural social work literature that the generalist method is the practice approach that is best suited to practice (Brown, 1980; Daley & Avant, 1999; Davenport & Davenport, 1998; Ginsberg, 1998; Southern Regional Education Board 1998; York, Denton, & Moran, 1998). It has been suggested that the generalist method is most appropriate because rural social workers are generalists (as opposed to specialists). However, rural social workers are a generalists because they work with all social systems including families, groups, individuals, organizations, and communities. The person-in-environment and strengths perspectives are also critical components of the generalist method for social work in rural communities and with rural individuals. Indeed, failure to understand the rural context and the strengths of the rural culture can create difficulties in providing social work services (McNellie, 2001).

SCHOOL MODEL

Advanced Generalist Conceptual Framework at SFASU

The primary motivation for our selection of the advanced generalist practice method was the nature of social work in our region. This was characterized by few advanced level practitioners who, by necessity, were involved with a wide variety of practice activities and with systems ranging in size from individuals to communities. Given the decision to pursue the advanced generalist method and the variety of models to deliver that method, we found it was important to clearly identify our definitions and conceptualization of advanced generalist practice in order to develop an integrated program.

Definitions

The advanced rural generalist program at SFASU is built upon three basic definitions that guide the development of the curriculum. These definitions address advanced generalist practice, generalist practice, and rural social work. The definitions used and their rationales are discussed below.

The first key definition for the program is that of *advanced generalist practice*. The definition of advanced generalist practice used in our MSW concentration is as follows:

> 1. Advanced generalist practice builds on the generalist foundation...but [is] characterized by a greater depth, breadth, and autonomy as demonstrated through specialized knowledge across problem areas, populations at risk and practice settings, with a greater selection of diverse interactions across practice levels. Briefly:
>
>   • Advanced practice requires the ability to differentially assess complex problems with systems of all sizes, with a variety of advanced assessment skills.
>
>   • Advanced practice requires specialized interventions with systems of all sizes.
>
>   • Advanced practice requires differential evaluation techniques with systems of all sizes.
>
>   • Advanced practice requires readiness for leadership in a variety of areas including: program development, coordination and administration, clinical and organizational supervision, policy creation, reform and implementation, leadership in research development and utilization, particularly in practice settings, and professional development.

The second key definition for the MSW program is that of *generalist practice*. This is the base upon which advanced generalist practice is built. The generalist practice definition used is identical to the one we use in our BSW program, thus providing a common thread in the professional foundation, both graduate and undergraduate. This definition of generalist practice is as follows:

> 2. Generalist practice involves the social worker in professional helping relationships with individuals, families, groups, organizations, and communities. This practice perspective serves diverse client systems and is not confined by a narrow cadre of theories; rather it is versatile enough

to allow problems and situations to determine the practice approach. Generalist practice employs a problem solving framework and a broad knowledge, value, and skill base with demands ethical practice and ongoing self-assessment.

- Practice is multi-level to include individuals, families, groups, organizations and communities.

- Practice is multi-theory, allowing for the free selection of theories as appropriate.

- Practice utilizes a problem identification and solving focus that follows a problem solving model.

- Practice utilizes multiple interventions at multiple levels, as appropriate.

- An ecological systems is utilized to reflect the complexity of individual, family, group, organizational and community system interactions.

- Practice requires an integration of awareness, sensitivity and professional response to issues of values, ethics, diversity, social justice and populations-at-risk.

The third key program definition is that of *rurality*. This concept provides the context for our practice model and is defined as follows:

3. Rural practice is social work both in and with rural communities, and it is also social work with rural people. Rural communities in a limited geographic sense are non-metropolitan, in that they have populations of less than 50,000 and are not adjacent to a metropolitan area. Social work with rural people is characterized by social exchange between people and systems that is less formal and more personal than that of urban environments. Social exchange theory and Gemeinschaft and Gesellschaft are appropriate theoretical bases for understanding these exchanges.

Social problems such as high poverty rates, inadequate housing, inadequate health care, scarcity of resources and professionals, socioeconomic underdevelopment, and physical distance from services and transportation are frequently identified as important problems and issues for rural communities. Development of resources, use of natural helping networks, and community development are often proposed as appropriate interventions in these communities. Important opportunities and strengths such as "sense of community," intimacy among community residents, orientations toward self sufficiency, and an abundance of personal space, often go unnoticed by outsiders.

Conceptualization of Advanced Rural Generalist Practice

Several concepts from the literature influenced our definition of both generalist and advanced generalist practice in our MSW program. For example, our generalist practice definition is consistent with that of McMahon (1996). McMahon delineated the five essential elements of the generalist curriculum:

1. An ecological systems perspective
2. A problem focus
3. A problem-solving focus
4. A multilevel approach
5. An open selection of theories and intervention.

Our definition emphasizes the following elements: a multilevel approach, an open selection of theories and interventions, a problem focus, and a problem-solving process. In addition, our generalist practice perspective is taught from an ecological systems perspective, as identified by McMahon.

Other authors support these basic concepts of generalist practice. Johnson (1989) states that social workers are generalists, and that this requires them to assess the situation and decide which system or systems are the appropriate level or levels of attention or focus of the work for the change effort, thus reinforcing the idea of multilevels and multisystems. She also supports the use of a problem-solving method and the use of multiple interventions. Schatz, Jenkins, and Sheafor (1990, p. 223) maintain that generalist practice consists of five elements: (a) the generic foundation, (b) a multilevel problem-solving methodology, (c) a multiple theoretical orientation, (d) a knowledge, value and skill base that is transferable between and among diverse contexts and locations, and (e) an open assessment unconstricted by a particular theoretical approach. Kirst-Ashman and Hull (1993) identify four major features of the Generalist Intervention Model: (a) the model is based on knowledge, skills, and values that reflect the unique nature of social work, (b) the model is oriented toward solving problems involving micro, mezzo, and macro systems as targets of change, (c) the problem may be analyzed and addressed from a wide range of perspectives, and (d) the use of a specific problem-solving method that is flexible in application.

One of McMahon's (1994) important contributions was in providing leadership in defining advanced generalist practice. Her definition states:

> Advanced generalists are expected to have the competence to practice independently in complex systems with a variety of problems and populations. In advanced generalist practice, identified foundation components and generalist practice elements are extended for greater breadth and depth. Central concepts that characterize advanced generalist practice… include ethical decision making, international social work and welfare, advanced theories and interventive models, advanced general method, advanced research and technology, and advanced ecological systems perspective. (pp. 5-6)

In addition, McMahon (1994) adds:

> The advanced (problem solving) method differs from the general (problem solving) method primarily in its application to indirect practice situations. Both advanced generalists and generalists use the six-stage process as they practice directly as line workers. At the advanced level, however, advanced generalists use the process also as they practice indirectly as supervisors, managers, administrators, advanced researchers in social planners. (p. 23)

These indirect practice activities require levels of autonomy and independent functioning. McNellie (2001) defines advanced generalist practice as follows:

> The advanced generalist practitioner is expected to have the skills necessary to advocate for the community at a macro level by meeting with individual clients, groups, or community leaders in the development of long-term resources, applying for grants, altering the way groups of clients are perceived, and identifying and removing systemic barriers, in order to meet the long-term needs of individuals, groups or community systems. (p. 16)

Gibbs, Locke, and Lohman (1990) add that advanced generalist practice: (a) "must provide depth in learning opportunities around the ...advanced curriculum," (b) requires the social worker to be able to use advanced curriculum content with multiple intervention levels, (c) requires problem or need identification to be focused on the person-in-environment experience and interventions framed within that context, and (d) is a preferred practice approach in rural areas and small towns.

Theoretical Underpinnings of the Rural Context

Two theoretical concepts helped us to shape our definition of the rural context. These are gemeinshaft and gessellschaft and social exchange theory.

Gemeinschaft and gesellschaft are appropriate as a theoretical model for understanding rurality in relation to social work because they focus on how people relate to their community and society. Martinez-Brawley (2000) has used gemeinschaft and gesellschaft to describe the differences between rural and urban environments in terms of the person-in-society perspective. Briefly, the gemeinschaft community is one in which there is more homogeneity and the standing of each person in society is clear. There is also limited mobility from the place of birth, social relations are intimate and relatively free of conflict, and the family and church are the moral custodians of the community.

Such characteristics are important components in explaining the behavior the person in a rural community. Gesellschaft is more characteristic of the urban community wherein there is more heterogeneity, person-community relations are more formal, and relationships tend to be more focused on economic versus social exchange. Thus, gemeinschaft can be an important theoretical base for understanding the behavior of and establishing helping relationships with rural people.

Social exchange theory was added as an important theoretical base because it deals with both the ties that bind people together and the effects of interactions between people (Collins, 1988). McDonell, Strom-Gottfried, and Burton (1998) have also pointed out that social exchange theory is useful for understanding human behavior at all system levels, but has received little attention in social work.

It is the nature of social relationships and exchange between persons and systems that make social work practice in rural settings different than practice in urban settings. Understanding the nature of these exchanges is critical to understanding the behavior in an environmental context that is so critical to social work practice. For example, social exchange in a rural context begins with a focus on "who the person is" as opposed to what their accomplishments might be or what position they hold. This focus is not limited to person-to-person interactions, but affects exchanges with families, groups, organizations, and the community as well. Since both "person centeredness" and being "landed" are very important concepts for rural communities, social exchange theory offers a useful base for understanding rural behavior and for practicing with rural communities.

The Advanced Generalist Curriculum at SFASU

Liberal arts perspective. The advanced generalist curriculum at SFASU is based on a liberal arts perspective consisting of a minimum of 24 semester credit hours that must be completed before clear admission to the program. The required liberal arts perspective content areas include multicultural studies, human biology, and statistics. The remainder of the liberal arts perspective includes course content drawn from the following areas: science, multicultural studies, sociology, social problems, English, math, psychology, economics, political science, and American history. Completion of this content enriches students' understanding of the person-in-environment context, which is essential to professional social work practice.

Knowledge related to the scientific method and critical thinking is provided by courses such as psychology, biology, math, and statistics. Students are prepared to use written and oral communication and to think critically through mastery of English, political science, math, social statistics, and human biology. Preparation in critical thinking about society, people, and the problems they face is provided by courses such as American history, economics, political science, sociology, social problems, and psychology. A base of knowledge about biopsychosocial determinants of human behavior, diverse cultures, social conditions, and social problems is provided through human biology, psychology, sociology, social problems, multicultural studies, political science, and economics. Students who are deficient in the liberal arts perspective must complete that content before achieving clear admission into the program.

Professional social work foundation. SFASU's professional foundation in social work is generalist in design and consists of 32 credit hours of course work, covering two semesters of full-time study. Each full-time student takes four classroom courses and concurrent field instruction in both the fall and spring semesters. This foundation contains two human behavior in the social environment, two generalist practice, and two field instruction courses. The foundation also includes an introduction to rurality, an introduction to the social work profession, an introduction to social welfare policy and services, and a social work research methods course.

In the fall semester full-time students enroll for the following courses: human behavior in the social environment, generalist practice, introduction to the social work profession, introduction to rurality, and field instruction. Full-time enrollment in the spring semester consists of human behavior in the social environment, generalist practice, social welfare policy and services, social work research methods, and field instruction.

The generalist practice, human behavior in the social environment, and field instruction courses are organized with a parallel structure that both reinforces and strengthens the integration of content. For example, in the first semester (fall), practice, human behavior, and field courses focus on individual, family, and group systems. The following spring these courses cover group, organization, and community content. Thus at any point in the foundation, students are learning content about both practice and human behavior related to the same system. In addition, field experiences are designed to encourage the application of this knowledge

One unique aspect of the professional foundation is the inclusion of a course on rural content (Introduction to Rurality). Students who enroll in the MSW program, including those who have lived in rural communities, rarely have any prior educational content in "rurality" upon which to build either the foundation or concentration. Thus, this course is essential for providing theoretical, behavioral, policy, and practice content that supports both the professional foundation and the concentration. The course develops the concept of rurality from a strengths-based, ecological systems perspective that is critical for developing practice skills in rural communities and with rural people.

Advanced rural generalist concentration. The advanced rural generalist concentration at SFASU consists of 31 semester credit hours taken over two semesters of full-time enrollment. The first advanced concentration semester (fall) includes

15 credit hours of classroom courses. The five courses taken during this semester include an advanced research methods course, a social policy analysis course, two advanced generalist methods courses, and one elective. In the advanced concentration, content on human behavior in the social environment and diversity are integrated into the practice methods courses.

Practice. The advanced practice methods courses are organized in a manner that is parallel to the structure of the generalist practice courses in the professional foundation. One advanced generalist practice course addresses individual, family, and group systems and the other deals with organizational and community systems. Both practice courses are built on the assumption that the generalist method is the overarching framework for practice. The ecological systems perspective and the rural context of practice are also key elements for both advanced practice courses. Within each practice course we teach specific interventive theories consistent with these basic principles of our advanced generalist perspective and related to appropriate client systems.

Advanced generalist practice is multimethod, yet some limitations must be selectively placed upon the advanced theories of intervention that are actually taught in the curriculum. In making selections of appropriate interventive methods for each system, we chose theories and methods of intervention that are based on consistent theoretical principles that could lend themselves to application across multiple systems. We were particularly focused on solution-based and problem-oriented theories and methods. For example, rational or system-based models exist for working with individuals, families, groups, organizations, and communities. Thus advanced interventive theories based on these principles were included in the practice curriculum. It was our belief that such theoretical consistency across interventive models would (a) assist students in integrating advanced methods into the generalist method, and (b) help them to view advanced generalist practice as a unitary concept, as opposed to a disconnected batch of specialized methods.

One of our advanced practice methods course addresses individual, family, and group systems. Students are first presented with the advanced generalist intervention model developed by McMahon (1994) as an integrating framework. Then they learn specialized interventive theories and methods for working with individuals, families, and groups. Theories and methods for practice with individuals that are included in this course are task-centered casework, cognitive, and behavioral interventions. The family-based practice methods covered are structural family interventions, social learning approaches, and solution-focused family intervention. Group process is then presented in relation to delivering one of the individual or family systems based interventions covered earlier in the course. The four assignments for this course require students to complete research papers about advanced generalist practice, and about advanced social work practice with individuals, families, and groups. An advanced generalist paper asks the student to compare and contrast advanced generalist and generalist practice, and to discuss the applicability of advanced generalist practice for rural social work. Each of the last three of these course assignments requires the student to apply concepts of advanced generalist practice, including the problem-solving method, in practice with a population of interest. In addition, within each paper each student must address issues of ethics, populations-at-risk, diversity, and rurality.

The other advanced practice methods course in our advanced concentration deals with organizational and community systems, as well as with task groups. The task group content was chosen for inclusion in this course because it is an important aspect of working with both systems. The course includes content in relation to organizational systems in social work supervision, and administration. The supervision content deals with administrative, educational, and supportive aspects of supervision. The administrative content addresses management, budgeting, human resources, and planning. The use of a systems model and a rational approach is emphasized in addressing methods of both supervision and administration. With regard to community systems, content on social planning, community development, and advocacy is presented from the systems and rational perspectives. Task group content deals with both group dynamics and procedural mechanisms for making groups an effective method for advanced practice with organizations and communities. The course has two major assignments. One requires students to apply an advanced organization practice method, either administration or supervision, to a social welfare agency with which they are familiar. The student must develop an appropriate theoretical base for the method through a literature review, demonstrate how this method could be applied to the agency, using the problem-solving method, and explain how the effective use of this method could benefit both the agency and its clientele. The second assignment is similar to the first, but looks at community systems. Students are required to apply social planning, community development, or advocacy methods to the same agency.

Research. The advanced research methods class builds on the knowledge base of research methods and statistics from the professional foundation and further develops student knowledge and skill in the areas of measurement, sampling, and data analysis, including the use of a computer-based statistical package. The major assignments for the course are the preparation of a social work research proposal and an abstract for the presentation of this research at a professional conference. Students will execute the research proposal during the subsequent semester through the collection and analysis of data, culminating in a written report and an oral presentation. However the beginning stages of the research execution are in this course, as students are required to submit the research proposal to the university's institutional review board for human subjects research. In so doing, students must deal not only with design, but also with ethical issues related to their research.

The research component of the curriculum is critical to our advanced rural generalist model because the analytical methods from both social research and critical thinking provide a strong, rational framework for selecting appropriate interventions from the multiple methods employed by advanced generalists. Given the nature of practice in our region, we know that our MSW graduates will not only be working autonomously, but often acting alone, likely with no other MSW in the work setting with whom to consult. Thus the ability to appropriately assess problems and select intervention methods is critical. The logical models for inquiry and decision making that are central to social research and critical thinking help the advanced generalists to make rational, data-based decisions that increase the effectiveness of their practice.

Policy. The policy analysis class builds on the knowledge of social welfare policy and services from the professional foundation and develops student knowledge and skill relating to the analysis of policy and policy modification or change. Students learn a specific policy analysis model (Gil, 1992) and its application to the analysis of policy and its resultant effects. The course also stresses the connection between policy and practice and the social worker's ability and responsibility to influence social change. Course content also assists students to learn about social movements and about appropriate strategies for affecting change, such as political action and social change strategies. The single assignment for this class is the analysis of an existing or proposed social policy relevant to social work in a rural context by utilizing a theoretical model of policy analysis. In this analysis students are required to identify relevant issues, analyze the effects of the policy on individuals, families, groups, organizations, and communities, and propose alternatives to the policy.

Electives. The elective course taken during this semester presents content either on a specific field of practice, such as child welfare or mental health, or on a method of social work practice such as administration or supervision. The electives taken by MSW students are intended to be supportive of the advanced concentration.

Final semester (field and research). The second advanced semester (spring) of full-time enrollment includes 16 credit hours of course work. Courses taken during this semester are a block field placement, a research practicum, and an elective. The block field placement is 500 hours and includes a 2-hour weekly integrative seminar. A comprehensive integrative paper focused on advanced generalist practice is a major requirement for the field placement and the seminar. Additional discussion of the advanced field placement is in the following section. The research practicum is a course in which students implement and complete the research project begun the previous semester. As part of the requirement for this course students collect data, analyze it, prepare a written report, and present this report at a meeting of faculty and students. The research report focuses on some aspect of advanced generalist social work in a rural context. The third course taken during this semester is an advanced elective. This elective delivers advanced content either on a specific field of practice, such as child welfare or mental health, or it focuses on an advanced method of social work practice such as administration or supervision.

FIELD APPLICATION AND INTEGRATION

The field instruction component of the MSW program at SFASU consists of 980 hours of agency placement. Four hundred eighty of these hours are in the foundation year and are completed as a concurrent placement of 240 hours per semester. In the professional foundation, students are in placement 16 hours (two days) per week and are required to attend a 1-hour weekly integrative seminar. Five hundred hours of field instruction placement are required in the advanced concentration. The concentration placement is in a block of 32 hours per week with a 2-hour weekly integrative seminar.

Since the context for our MSW concentration is rural, students are placed in settings located in small towns, rural areas, or regional centers that serve primarily rural populations. In the foundation placements, students experience working with individuals, families, groups, organizations, and communities. In the first-semester placement more emphasis is placed on working with smaller systems such as individuals, families, and groups. In the second semester emphasis is placed on work with groups, organizations, and communities. This emphasis facilitates integration by coordinating type of experience with the practice and human behavior content that are taken concurrently.

The concentration placement is also rural in design. In the advanced placement, students are also expected to work with all five systems. These students obtain advanced experiences in working with as many of these systems as possible within the context of the agency. The seminal project, which the students are required to complete as part of the integrative seminar, demonstrates the application of advanced rural generalist methodology in the agency setting. Briefly this integrative paper requires students to identify their professional work in the agency with two specific systems, one at the micro level and the other at the macro level. The paper requires content on the ecological systems perspective, diversity and populations at risk, rurality, and advanced intervention—from establishing relationships to termination with both a micro- and macro-level system. Preparing and presenting this paper is a critical part of the curriculum integration process and is considered part of the comprehensive examination required for graduation.

TRIALS AND TRIBULATIONS

Conceptual Issues

While the choice of an advanced generalist practice model and a rural context for practice was relatively straightforward and promising as a way to address the needs of our service region, it was a daunting choice nonetheless. When we began the development of our advanced generalist concentration, neither the concepts of advanced generalist nor rural social work presented themselves in either the literature or in practice as being clearly defined in terms of models that were broadly accepted. Few accredited advanced generalist MSW programs existed, and there were a number of significant differences in how those programs were designed. In addition, there were almost no MSW programs that focused extensively on the rural context of practice we were considering. Therefore our advanced generalist model in a rural context program, while exciting from an innovation and creativity perspective, was challenging to develop.

The first major issue addressed was how to approach the idea of advanced content within the generalist framework. This represented a significant conceptual hurdle, in large part because of the prevailing use of language related to both the concepts of *generalist* and *advanced*. The use of either the generalist method or generalist practice as synonymous with the professional foundation at the baccalaureate level, and to some degree with the foundation of the MSW degree, created the erroneous assumption that generalist might not be an advanced practice method. Furthermore, the common practice of associating *specialization* with advanced practice created an apparent contradiction. If specialized was advanced, and if the method of practice was general, then how could these apparent opposites be reconciled into an advanced social worker who was a specialized generalist?

After much reflection, we rejected the position that generalist and specialist social work were divergent ends of a dichotomy. After examining another profession, medicine, we were able to conclude that advanced interventions and skills were employed within the framework of the "general practitioner" and decided that this held true for social work as well. As a result, we came to view generalist social work as "basic" social work and advanced generalist social work as "advanced" social work. We then understood that specialized or advanced interventions could occur within the context of a generalist method.

Given these assumptions, the common link between generalist practice and advanced generalist practice was the conceptual framework of the generalist method. Where they differed was in terms of the specific intervention methods used within that framework. The advanced generalist would employ more advanced or "specialized" methods, and the generalist would use more "basic" methods. Indeed, the professional activities for the generalist and advanced generalist were not seen as a dichotomy but rather as laying along a continuum. In practice, there were clearly some areas of overlap in which the generalist BSW practitioner would provide services very similar to those of the advanced MSW practitioner.

Faculty Issues

Perhaps the most significant challenge was how to bring the faculty together to reach common agreement about advanced generalist practice. Ours was a new program built on an existing BSW program. To build the program we had to hire not only additional faculty, but also faculty with prior teaching experience in graduate social work. The preparation of the faculty members in this area is a significant issue in developing the advanced generalist curriculum. Many faculty members have no prior exposure even to generalist practice, as many enter the profession with an MSW degree from institutions in which generalist or advanced generalist practice was not a strong element of the curriculum. Additionally, generalist and advanced generalist practice models do not tend to be developed either through doctoral education or graduate teaching experience, where specialization tends to be emphasized. In some respects, faculty members who held a BSW degree and those with undergraduate teaching experience in social work were better prepared conceptually for developing an advanced generalist curriculum. However, they too had to struggle in grappling with "greater breadth and depth" concepts and how that could be defined for the advanced generalist method.

We were able to develop faculty consensus on the advanced generalist method for our program only through frequent faculty meetings that focused on our key curriculum concepts and how to implement them in the curriculum. On average, the faculty met weekly to discuss matters related to the advanced generalist curriculum. While these meetings were sometimes tense and lengthy, ultimately a fairly diverse group of faculty came to a common agreement about how to define and implement the program.

Field Issues

Initially, implementation of the advanced generalist concentration proved difficult to implement in the field. Our agency supervisors were primarily community-based MSWs who had been educated in traditional "specialized" MSW programs and often lacked a strong understanding of generalist practice, especially at the advanced level. Typically these agency instructors were strong in providing advanced experience related to individual and family systems, but were less comfortable in providing group, organizational, and community experiences for students. This was addressed through extensive field instructor training, which both reinforced the generalist method and helped agency instructors to identify appropriate experiences with the larger systems.

OUTCOME ASSESSMENT

The rural advanced generalist program at SFASU has achieved its goal of preparing MSWs to practice in our service region. The placement of our students in social work jobs after graduation has been very successful, in that many students have positions prior to graduation and the typical wait between graduation and employment is only two to three months. The annual focus groups with our field instruction advisory committee indicate that our students are desired as employees by local agencies and that they are prepared for advanced level practice. In addition, exit interviews with graduating students tell us that the MSW program has achieved its objectives in preparing students for advanced level generalist practice in a rural context.

Further data about the preparation of our MSW graduates for practice in our rural service region indicate that an advanced generalist approach was highly appropriate. Surveys of alumni reveal that while most obtain initial employment primarily in direct practice with individuals and families, they move rapidly into working with other systems. Many move into supervisory and administrative positions within one or two years. This rapid movement into administrative and supervisory positions is probably related to the shortage of MSWs (Daley & Avant, 1999), the small size of the agencies, and need to be flexible in addressing the variety of social problems in the region.

Another factor in this job movement is the generalized nature of advanced social work positions in this rural region. Surveys of job responsibilities carried by MSW social workers in our service region indicate that advanced practice is generalist in nature, in that they work with all systems. On average, MSWs report that 60% of their job responsibility lies in working with individuals, and 20% each in working with family, group, organizational, and community systems. Alumni surveys also indicate that our graduates often continue to retain some direct practice responsibility after being placed in administrative and supervisory positions.

Graduates of the MSW program have also been very successful in passing the state licensing examinations, as indicated by their 97% pass rate on the intermediate-level licensing examination during the last three years. Initially the faculty had expressed concerns about the compatibility of our advanced generalist concentration with the state exam, which contains a great deal of direct practice and clinical content. However, given the success of our graduates on the examination such concerns appear to have been groundless. Indeed, the generalist method that is central to our curriculum seems have prepared our students well for state licensure.

GRADUATE SOCIAL WORK EDUCATION AND THE FUTURE OF ADVANCED GENERALIST PRACTICE

Advanced generalist practice holds a great deal of promise as a methodology for preparing advanced level social workers for work in a rural context. Rural social workers tend to work with a broader range of systems and problems than their urban counterparts, in large part because of the size of the rural communities and agencies rural practitioners live and work within. These community-based agencies tend to be smaller than their urban cousins and possess low percentages of advanced level practitioners as employees. Given these factors, highly specialized social work jobs are not very functional for rural agencies, since practitioners who deliver direct services are often needed to fill supervisory and administrative functions. Since preparation in advanced generalist practice produces social workers with advanced level knowledge, skills, and values for working with multiple systems, advanced generalists are more flexible and better able than specialists to respond to the diverse needs of the rural agencies and clients they serve.

The advanced generalist and generalist methods of social work practice are well matched to working with a rural population. Rural people tend to be "traditional" in that they are steeped in the ways of the family and the community. Thus any effective change effort with an individual client must take into account at least three systems: the individual, the family, and the community. Work in a rural environment tends to be much more personalized than work in an urban environment, i.e., the "who" of the person a social worker deals with in a rural community is much more important than the "what" of the person. Multiple systems and their interaction with that person make up the key concept of "who" a person is and must be taken into account to be effective. Even the social agencies and other community organizations are strongly influenced by community traditions and individuals. Therefore, to be effective in rural practice, it is essential for the social worker to have a multiple-system perspective.

Survey data from our region indicates that the nature of advanced practice in our rural service region is, in fact, generalized because MSW social workers tend to work with all five systems on a regular basis. Advanced skills are used with these systems and are not diminished by the fact that at one point the social worker may be using direct intervention skills with an individual and later that day may be using task group and community skills with a community resource planning group. Advanced generalist practice offers excellent preparation for the skills and flexibility needed to engage effectively in this type of practice.

The real challenge ahead for advanced generalist practice is in gaining an understanding of and acceptance for this method of practice within the profession. We have seen a bias in some of our community-based social workers that "generalist," even advanced generalist, is something less than "specialist" social work. This view reflects a lack of understanding of the underpinnings of generalist and advanced generalist methodology and an egocentrism that stems from their own preparation as advanced specialists. While intensive educational efforts on behalf of advanced generalist practice have begun to mitigate this bias, such efforts must continue to gain acceptance of the concept of advanced practice as multisystem.

Our experience is that the advanced generalist practice method is effective in producing productive MSW social workers for rural practice in our region. Our graduates are desirable employees for area agencies and have little difficulty in finding employment. The advanced generalist framework prepares them well for the broad-based job responsibilities that they will find in the social welfare sector. These advanced generalists are prepared to work with multiple systems and have the flexibility to adapt to new responsibilities and opportunities as they emerge, either in their agencies or in their careers. The advanced generalist preparation also has proven effective in preparing graduates for MSW licensure. Undoubtedly we will learn more about the strengths of the advanced generalist method as our graduates move through their social work careers. Clearly, what we have seen to date offers a strong endorsement for the advanced generalist method in social work practice in the rural context.

REFERENCES

Brown, P. (1980). Our rural past: May 11, 1935, the New Deal lights up seven million farms. In H. W. Johnson (Ed.), *Rural Human Services: A book of readings*. Itasca, IL: F. E. Peacock.

Collins, R. (1988). *Theoretical sociology*. Washington, DC: Harcourt Brace Jovanovich.

Daley, M., & Avant, F. (1999). Attracting and retaining professionals for social work practice in rural areas: An example from east Texas. In I. B. Carlton-LaNey, R. L. Edwards, & P. N. Reid (Eds.), *Preserving and strengthening small towns and rural communities* (pp. 335-345). Washington, DC: NASW Press.

Davenport, J., III, & Davenport, J. A. (1998). Rural communities in transition. In L. H. Ginsberg (Ed.), *Social work in rural communities* (pp. 39-54). Alexandria, VA: CSWE.

Gibbs, P., Locke, B. L., & Lohman, R. (1990) A paradigm for the generalist-advanced generalist continuum. *Journal of Social Work Education, (26)*3, 238.

Gil, D. G. (1992). *Unraveling social policy* (5ᵗʰ ed.). Rochester, VT: Schenkman Books.

Ginsberg, L. H. (1998). *Social work in rural communities* (3ʳᵈ ed.). Alexandria, VA: CSWE.

Johnson, L. C. (1989). *Social work practice: A generalist approach* (3rd ed.). Boston: Allyn & Bacon.

Kirst-Ashman, K., & Hull, G. (1993). *Understanding generalist practice*. Chicago: Nelson-Hall.

McDonell, J., Strom-Gottfried, K., & Burton, D. (1998). Behaviorism, social learning, and social exchange theory. In S. P. Robbins, P. Chatterjee, & E. R. Canda, (Eds.) *Contemporary human behavior theory: A critical perspective for social work* (pp. 336-358). Boston: Allyn & Bacon.

McMahon, M. O. (1994). *Advanced generalist practice with an international perspective* (pp. 6-10). Englewood Cliffs, NJ: Prentice-Hall.

McMahon, M. O. (1996). *The general method of social work practice* (3rd Ed., p. 23). Needham Heights, MA: Allyn & Bacon.

McNellie, R. B. (2001). The advanced rural generalist. *The New Social Worker, 8*(1), 17.

Martinez-Brawley, E. E. (2000). *Close to home: Human services and the small community*. Washington, DC: NASW Press.

Schatz, M. S., Jenkins, L. E., & Sheafor, B. W. (1990). Milford redefined: A model of generalist and advanced generalist social work. *Journal of Social Work Education, 26*(3), 217-231.

Southern Regional Education Board (1998). Educational assumptions for rural social work. In L. H. Ginsberg (Ed.), *Social work in rural communities* (pp. 23-26). Alexandria, VA: CSWE.

York, R. O., Denton, R. T., & Moran, J. R. (1998). Rural and urban social work practice: Is there a difference? In L. H. Ginsberg (Ed.), *Social work in rural communities* (pp. 83-97). Alexandria, VA: CSWE.

Chapter 4

Model Four: Louisiana State University

RETHINKING THE LSU INNOVATION

Brij Mohan and Priscilla D. Allen
Louisiana State University

> Foundationalism is an epistemological view which can be adopted by those who suspend judgment on the realist's claim that reality has an intrinsic nature. A foundationalist need only claim that every belief occupies a place in a natural, transcultural, transhistorical order of reasons—an order which eventually leads the inquirer back to one or another "ultimate source of evidence."...Pragmatists object to foundationalism for the same reasons as they object to realism. They think that the question of whether my inquiries trace a natural order of reasons or merely respond to the demands for justification prevalent in my culture, like the question whether the physical world is found or made. One to which the answer can make no practical difference. (Rorty, 1999, p. 151)

"Which moral or political alternative is *objectively* valid?" Richard Rorty answers: "For a Deweyan pragmatist like me, history and anthropology are enough to show that there are no unwobbling pivots, and seeking objectivity is just a matter of getting as much intersubjective agreement as you can manage" (Rorty, 1999, p. 15). He concludes: "The new social hopes which filled the nineteenth century helped them accomplish this transvaluation of traditional philosophical values, and the resulting philosophical pluralism reinforced the sense that a perfected society would make possible ever-proliferating human diversity" (Rorty, 1999, p. 270).

Modern social work—its theory and practice—has evolved from a dualist tradition without resolving its essentialist fixations about human nature and social reality. The advanced generalist practice model is an inadvertent revolt against the fallacies of innate beliefs and assumptions that undergird contemporary professional practice. This chapter is an attempt to unravel the ontology of this quest "without alibi" (Derrida, 2002). The authors postulate certain epistemological formulations, theorize basic tenets, examine the framework of an evolving experiment, and critique the validity of advanced generalist practice as the answer to our current inanity.

THE ONTOLOGY OF SOCIAL GENERALIST PRACTICE

Social practice per se is an unrecognized concept in the social work literature. Our essentialist notions of "practice" constrain the power and mystique of social work as a dynamic professional endeavor committed to social hopes. Extant epistemologies and practicism shaped by the *logos of societas* have nearly atrophied in search of a perfected system that does not exist. The rise and fall of social practice is a monumental event of the twentieth century (Mohan, 2000).

"To date, there are few outcome studies of generalist or advanced generalist practice....As yet there is no single accepted model of generalist social work....Progress toward an accepted model awaits the solution of difficult issues," concluded Pamela S. Landon (1995, 1101-1108). Landon's summary of curricular refinements, research, and evolution of generalist literature offers an amalgamated identity of varied strands that constitute the parasitic-schizophrenic ontology of social work.

We offer a framework to construct a paradigmatic view of an advanced generalist practice model with three a priori postulates (see Figure 4.1):

1. Philosophical of Pragmatic Practice
• The pragmatist theory of truth helps unravel human reality as an "intersubjective matter."[1] • Anti-Platonism validates antiauthoritarian thrust in support of a dialogical social praxis (Mohan, 1992). • The nascent influence of Derrida, Dewey, Foucault, Habermas, Nietzsche, and Wittgenstein on social practice and its advocates (Mohan, 1999, 2002) posits advanced generalist practice in a contextualized epistemic "person-in-environment" whole.
2. Basic Postulates and Formulations
• Advanced generalist practice is a pragmatic adaptation of scientific approaches to social problems. • The crisis of social work calls for a radical transformation. • Advanced generalist practice rests on the basic premises of *unification of social work* (Mohan, 1999).
3. Conceptual-Structural Reorganization
• Conceptual congruence involves reformulation of curriculum designs; • Transformation of existing models of pedagogical delivery systems; and • Reorganization of SW-EPR (social work education, practice, and research) as a system (Mohan, 1988).
[1] "The foundation of Truth is freedom. Thus [people] can choose non-truth. This non-truth is ignorance or lie" (Sartre, 1992, p. 13). See Figures 4.2 and 4.3.

Figure 4.1 Conceptual contours of advanced generalist practice: A holographic view

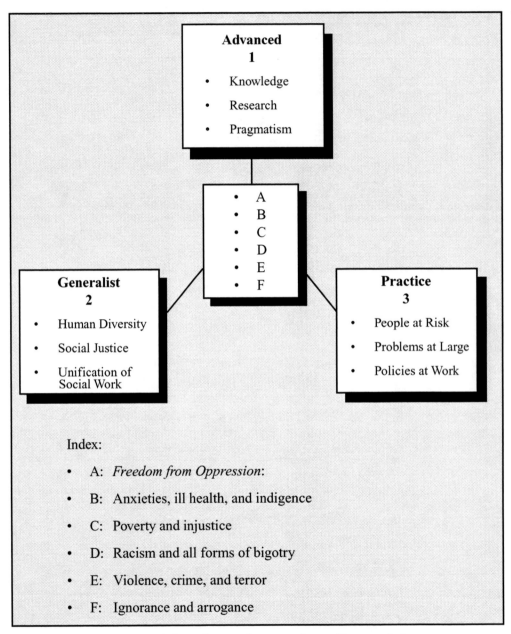

Figure 4.2 Anatomy of the advanced general practice model

Figure 4.2 represents a synthetic view of three essential components of advanced generalist practice: each one is both independent of and interdependent with the other. As a unified construct they assume a new identity and their alchemy reinvigorates a symbiosis that infuses new meanings to the concept of practice. Implicit here is the notion that each of these components *of itself* and *by itself* as an incomplete conceptual tool atrophies in inanity and waste.

At the heart of this conceptualization is the focus of advanced generalist practice on individual and societal problems that cause misery and despair. As premised elsewhere, social work's ideal goal is: *end of itself* (Mohan, 1999; 2000). These problems and conditions dehumanize human beings who suffer perpetually without an enduring solution. Human beings, for example, are not born racists; nor do they deserve poverty because they are "lazy" or "unworthy." Ideologies of social pathology have created a dubious mythology that ought to be deconstructed. We modestly seek that goal through this perspective.

In Figure 4.3, a curriculum design is presented that offers a new perspective on the structure and function of our pedagogical tools and systems of delivery.

The pedagogical automata are viewed as a network of varied curricular linkages holistically reinforcing each other in a uniquely responsive-reflexive problem-solving system. We have included all the elements of existing social work education as required by the Council on Social Work Education (CSWE). However, we have consciously divorced the hierarchical concepts of foundation and specialization. Each of the nine blocks represents a subsystem of a dynamic whole without being dependent on each other. Their lack of interdependence is mutually self-liberatory in the sense that none is exclusive of the other. In other words, the age-old dualism of micro and macro, clinical and nonclinical, is simply nonexistent. Blocks 1, 3, 7, and 9 and blocks 2, 4, 6, and 8 around block 5 depict a confluence of varied curricular strands that enrich pedagogical impact on the learners. The notion of advanced generalist practice (block 5) is a logical culmination of the cumulative cognitive force that the teaching-learning process seeks to impart beyond the existing frameworks of ossified dualism that represent fragments of fractured social realities. If post September 11th depression, for example, is a cause of concern, it is the totality of evil that must be of concern without counterproductive outcomes. Oppressive, insurmountable conditions—loss of job and massive discrimination in the job market—will not only cause individual depression, they will also result in a cultural chaos. It is therefore scientific to look at human failings from a different perspective if age-old problems, such as poverty and discrimination, are to be targeted for good. There is an element of customary wisdom in a "multimethod," "holistic," "unitary" practice perspective that reinvented "social work intervention." But advanced generalist practice must rise above this "generalist" intervention.

1 Human Behavior & Social Environment	2 SOCIAL & ECONOMIC JUSTICE	3 Social Welfare System & Social Policy
4 OPPRESSED POPULATIONS	5 • *Advanced* • *Generalist* • *Practice*	6 FIELD EDUCATION
7 Social Work Practice	8 VALUES & ETHICS	9 Social Practice Research

Confluence of Core and Advanced

[2] The reference to "a new kind of" automata is owed to Stephen Wolfram (2002).

Figure 4.3 A curriculum design for advanced generalist practice pedagogical automata: A new kind of system [2]

Finally, we seek to identify the elements of the model itself. The ABC model (see Figure 4.4) primarily involves a dynamic interface of three basic components: (a) curriculum objectives, design, offerings, and pedagogical approaches; (b) cognitive-behavioral-normative elements that define our knowledge, skills, and values relative to curriculum, and; (c) field education, which helps us transform social reality by the application of curriculum intervention. The combination of all three components results in (d) the focal arena where all elements meld as a unified whole in the process of social transformation (Mohan, 1999).

Of special interest and significance here is our assumption that theory and practice (of social transformation) and organizational contexts are intrinsically intertwined to achieve common objectives. Noble and pious goals, unless attempted through a dialogical, constructive process, will remain rhetorical ideas signifying nothing, unless our tools and modalities are uncorrupt, nondiscriminatory, and universally applicable. The ultimate truth, as Sartre said, is freedom. We question the organizational characteristics and rationale of academic units that are designed to produce graduates. We sincerely doubt if modern social work is a vehicle of human emancipation. Our professional identity and intraprofessional strivings have become dysfunctional (Mohan, 2002). Conceptualization and reorganization of advanced generalist practice is not a panacea; it is a first step toward a new worldview.

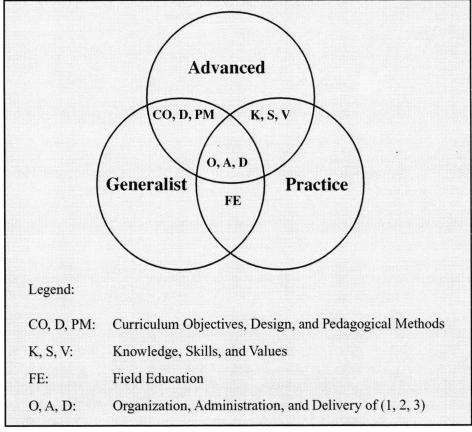

Legend:

CO, D, PM: Curriculum Objectives, Design, and Pedagogical Methods

K, S, V: Knowledge, Skills, and Values

FE: Field Education

O, A, D: Organization, Administration, and Delivery of (1, 2, 3)

Figure 4.4 Elements of the advanced generalist practice model

EVOLUTION OF AN EXPERIMENT: RETHINKING ADVANCED GENERALIST PRACTICE

Rethinking curriculum renewals is difficult, involving a paradoxical sense of accomplishment and frustration. The experiences of faculty and students at Louisiana State University (LSU) are both unique and common. The promulgation and evaluation of a credible system is quite an achievement. Yet, we seem to be at square one in terms of offerings, sequencing, and contents. Before we make some concluding observations, we would like to share our "story" with others in hope to learn more from each other.

Overview: Rationale for an Advanced Generalist Perspective

The LSU model, like that of many other schools, evolved though a fascinating journey with innovative and creative curricular designs. However, its main thrust is a product of the frameworks that were conceptualized in the 1970s and 1980s. While major changes have occurred during five reaffirmation phases, a problem solving, capacity building, empowering model describe current practice. Ecological and systems frameworks are generally employed to unify varied strategic combinations and to address complex and challenging problems.

Thus, the development of LSU's social work practice model goes back to a systems framework integrating both fields and methods. In the eighties, this dualism was pragmatically resolved by consolidating all methods into two direct and indirect practice areas with a "realigned" alternative integrating the basic offerings of the two. Historically, this development marks the beginning of an advanced generalist model, though it was not named as such. During the nineties, these direct/indirect/integrated options were revamped to develop fields of practice in the child welfare and health and mental health areas. The awareness that these two concentrations were not mutually exclusive spurred the development of advanced level courses in both foundation and concentrations. The current advanced generalist practice model is an outcome of this evolutionary process.

Social work as a discipline often diminishes the necessity of borrowing from other sciences, fearing that it weakens, rather than defines, the profession (Mohan, 2002). However, "One of the profession's greatest needs at present is an organizing framework for its knowledge base" (McMahon, 1994). The generalist school of thinking embraces the reality that to be effective, we must include other sciences in our knowledge base, such as psychology, sociology, biology, anthropology, and philosophy. Heavily relying on a liberal arts base, advanced generalist practice allows the student a broad exposure to the science of social work. By its very nature, social work is, and always has been, "generalist" based on the fact that it focuses on placing the person in the environment, addressing issues that range from the individual to the family and the group within both the societal and policy level (Derezotes, 2000; Sheafor & Landon, 1987). Rather than providing clear divisions between the clinical, organizational, administrative, planning, and policy arenas, advanced generalist practice provides a holistic approach, focusing on a multicultural, diverse perspective. It considers how systems, economic forces, and environmental factors work in concert. Areas including values, ethics, social justice, diversity, and multiculturalism are incorporated into the coursework with special emphasis on human oppression. A strong focus lies on a "dialogical approach to diversity and oppression" (Mohan, 1993), "undoing racism," strengths, ecological, and global-comparative perspectives.

Background and Evolution

Established in 1937, the LSU School of Social Work was largely influenced by New Deal legislation, which encouraged states to meet the social reform needs of the time. Located in Baton Rouge, the state's capital, LSU's School of Social Work is one of only four accredited graduate programs within the state With an enrollment of more than 200 students, and 14 full-time, and 12 adjuncts and part-time faculty, the school produces the majority of the state's social workers. The school also houses the Office of Social Service Research and Development, which employs a dozen additional research associates and staff with an annual funding of approximately $1 million.

In 1996, the school accepted its premier doctoral class of 15 students. Since then, the typical number of annual admissions has ranged between two and five students. As of September 2002, LSU has awarded eight Ph.D.s in social work.

Reasons Leading to Change: Competing Issues

Prior to the implementation of the advanced generalist practice model, two concentrations were offered as advanced practice: Families and Children (F&C) and Health and Mental Health (H/MH). The foundation curriculum involved a horizontal sequencing of five content areas: Human Behavior and the Social Environment, Social Policy, Social Work Practice, Social Research, and Generic Field Internship.

Many attribute the genesis of advanced generalist practice at LSU to a 1996 faculty retreat. Nancy Humphreys, the former Dean of the University of Connecticut's School of Social Work, facilitated a session during which a host of issues were discussed, not the least of which was the need for an improved model that better suited the needs of our graduates. Interestingly, the retreat was not developed to introduce advanced generalist practice. The advanced generalist practice model was gaining force in graduate social work programs, and the idea of exposing students to a broad-based model was felt to be an ideal solution to what was described as a disconnect between what the school offered and what the faculty, staff, and community felt was missing in the program. In reviewing earlier self-study documents, it is clear that the school had been heading toward the advanced generalist practice arena for some time.

Once the decision was made, steps toward the implementation of advanced generalist practice were taken with measured caution. It was an active time, presenting programmatic and curriculum changes to the faculty senate, aligning faculty with areas of expertise, restructuring pedagogy, combining and deleting classes, and reshaping curricula themes such as policy, diversity, ethics, research, and social justice, advocacy, macro practice, into the fabric of the program. The former dichotomy of the two concentrations was dramatically altered.

Generalists vs. specialists. In many senses, advanced generalist practice speaks to the reality of what the community needs of its social workers while reshaping the belief of many incoming students that social work is intended primarily to train private practitioners. The irony of many social work programs is that many students expect to become specialized private practitioners in two years, which generalists feel is an impossibility. Advanced generalists believe that true specialization cannot occur within the classroom, but is gained through experience built upon the foundation of a generalist base (Schatz, 2000). Social workers must understand human relationships, environmental, economic, and social influences, and the dynamic interaction between self and client before they enter a clinical relationship. Private practice is an initial goal that many students, through valuable exposure to the reality of social work, find themselves altering. Although clinical training is a critical part of social work, LSU would fail the people of Louisiana and beyond if we failed to produce generalist practitioners first. We have discovered through our own experience that problems arise when we try to develop specialists first, only to learn that a critical prerequisite of skills and knowledge is needed to effectively practice in the larger community. Advanced generalist practice has balanced the mission of the profession with the needs of the community.

Regional market realities. A most important factor when considering a change in curriculum is the student population and the needs of the larger community the students will likely serve. The overwhelming majority of LSU students remain in Louisiana long term, the state is largely rural, and the majority of its social service administrators are trained by LSU. Many alumni have found themselves working in roles of administration, community development, and supervision rather than in direct clinical practice. A primary reason for LSU embracing the advanced generalist model was to better prepare future organizers, supervisors, and leaders to meet the demanding roles within Louisiana.

Integrating and maximizing faculty expertise. The numbers of faculty focusing on clinical and direct practice outnumbered those focusing on research, policy, and indirect practice. With such a modest number of faculty in the school to begin with, the dichotomy between H/MH and F&C was inadequately sustained. Utilizing a multidimensional interplay between the micro-level and mezzo-level courses maximized the resources within the department. The experts in clinical and direct practice, and those specializing in the policy arena, research, organizational behavior, theory, and philosophy offered courses with a mutually inclusive perspective.

Knowledge limitations in the concentration method. With the earlier bifurcated program, students trained in the F&C concentration were often left without a solid background in mental health issues and, similarly, those trained in H/MH were missing critical areas in working with families and children. Students needed across-the-board training as the two are anything but mutually exclusive. Further, both concentrations lacked the fullness of working with organizations and systems, a logical component of social work practice. The distribution between the concentrations was not balanced. At one point there were only 25% in the F&C concentration, with the remaining 75% in the H/MH concentration. The composition was likely based on the students' predilection to choose mental health, thinking they would become private practitioners after graduation. Given that less than half of LSU graduates reported mental health as their primary area of practice in a recent survey, the concentrations were not suited to meet the needs of the larger community. Therefore, the concentrations were too limited in scope, chosen for the wrong reasons, and not reflective of the reality of practice that students would face in Louisiana. As Teigiser (1983) suggests, the generalist practitioner must be trained to utilize a multilevel assessment, considering both individual and environmental factors in concert.

LSU has embraced change and fluidity in its social work program throughout its history. A unique relationship exists between LSU and the outside community, as the community is very invested in the status of the school's social work program. LSU realizes the necessity to respond to the external needs of its state and of the stakeholders. Through reflection regarding the needs of the community, advanced generalist practice made complete sense.

Frameworks and Curriculum Design

The LSU model demonstrates an advanced generalist practice model by layering a complex system of choice, expertise, and problem solving at the foundation level. Course offerings represent this model by use of requisite courses including advanced policy, advanced practice, advanced research, and electives such as family therapy, medical social work, and social work with older persons in which a wide range of analytic techniques within the ecological and systems framework are explored. The curriculum concentrates on the interaction between individuals and social institutions emphasizing dignity, ethical standards and the promotion of individual, organizational, and systemic well being.

The true challenge with any advanced generalist practice model lies in delineating the first- and second-year curriculum, bridging the generalist foundation to the advanced generalist level of practice. It seems LSU adheres to Timberlake, Farber and Sabatino's (2002) principle that generalist practice refers to what social workers *bring* to a problem-solving situation, and advanced generalist practice refers to what social workers *do* as problem solvers. The school works to promote effective problem solvers in the micro, mezzo, and macro arenas by building on an earlier educational career, adding substance to the education through intensive practice, theory, research, and field experiences.

The first 30 credits of the master's program are considered the foundation year. In this first year, students are immersed in social work practice and history, research methods, social policy, human diversity, human behavior in the social environment, and field instruction. The second (or advanced instruction) year consists of courses in advanced direct practice, advanced social policy, advanced indirect practice, and program evaluation. Advanced standing is granted to students who meet the admissions criterion of successfully completing foundation courses in an accredited baccalaureate social work program. This status avoids duplication of coursework. Students supplement the required course electives in the areas of mental health, aging, medical social work, spirituality, and family therapy. In 2001-2002, the school offered three optional emphases: corrections, medical social work, and aging.

Field Linkage to Advanced Generalist Practice

The linkage between field practice and the advanced generalist practice model has undergone an important evolution. Historically, the school offered either foundation or classified internships. This often left students without exposure to the scope of practice necessary within largely rural, poor, and diverse populations. For example, Family Services of Greater Baton Rouge was classified as an F&C agency despite the fact that much of the work was focused on mental health, counseling, and intervention. The natural overlap between health and mental health within children and families was ignored in favor of cleanly classifying placements.

Despite the distinction between placements, to be effective as practitioners students needed training in both direct and indirect practice, policy and planning, diagnosis and assessment, children and families, *and* group and individual counseling. The field office was responding on a regular basis to concerns regarding deficient basic skills in clinical assessment, administrative duties, and basic community organization skills from students, agency supervisors, and faculty liaisons. At the commencement of each placement block, the student, faculty liaison, and agency supervisor evaluate the field experience. Factors include whether the field experience meets the students' needs, fits in the school's philosophy, and fulfills an advanced generalist practice model.

The field office strives to expose students to a variety of populations to mirror the reality that exists in Louisiana. One skill that has been successfully incorporated is moving beyond the students' choices and preferences, thereby broadening their perspective about dealing with a diverse population. The advanced generalist practice model was a solution to provide the skills necessary for meeting the needs of the state's population. With any successful school of social work, the field office provides a critical role directly related to the success of the entire program. The LSU field office is an example of integrating skill between practice and theory in the most practical manner.

All students are interviewed before placement determination. The interview is a critical time, when students' strengths and attitudes are demonstrated. Often students express an initial level of discomfort with the prospect of working with a particular population, such as older persons or the mentally ill. Using this information, and with careful screening and supervision, the field staff expertly incorporates the area into the student's learning. Students are often surprised to find that they enjoyed the experience and possess the skills to work with a population about which they were initially uneasy. Several placements allow exposure to a variety of populations, such as a hospital setting. Discharge planning is described as a classic need for generalist training. The school practices the philosophy that there is a responsibility to prepare students for the variety of clients they will likely encounter. Changing bias among students from reluctance to advocacy is an active part of field and classroom linkage. The field component solidifies the ethical and practical dimension of our profession: serving those most vulnerable, in placements where students are valued, properly supervised, and nurtured as future practitioners.

Application and Integration Between Theory and Practice

McMahon (1994) refers to the advanced generalist methodology as the ways in which the generalist employs techniques to process theories and utilize expertise for indirect and direct practice. Schatz, Jenkins, and Sheafor (1990) indicate students must possess knowledge to "engage in theoretical and practice research and evaluation." LSU's advanced generalist practice model serves to synthesize theory, practice, and research.

The advanced generalist practice model rests on the premise that practice theory and methods can be applied to diverse fields and populations in varied problem-solving processes. This pragmatic application posits social work practice in a dynamic mode to transform social reality in a systemic design with emphasis on integration and synthesis of diverse tools and interventive skills. The school largely utilizes the ecological (person-in-environment) theory (Germain & Gitterman, 1986) and systems theory incorporating a holistic approach.

OUTCOME ASSESSMENT

Outcome assessment is a time-tested tool to demonstrate the evidence of successes and failures. The school continues to rebuild on evidence-based practice outcomes in its quest for improvement and quality without any pretensions and complacence.

The school describes three domains of outcome measurement: (a) outcomes through student evaluation while in the program, (b) outcomes measured once students leave the program, and (c) broader outcomes measured by faculty, field, and community response and through the achievement of research and service in the community (School of Social Work, 1988; CSWE, Vol. 1, p. 12)

Students change, times change, perspectives change. Once preferring the thesis to demonstrate cumulative knowledge, the majority of students in 2002 opted to take the comprehensive exam, a multiple-choice test, to demonstrate their knowledge of social work. Expedience, information revolution, youthful years, and pressure of economic realties tend to encourage a pragmatic attitude toward career goals and choices.

Another method of evaluation is the image of the school through its students. In 2001, Dr. Millar's and Professor Pogue's Advanced Indirect Practice sections received a national award for their contribution to community activism surrounding gun violence—uncritically representing the partnership between direct and indirect methods in complexly overlapping fields while representing the school's success in community organization. The school shares a close relationship with more than 50 field supervisors. Regular monitoring, interaction, and inservicing is offered to routinely monitor the school's goals and objectives as well as the fit between the academy's offerings and the community's needs.

In the spring of 2000, a survey was distributed to collect data based on graduates' perceptions of the school (Grenier, 2002). The overwhelming majority of respondents reported a high level of satisfaction with the School of Social Work utilizing an advanced generalist approach. Advocacy and direct practice were the most common methods used in the students' work roles. Forty-six percent of respondents reported mental health as their primary field of practice, followed by children and youth services (25%), health (24%), geriatrics (14%), and family services (14%). Other categories with lower frequencies included corrections, substance abuse, education, disabled services, women's services, community development, employee assistance, research. and legal services.

It may be noted here how the school faculty established and implements its goals and objectives. Of the seven goals, the second reads: "The School aims to offer second-year concentration emphasizing advanced practice grounded in a generalist framework and building on a clear understanding of social work history and its professional mission" (School of Social Work, 1996, p. 5). It continues as follows (emphasis added):

> The School of Social Work curriculum is a dynamic whole based on the concept of person-in-environment, with an emphasis on contextual realities, empowerment, and social justice. *The two-year program of advanced education offers a solid professional foundation upon which the advanced concentrations are built. The first-year foundation is clustered around five major content areas: Human Behavior and Social Environment, Social Policy, Social Work Practice (both direct and indirect), Social Research and Generic Field Internship.* (School of Social Work, 1996, p. 9)

TRIALS, TRIBULATIONS, AND CONTINUING CONUNDRUMS

The contradictions, continuing dualism, and the resulting conundrums of an evolving advanced generalist model are self-evident in the analysis of the above statements. As we await our upcoming reaffirmation of accreditation in 2004, we feel strong and positive in our ability to demonstrate the efficiency and practicality of the first years of advanced generalist practice at LSU. Years of considered experiences and assessments have reaffirmed our conviction about the falsity of dichotomous concentrations that deal with intrinsically related problems.

Graduate social work education at LSU is at a crossroads. Recently the school's independence was gravely threatened. In the fall of 2002, the university's administration nearly moved the School of Social Work under the College of Education. The proposed change was met with strong opposition by the faculty and larger social work community. Today the school continues to enjoy its status as a free-standing school led independently by a dean (versus a proposed director). Its academic material existence in the university system still remains intact—thanks to the support it enjoys from the community at large. In other words, we must rethink our purpose and mission as a credible member of the academic community as well. No one knows the impact of Sept. 11th on the future of the welfare state that sustains social work's pulse. Threats to the school continue. Louisiana's dependence on oil revenues and the local politics of allocations routinely threatens the university's budgetary provisions. Therefore our institutional demise is only a fiscal crisis away. Should that happen, the university's commitment to academic units not considered central to its mission will vanish. We have gone through this traumatic ritual many times during the last two decades.

Some other allied conditions and forces may affect the future of graduate social work education. A fission between two existing programs (MSW and Ph.D.) may threaten a fledgling doctoral program that is hopelessly underfunded and painfully neglected. This has direct and indirect implications for the master's program. To support one at the expense of the other is both myopic and foolhardy. The authors strongly believe in the symbiotic relationship of the two, which bodes well for the future of an innovative advanced generalist practice model. In a Research- Extensive University, any practice innovation that is well grounded in scholarly rationale will receive generous support. This augurs well for both students and faculty as a whole.

Social work's position in the hierarchy of university departmental units has never been very high. Despite very strong support from the community, we still need a credible, self-sustainable academic base independent of political linkages. A perpetual leadership crisis simply aggravates this situation. An outsider's view of the world of social work is presented below to demonstrate how we are perceived by the scientific community:

> Social work as a profession has not yet established an authentic foundation for its future. Its crisis of legitimacy is an outcome of conceptual bastardization of noble constructs without meaningful commitment to annihilate the forces of oppression....How can delivery of an otherwise noble profession be so alienated from its avowed mission? Social work's mission is egalitarian in nature which must be achieved with a commitment to equality and justice. This should ultimately lead to achieving a fair and just social order. If social work is the torchbearer of freedom and justice, it must be saved from its own trappings. This assertion is premised on the basis of multi-faceted crises that bedevil social work as an academic endeavor. The practitioners who enter academia without adequate research background and intellectual commitment see academic obligations as secondary to their mission. They—by using the politics of race and gender as a tool for power—demean academic pursuits which reduces social work to a second-class citizenship. (Singh, in press)

The future of social justice is the future of social work. The future of advanced generalist practice or its successors depends on the extent to which social work as a discipline is committed to both academic and professional mandates. This is both a general and particularistic observation borne out by hard realities. We believe in what we do. We remain cautiously optimistic about innovations and their outcomes. While advanced generalist practice per se may undergo further transformation—if not demise—we continue to learn with hopes for a better future. If we falter, we will have none to blame but our own cultural trappings.

In closing, it may be said that advanced generalist practice is a quintessential vehicle of social transformation. As such, all-functionalistic flawed frameworks (strength perspective to capacity/evidence-based practice) seem counterproductive at best. To insure humanity's fate in history, we have no choice but to be free of ourselves. Search for truth is a self-purifying human reality. Sartre sums it up best:

> Thus truth is not a logical and universal organization of abstract "truths": it is the totality of Being to the extent that it is manifested as a *there is* in the historialization of human-reality....And Free human-reality must necessarily assume its responsibilities vis-à-vis the truth....The unveiling of truth has stopped for certain societies or people because they perpetually move in the same circle of traditions. (Sartre, 1992, pp. 5, 16, 19)

ACKNOWLEDGMENTS

The authors wish to express their sincere gratitude to Dr. Kristin Gansle, Louisiana State University, for her technical artistry on *Elements of Advanced Generalist Practice Model* and editorial support. We also extend our appreciation to Denise Chaisson-Breaux, Director of Student Services, and Traci Lilley, Director of Field Education, for sharing historical information and constructive comments on earlier versions of this manuscript.

Correspondence concerning this chapter should be addressed to Dr. Brij Mohan, School of Social Work, Louisiana State University, 311 Huey P. Long Fieldhouse, Baton Rouge, Louisiana 70803, (225) 578-1345. Email: swmoha@lsu.edu.

In 1984 the school launched the world's first *Journal of International and Comparative Social Welfare*. It continues to be edited by the authors of this chapter as *New Global Development: JI&CSW* (www.newglobaldevelopment.com).

REFERENCES

Ackerman, F., Goodwin, N. R., Dougherty, L., & Gallagher, K. (Eds.). (2000) *The political economy of inequality.* Washington, DC: Island Press.

Anderson, J. D. (1982). Generic and generalist practice and the BSW curriculum. *Journal of Education for Social Work, 18*(3), 37-47.

Council on Social Work Education. (2001). *Educational policy and accreditation standards.* Alexandria, VA: Author.

Derezotes, D. S. (2000). *Advanced generalist social work practice.* Thousand Oaks, CA: Sage.

Derrida, J. (2002). *Without alibi.* P. Kamuf (Ed. & Trans.). Stanford, CA: Stanford University Press.

Germain, C., & Gitterman, A. (1980). *The life model of social work practice.* New York: Columbia Press.

Grenier, C. (2000). *Social work alumni analysis.* Baton Rouge, LA: LSU School of Social Work.

Landon, P. S. (1995). Generalist and advanced generalist practice. R. L. Edwards (Ed.), *Encyclopedia of social work,* 19th Ed. (Vol. 1, pp. 1101-1108). Washington, DC: NASW Press.

McMahon, M. O. (1994). *Advanced generalist practice with an international perspective.* Englewood Cliffs, NJ: Prentice Hall.

Mohan, B. (1988). *The logic of social welfare: Conjectures and formulation.* New York: St. Martin's Press.

Mohan, B. (1992). *Global development: Post-material values and social praxis.* New York: Praeger.

Mohan, B. (1993). *Eclipse of freedom: The world of oppression.* Westport, CT: Praeger.

Mohan, B. (1999). *Unification of social work: Rethinking social transformation.* Westport, CT: Praeger.

Mohan, B. (2000). The rise and fall of social practice: Epistemologies of change. *International Journal of Contemporary Sociology, 37*(2), 140-157.

Mohan, B. (2002). *Social work revisited.* Philadelphia: Xlibris.

Rorty, R. (1999). *Philosophy and social hope.* New York: Penguin.

Sartre, J.-P. (1989). *Truth and existence* (Adrian van den Hoven, Trans.). Chicago: The University of Chicago Press.

Schatz, M. S. (2000). Colloquium on Advanced Generalist Practice. Kean University, Union, NJ.

Schatz, M. S., Jenkins, L. E., & Sheafor, B. W. (1990). Milford redefined: A model of initial and advanced generalist social work. *Journal of Social Work Education, 3,* 217-230.

Schatz, M. S., & Simon, S. (1999). The portfolio approach for generalist social work practice: A successful tool for students in field education. *The Journal of Baccalaureate Social Work, 5*(1), 99-107.

School of Social Work (1978). *Self study and evaluation report* (Vol. 1, p. 98, submitted by B. J. Wiest). Baton Rouge, LA: Louisiana State University.

School of Social Work (1982). *Self study report: Objectives, curriculum, organization, administration, faculty, students, finances and facilities* (Vol. 1, p. 159, submitted by B. Mohan). Baton Rouge, LA: Louisiana State University.

School of Social Work (1988). *Self study report* (Vol. 1, p. 276, submitted by J. O. Midgley). Baton Rouge, LA: Louisiana State University.

School of Social Work (1996). *Self study of the school of social work* (Vol. 1, p. 174, submitted by K. I. Millar). Baton Rouge, LA: Louisiana State University.

Sheafor, B. W., & Landon, P. S. (1987). Generalist perspective. In A. Minahan et al. (Eds.) *Encyclopedia of social work* (18th ed., pp. 660-669). Silver Springs, MD: National Association of Social Workers.

Singh, Vijay P. (in press). [Review of the book *Social work revisited*]. *Journal of Ethics in Social Services.*

Teigiser, K. S. (1983). Evaluation of education for generalist practice. *Journal of Education for Social Work, 1,* 79-85.

Timberlake, E. M., Farber, M. Z., and Sabatino, C. A. (2002). *The general methodology of social work practice: McMahon's generalist perspective.* Boston: Allyn & Bacon.

Wolfram, S. (2002). *A new kind of a science.* Carbondale, IL: Wolfram Media.

Chapter 5

Model Five: Wichita State University

ADVANCED GENERALIST PRACTICE MODEL

Cathleen A. Lewandowski, Linnea F. GlenMaye, and Brien L. Bolin
Wichita State University

This chapter seeks to describe the advanced generalist practice model developed at Wichita State University, to provide examples of how it can be applied to practice, and to discuss how it can meet the needs of clients in complex, ever-changing service delivery environments. Prior to describing the model itself, we discuss the trends in social work practice, education, and in the social and political environments at both the national and local levels that provide the rationale for developing an advanced generalist approach to practice. This is followed with a description of the model, the perspectives underlying the model, issues in implementing the model, and its application to practice.

RATIONALE FOR AN ADVANCED GENERALIST PERSPECTIVE

The rationale for implementation of an advanced generalist perspective is based on both current trends within the profession, and on trends in local social concerns and community and agency responses to these trends. Professional trends include the ongoing debate on class versus case advocacy, the perceived fluidity of professional boundaries, and the increased emphasis on interdisciplinary practice. Local trends include privatization, agencies that consistently change over time, increased immigration, and economic inequality. Following is a description of these trends, which led the School of Social Work at Wichita State to implement an advanced generalist curriculum as the most appropriate response.

Current Trends in Social Work Practice

In 1998 and 1999, *Social Work* published two special centennial issues that focused on what social work "has meant, what it means, and what it should mean" in the next millennium (Witkin, 1998, p. 483). Though the authors in these issues do not use the term "advanced generalist" in describing what practice should mean, both issues call for a model of practice that reflects the historic commitment of the profession to individual and social change. There are endorsements for a both/and posture toward individual and social change and moving away from an either/or position (Witkin, 1998), the adoption of a guiding vision for a just and civil society (Stuart, 1999), and the idea that people cannot be understood apart from their cultural, political, and social contexts (Witkin, 1998). Witkin (1999) further notes that the social context cannot be taken for granted, as it is dynamic and constantly changing. It is this emphasis on both/and, a commitment to social justice and other core social work values, and an incorporation of the changing context of human relationships that characterizes Wichita State's advanced generalist model. We are in agreement with the viewpoint of Karen Haynes (1998) who states that "to do social work and to be a social worker requires commitment both to the goals of social justice as well as to the goal of healing individual pain" (p. 509). And, we believe that the advanced generalist model as developed at Wichita State prepares practitioners to meet the practice challenges of this new millennium.

Regardless of their approach, several authors in the centennial issues of *Social Work* call for a more unified approach to practice that undoes the false division between micro and macro practice (Abramovitz, 1998); that promotes exchange of integrative psychosocial, economic, occupational, employment, and enfranchisement practices (Briar-Lawson & Lawson, 1998); that recognizes the dual focus on person and environment (Stuart, 1999); and which honors the unique calling of social work that does not allow unidimensional or comfortable thinking (Schneider & Netting, 1999, p. 356). The Wichita State model and other advanced generalist models provide a holistic perspective that addresses these concerns. The concerns or issues raised include the need to be focused on both case and class advocacy (Haynes, 1998), the recognition of the interactive, interdependent relationship the profession has with society requiring a more fluid professional boundary (Gibelman, 1999), and the need for a dual focus on the person and the environment (Stuart).

Case Versus Class Advocacy

The case versus class advocacy debate within the profession is perhaps as old as the profession itself (Specht & Courtney, 1994). This debate has taken many forms. Should social work be practiced in agencies or can social workers practice independently? Is practice with individuals as valid as practice with communities? Should social work seek to address individual dysfunction and problems or work to change the conditions that created the problem? An either/or approach to practice requires practitioners to choose one side of each of these questions, abandoning the other as inauthentic practice.

In examining this debate, Haynes (1998) suggests that rather than either/or choices, social work needs to recognize that there is a place for both case and class advocacy, for social justice as well as individual concerns. The advanced generalist model seeks to bridge the historical divide by offering a practice perspective that allows social workers to hold both case and class advocacy in equal regard, and to consider them both in all practice settings.

Fluid Professional Boundaries

An advanced generalist practice perspective "fits" with a social work practice perspective that views professional boundaries as fluid and that holds an appreciation for the interdependence of social work and its larger professional environment. Gibelman (1999) explains that while social work has sought to define itself, the profession has been influenced by the sociopolitical environment that helps to define what is considered social work practice at any point in time. Consequently, professional boundaries have remained rather fluid, which in fact is one of social work's strengths, allowing it to flourish and to become an increasingly diverse and, therefore, complex profession. Because of the interdependent and broad-ranging interaction with many disciplines and professional contexts, social work practice requires a perspective that is solid, yet flexible, allowing for change over time without losing track of direction or of the profession's core values and commitments. As will be described later, the advanced generalist practice perspective allows for such flexibility, precisely because it is grounded in the core values of social justice, respect and appreciation for diversity, and empowerment (being more a perspective than a technique).

Finally, Stuart (1999) argues for the continued person and environment emphasis, an idea that has been consistently present in social work's history. Briar (1981) pointed out that the person-environment focus has been part of social work's conceptual framework since its beginnings and suggested that social workers want to perceive the person-interacting-with-environment as a whole, without an arbitrary division between person and environment. In keeping with this long-standing perspective, Stuart identified several trends that call for a continued dual focus on both the person and the environment, holding them both in view without losing sight of the other. Such trends include the devolution of federal programs, increased privatization and managed care, negative attitudes toward government and public assistance recipients, globalization, increased immigration, and the continued persistence of social and economic inequalities that negatively affect minorities, women, children, the disabled, the elderly, and other vulnerable groups (Stuart). None of these trends can be effectively addressed without examining the "whole," as Briar suggested, since the profession's core values and commitments require that we seek to address social concerns while caring for and empowering those that are most affected by those concerns. Again, as will be described in the next section, the advanced generalist practice perspective is a holistic perspective that provides the framework needed for practitioners to take stock of the "whole" person and the environment in all practice contexts.

The Trend Toward Interdisciplinary Practice

The increased emphasis on interdisciplinary practice within social work is one example of a way that policies and trends influence the way practitioners conduct their practice. The trend toward interdisciplinary practice is emerging in response to persistent, newly emerging, and complex issues. As we move into the new millennium, the complexity of this era's social problems requires collaborative practice strategies that draw upon the expertise of other disciplines (Corney, 1995; Elwyn, Rapport, & Kinnersley, 1998; Franklin & Streeter, 1995; Kinder & Cashman, 1998; Mitchell, Harvey, & Rolls, 1998; Pohl, 1998; Smith & Stowitschek, 1998) and the input of multiple social service agencies (O'Brien, 1998). Interdisciplinary collaboration integrating multiple knowledge and practice bases is a key component of efforts to improve the quality of interventions (Marett, Gibbons, Memmott, Bott, & Duke, 1998). Today's practitioners need skills in the dynamics and structure of team-based, collaborative services to provide effective interventions in the current practice reality (Lewandowski & GlenMaye, 2002).

Because of their emphasis on both/and, social workers with an advanced generalist perspective are prepared to move into an interdisciplinary, collaborative practice environment, as this perspective allows for the incorporation of new ways of practicing without losing a sense of professional identity. Further, as is explained below, the model proposes a nonlinear approach to intervention, which allows practitioners to appreciate and work with the complexity of any given practice context.

Local Trends

The trends identified at the national level were also seen at the local level in the community needs assessment undertaken before implementation of the school's advanced generalist program. These trends include the transforming of agency boundaries, the impact of privatization, increased immigration, and economic inequalities. Just as the profession's boundaries are fluid, local agency boundaries are also fluid. This fluidity is evidenced by the fact that most of the agencies participating in the needs assessment survey indicated that both the type of services they offered and the structure of the agency are undergoing rapid change. Within the last 10 years, many agencies reported that they had changed the population of clients served, the services provided, and/or had undergone a major organizational shift. For example, several agencies participating in the needs assessment were less than 10 years old, having come into being as a result of new funding opportunities or reorganization of a previous agency.

Within this context of organizational change, the onset of privatization in state social services has further increased the extent of organizational change, as agencies shift to meet contractual requirements and restructure to survive (or attempt to survive) the financial pitfalls of contracted services. In Kansas, some agencies faced bankruptcy after being contractual providers for only a few years.

The needs of diverse groups are unevenly met in this changing service environment. Ethnic and racial minorities, the poor, the elderly, and the young are the most vulnerable to difficulties arising out of economic and social change. In Wichita, as in many communities, there is an unequal distribution of goods and services, and discrimination and oppression contributes to these inequalities.

Two primary goals of advanced generalist practice are to empower individuals and communities and to foster social justice. Such goals cannot be accomplished without culturally competent practice, since such cultural competence lays the groundwork for empowerment-based practice to foster social justice. Empowerment-based practice seeks to increase personal and political power so that people can take action to improve their life situations (Gutierrez, GlenMaye, & DeLois, 1995). This definition carries the implication that the advanced generalist practitioner seeks to effect change at all levels. Though distinct in many ways, cultural competency, empowerment, and social justice are mutually supportive and interrelated dimensions of practice. The concept of multidimensionality provides a framework for appreciating the interrelated dimensions of these core social work values. As explained in the following paragraphs, the advanced generalist practice model is able to address these national, local, and values issues and to serve the profession in the new millennium of service and practice.

IMPLEMENTATION

The decision to implement an advanced generalist model was made after faculty reviewed data from the community needs assessment. As described previously, community trends in the growth of social problems and the evolution of the practice community called for a perspective of practice that could encompass the complexity of micro and macro practice concerns within a practice community that was constantly changing. The faculty agreed that basing the MSW curriculum on a more narrow specialization would ill-prepare graduates for a complex and unpredictable practice environment. For example, no one could have predicted the vast and far-ranging impact of managed care and privatization on social work service provision. In a climate of complexity and uncertainty students need to learn how to think, how to process information, and how to make ethical decisions within complex practice situations. The faculty determined that an advanced generalist perspective could best meet these educational objectives. Prior to fully developing the curriculum, faculty organized a colloquium for social work practitioners and agency administrators to get their feedback on the proposed advanced generalist model. Practitioners and administrators who attended were in complete support of the development of the advanced generalist model.

There has been little dissension or disagreement with the model among faculty or within the local practice community. Perhaps one reason for the consensus is that the model does not require anyone to make either/or choices about what constitutes social work practice. More importantly, however, the model addresses the emerging needs of the community, within the context of dynamic change. In the following sections, the Wichita State model of advanced generalist practice will be delineated.

OVERVIEW OF THE MODEL

The advanced generalist practice model at Wichita State can be illustrated as a three-dimensional cube, with the sides being defined by the levels of social work practice, the practice process, and the three thematic values of cultural competency, empowerment, and social justice (Figure 5.1). Social work processes include assessment, intervention, and evaluation. Cultural competency, empowerment, and social justice, the program themes, are the third face of the cube. As shown in Figure 5.1, these dimensions are interdependent and simultaneously present, forming equal sides to the cube.

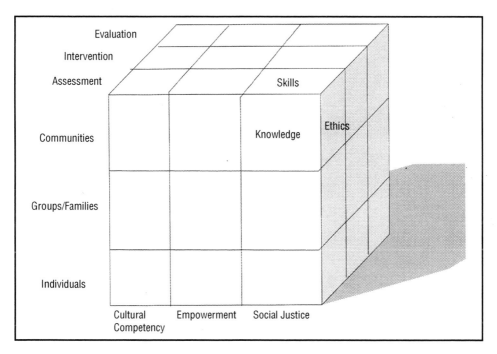

Figure 5.1 Multi-Dimensional Building Blocks of Advanced Generalist Practice

Within this whole cube are 27 smaller cubes, each of which represents the knowledge, values, and skills needed to practice within that area of practice. An example of one of the cubes is found in Figure 5.2. Here, a cube has been unfolded to show its six sides: three are the dimensions of practice (process, level, theme), and the other three are the knowledge, skills, and professional ethics needed for practice within that domain. The model presents a holistic and nonlinear approach to practice where the dimensions, created within each of the smaller "cubes" within the model, are not independent, nor are they separate from the other. The perspective encourages practitioners to view these dimensions as interrelated, and to foster a multidimensional, nonlinear perspective of practice.

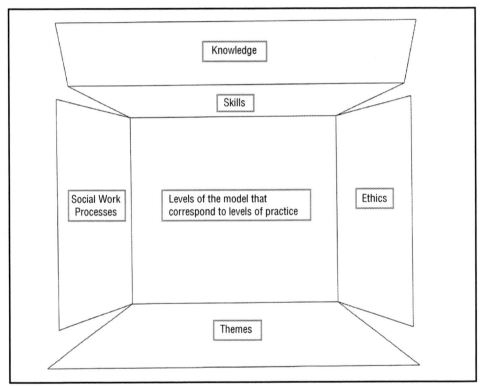

Figure 5.2 An Expanded Cube

Multidimensionality

This advanced generalist model is fundamentally multidimensional in perspective. The multidimensional perspective means that the advanced generalist social worker must be able to appreciate that change occurs at multiple levels simultaneously and that a change in one system affects change in others. This multidimensional perspective suggests that change and human interactions occur in and affect several levels simultaneously.

Within an individual, the levels consist of the multiple levels of development and function, including biological, social, psychological, and spiritual development (Towle, 1957). As individuals interact with their environment, multiple levels include the variety of levels of social organization, such as family, groups, and organizations. Rather than assuming an either/or linear approach, the multidimensional perspective suggests a both/and approach to understanding human interactions. As described by Derezotes (2000), a change in one level affects other levels simultaneously. From a multidimensional perspective, a change in the community effects a change in individuals within that community. Similarly, individual change has an effect on the community. At the micro level, individuals who improve their physical development will simultaneously affect other areas of functioning.

Carroll (1977) described a three-dimensional model of practice that sought to bridge the divide between debates over whether practice should be organized by methods or field of practice and to provide a rationale for social work specializations. In Carroll's model, the domain of practice is delineated by the convergence of social problems, social units of concern, and social technologies. Social problems represent the primary concerns that are usually addressed in social work, such as drug abuse, mental illness, and child abuse and neglect; social units range from the individual to society; and social technologies include casework, group work, supervision, research, and social planning. In this model, each dimension can be selected and reassembled to form a social work practice specialization. For example, "a specialization in community mental health would include mental illness from the social problem dimension, community from the social unit dimension, and community organization from the social technology dimension" (Carroll, p. 431). Thus, rather than providing a unifying framework for the profession, the model sought to provide a rationale for diversification through development of sub-fields of practice, or specialties.

In contrast to providing a rationale for a variety of distinctive specializations, our model provides a perspective on practice that encompasses the breadth of practice and provides a holistic view of its many dimensions. The advanced generalist practice model encourages the practitioner to understand that any given practice context may require them to intervene at a variety of levels and to apply a wide array of skills. The model is not to be viewed as encompassing discrete practice dimensions that are specialties in and of themselves. Rather, our advanced generalist model proposes a perspective of practice that is common to all social work intervention, regardless of the level or target of intervention. The specific skills, or technologies, required for intervention are identified within each of the cubes that are formed by the intersection of a given level, process, and theme, but the practitioner brings the wholeness of the advanced generalist perspective to each practice situation. Most importantly, the model argues that values and ethics, along with social work's core commitments, are inextricably connected to social work knowledge and skills, and are present in any given practice situation, regardless of the extent to which the practitioner is conscious of the value implications of the chosen intervention.

Levels of the Practice

The dimension describing levels of practice includes the levels of individual, group/ family, and community/organization. These levels appear to correspond to micro, mezzo, and macro levels of social work practice. The key difference from traditional understanding, though, is that this model encourages practitioners to view the micro and macro dimension of practice in a nonlinear manner. By this we mean that micro, or individual concerns, are present in any macro practice context, and macro, or larger system concerns, are present in any micro practice context. Because of the interrelatedness of systems, intervention with larger systems, such as a community, simultaneously impacts smaller systems, such as individuals and families. The key concept in this understanding is in the term *simultaneous*. When a social worker engages in practice at any level, the impact of this engagement is not sequential, but is for all practical purposes simultaneous, because individuals are embedded within a complex web of social interactions.

In contrast, a linear model would portray these interactions as sequential and predictable, capable of being understood through mechanistic, cause/effect typologies. We are suggesting that change is sudden and unpredictable. When the individual changes, the family changes as well. Further, social work practitioners are part of the multidimensionality and simultaneity of interaction within systems and levels. They become a part of the system in which they interact. They must assess and intervene on multiple levels, keeping the "whole" picture in view, and with awareness of their own impact on systems, whether at the micro, mezzo, or macro level.

Social Work Processes

The social work processes included in this model reflect the three phases of the problem-solving process of assessment, intervention, and evaluation (Compton & Galloway, 1989). Social work's problem-solving model reflects Dewey's (1933) rational problem-solving model. The steps in this model are: deciding on a problem, gathering information about the problem, generating alternative solutions, comparing alternatives, selecting the best solution, developing a strategy or plan of intervention, implementing the solution, and evaluating the results (Brueggemann, 2002). Compton and Galloway (1989) describe this problem-solving model as a spiral process, to suggest that the process does not necessarily move in clearly defined ways. They also suggest that assessment continues from the initial contact to termination. Though the process is not strictly linear, Compton and Gallaway present each step as its own entity, so that the social worker is doing assessment, intervention, or evaluation.

In contrast, this model draws upon phenomenology to explain the relationship between the stages in social work's problem-solving model and how we can understand our clients' experiences of the intervention. According to phenomenology (Ellenberger, 1958), (a) one attempts to use an absolutely unbiased approach to the understanding of self and others, and (b) phenomena are observed only as they manifest themselves, and this would include our observations of a client's perceptions of the "flow" of the intervention. To accomplish this observation, the observer puts the "world in brackets." By doing this, the observer (in this case the social worker) excludes judgment from her mind, to exclude making any value judgment about the phenomena, about cause and effect, subject and object, and even whether the object and subject actually exist. In this way, observation is enhanced and previously unnoticed structures of phenomena may become apparent (Ellenberger, p. 96). In advanced generalist practice, this means refraining from making any predisposed judgments about the intervention, plan for what should be done, the causes of the client's situation, and the existence of the situation. By avoiding all prejudgments, the social worker can more readily observe what actually occurs during the interaction with clients.

Phenomenology's description of time as a multidimensional subjective experience is also helpful in understanding the relationship between stages in social work intervention. According to phenomenology, the concept of time has at least two attributes: duration and simultaneity. Duration is for some, the stuff of reality, as it is a way of perceiving and measuring existence. Simultaneity, however, is the acknowledgement that each moment, or instant, can contain several events at the same "time" (Ellenberger, 1958). Thus, each instant is situated at the intersection of duration and simultaneity. The assumption is that individuals have their own way of experiencing time, or the intersection of duration and simultaneity, and that it is the total of these experiences that sheds light on understanding of the inner world. According to Ellenberger (p. 103), the most subjective experience of time is the "flowing of life experienced as a spontaneous, living energy." Time is experienced as flowing with a certain speed, and individuals may begin to feel less certain about their place in the world when time seems to be either slowing down or speeding up.

When applying these concepts to advanced generalist practice, all stages of the process are present in any given moment of interaction as past and future interactions are part of the present interaction. For example, the social worker and client consider assessment and anticipate evaluation while engaged in the intervention. Thus, the process itself is multidimensional. Because the social worker and client each have a unique, subjective experience of the interaction, the social worker's goal is to seek understanding of the client's experience, without any predisposing views or judgments. The worker seeks to understand the client's experience of the "flow" of the social work process. Such an unbiased perspective is supported by cultural competency, social justice, and empowerment.

Program Themes

Cultural competency. Cultural competency includes the acquisition of the awareness, knowledge, sensitivity, and practice skills necessary to effectively understand and address the cultural/racial/ethnic worldviews, strengths, issues, and needs of diverse populations. The ultimate goal in the development of cultural competency is to actively utilize the appropriate practice methods that foster enhanced cultural identity and cultural/racial/ethnic empowerment.

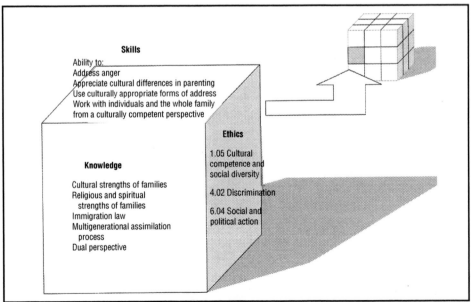

Skills
Ability to:
Address anger
Appreciate cultural differences in parenting
Use culturally appropriate forms of address
Work with individuals and the whole family
from a culturally competent perspective

Ethics
1.05 Cultural competence and social diversity
4.02 Discrimination
6.04 Social and political action

Knowledge
Cultural strengths of families
Religious and spiritual
  strengths of families
Immigration law
Multigenerational assimilation
  process
Dual perspective

Figure 5.3 Cultural Competency with Families

The literature in the human services contains many terms for cultural competency, including multiculturalism, cultural literacy, cultural sensitivity, ethnic sensitivity, cultural awareness, and interculturalism, (Cohen, 1992; Devore & Schlesinger, 1999; Gutierrez & Lewis, 1999; Hirsch, 1987; Sue et al., 1998). Whatever the term, cultural competency calls for an acquisition of the awareness, knowledge, sensitivity, and practice skills necessary to effectively work with diverse individuals, groups, and communities.

Social justice. To be just means to treat all people fairly. In its most basic meaning, social justice refers to equal rights, opportunities, protection, and treatment under the law for all people. Social justice is linked to advocacy and efforts to ameliorate and eliminate discrimination and oppression, and must include substantive forms of equality. These efforts are often put into the context of macro-level advocacy. However, Pelton (2001) contends that justice "should properly be considered on an individual level; just actions respect the dignity and worth of each and every individual" (p. 433).

From an advanced generalist perspective, social justice is a part of every social work interaction. As Swenson (1998) states, "social justice is increasingly described as the organizing value of social work" (p. 527). Figure 5.4 illustrates the knowledge, values, and skills social workers bring to a situation for socially just evaluation processes with clients.

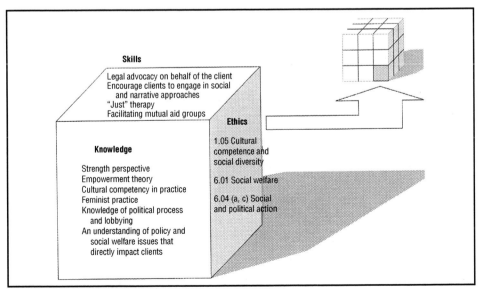

Figure 5.4 Social Justice with Individuals

Empowerment. Empowerment is a concept that may be defined in a variety of ways and that reflects a variety of perspectives and practices, describing both the process and outcome of gaining power over one's own life and actions (Gutierrez & Lewis, 1999; Payne, 1997). Empowerment includes and refers to personal, inter-personal, and political power (Gutierrez, DeLois, & GlenMaye, 1995). Empowerment practice is participatory with shared power and active involvement of clients in the change process (Gutierrez, GlenMaye, & DeLois, 1995). Figure 5.5 provides an example of the knowledge, values, and skills a social worker may bring to an intervention for empowerment-based assessment with clients.

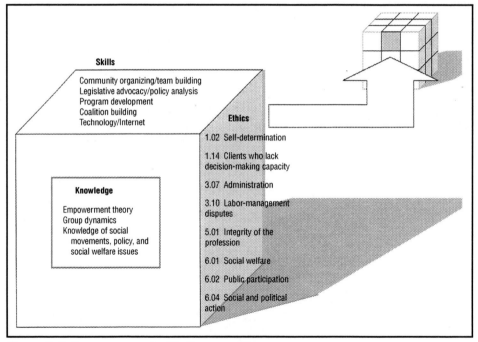

Figure 5.5 Empowerment with Communities

The Heuristics of Advanced Generalist Practice

Social work students come to understand the advanced generalist model through a heuristic process of learning, doing, and reflecting on their experiences. Heuristics is based on the assumption that the experience of the world is always a uniquely individual experience of the world, a notion put forth by Husserl, the founder of phenomenology (Lewin, 1992, p. 144). Consequently, there is no privileged reality and no way to include all relevant information in the process of data collection and analysis (Heineman Pieper, Tyson, & Heineman Pieper (2002). Heuristics challenges the knower, or the one who would seek knowledge, to continually examine one's own assumptions, biases, and prejudices at each step of the process.

When applied to learning, heuristics is an educational method where learning takes place through discoveries that result from investigations made by the student. Students learn a process as well as a model when learning the advanced generalist model. In addition to content, students are presented with a way of viewing practice that allows them to think critically about themselves as practitioners in relationship with clients. They learn to examine their own assumptions and biases on an ongoing basis. In the process of grasping the multidimensionality of the model, students can begin to appreciate the full complexity of practice and can become more comfortable in partnering with clients and other professionals as the process unfolds. As they come to understand that with complexity comes a degree of unpredictability in outcomes, they can more readily empower clients to create their own definition of a socially just outcome. These experiences are shaped by both the workers' and the clients' cultural, political, and social contexts. Through this heuristic process of learning, students come to understand that professional knowledge, including this model, is one way of knowing among many. Thus, they should constantly seek to reassess their skills and evaluate their practice.

Field Practicum

As in most social work education programs, students' classroom learning is applied and integrated in their field practicum courses. The advanced generalist model (Figure 5.1) is used to organize the competencies for the advanced generalist concentration so that students and their field instructors can plan the field practicum educational experience to develop these stated skills. Field practicum approaches the model from the inside; that is, it focuses on the advanced generalist knowledge, values, and skills needed for that practice setting, as illustrated by the expanded cube in Figure 5.2. Field practicum competencies are first organized into the three broad areas of advanced generalist knowledge, values and ethics, and skills. Within each of these areas, competencies relevant to empowerment, social justice, cultural competency, and multidimensionality are listed. For example, one multidimensional competency is to develop skill in applying an integrative theoretical perspective to diverse client systems across multiple settings. For cultural competency, one of the competencies is to integrate and apply culturally competent knowledge, sensitivity, and skills to develop a positive working rapport with clients across cultures.

Training for field instructors is another critical component in implementation, since most of them are unfamiliar with advanced generalist practice. During field instructor training, field instructors are asked to identify critical tasks that they perform as social workers in their work setting. Once these tasks are listed, they are compared with the advanced generalist field practicum competencies that guide the advanced generalist field practicum experience. Through this process, field instructors are able to see that much of what they are currently doing as practitioners coincides with the practice competencies established as goals for the advanced generalist field practicum. Regardless of their education or previous specialized trainings, most field instructors agree that the work environment calls for the ability to address complex situations from a broad, multidimensional perspective.

Outcome Assessment

One of the most significant methods for evaluating the skills students have developed in applying the advanced generalist perspective is through the final integrative project that students complete during their last semester. As with other aspects of the model, the Advanced Generalist Integrative Project is both process and outcome, as the goal is for students to develop advanced generalist skills while engaged in the process of ongoing critical thinking and reflection, assessment, and evaluation. Some of the key learning objectives of the Integrative Paper are to:

1. differentially apply advanced generalist skills with complex systems;
2. develop and apply contextualized interventions using a multiple systems framework;
3. analyze and incorporate values and ethics in ambiguous and complex interventive situations; and
4. integrate, synthesize, and apply theories of practice that maximize empowerment, social justice, and cultural competency.

The project includes three major components that are completed as part of the course assignments in the three required courses of the final semester: practice, research, and practicum. The Integrative Project includes a client assessment, a literature review of practice interventions, and an intervention plan that incorporates the advanced generalist perspective. In the research component, the student designs and conducts a practicum-based research study in an area of practice and program evaluation relevant to the issues addressed in the practice section. Recommendations for practice and policy change proceed from the research findings and are presented in practicum seminar.

This project is then presented at the Advanced Generalist Colloquium, held on the last day of classes at the end of the semester. All MSW students, BSW students, and field practicum instructors are invited to attend. In their presentations, students describe how they have synthesized coursework into their own advanced generalist practice perspective and applied it to their client population of interest.

Through the ongoing dialogue that occurs during the presentations, students, faculty, and practitioners have been able to further the development of the advanced generalist perspective. The faculty have incorporated knowledge from the evaluation of students' Integrative Projects and the feedback from the colloquium into planning and developing the curriculum for the upcoming year. Thus, development of the advanced generalist perspective is a dynamic, evolving, and mirroring process like that described in complexity theory and the heuristic process of learning.

THE FUTURE OF ADVANCED GENERALIST PRACTICE

This chapter described the advanced generalist model as complex and multidimensional, incorporating the dimensions of levels and processes of practice and the themes of cultural competency, social justice, and empowerment. We discussed the trends in social work practice, education, and in the social and political environments at both the national and local levels that provide the rationale for implementing an advanced generalist model. We discussed how the advanced generalist model can meet the needs of a practice environment that is complex, dynamic, and constantly changing in unpredictable ways. Finally, we described the heuristics of advanced generalist practice and discussed some implementation issues.

In conclusion, this chapter is meant to further discussion of the advanced generalist model. We sought to articulate our present understanding of the learning and doing of advanced generalist practice which, by definition, will continue to develop and change.

REFERENCES

Abramovitz, M. (1998). Social work and social reform: An arena of struggle. *Social Work, 43*(6), 512-526.

Briar, S. (1981). Needed: A simple definition of social work. *Social Work, 26*(1), 83-84.

Briar-Lawson, K., & Lawson, H. A. (1998). Collaboration and integrated community-based strategies on behalf of individuals and families. In S. J. Jones & J. L. Zlotnik (Eds.), *Preparing helping professionals to meet community needs* (pp. 111-125). Alexandria, VA: Council on Social Work Education.

Brueggemann, W. G. (2002). *The practice of macro social work* (2nd ed.). Belmont, CA: Wadsworth.

Carroll, N. K. (1977). Three-dimensional model of social work practice. *Social Work, 22*(5), 428-432.

Cohen, N. A. (1992). *Child welfare: A multicultural perspective*. Boston: Allyn & Bacon.

Compton, B. R., & Gallaway, B. (1989). *Social work processes* (4th ed.). Belmont, CA: Wadsworth.

Corney, R. (1995). Mental health services. In P. Owens, J. Carrier, & J. Horder (Eds.) *Interprofessional issues in community and primary health care*. London: MacMillan.

Derezotes, D. S. (2000). *Advanced generalist social work practice*. Thousand Oaks, CA: Sage.

Devore, W., & Schlesinger, E. G. (1999). Ethnic-sensitive social work practice (5th ed.). Boston: Allyn & Bacon.

Dewey, J. (1933). *How we think: A restatement of the relation of reflective thinking to the educative process*. Boston: Heath.

Ellenberger, H. F. (1958). A clinical introduction to psychiatric phenomenology and existential analysis. In R. May, E. Angel, & H. F. Ellenberger (Eds.), *Existence* (pp. 92-126). New York: Simon and Schuster.

Elwyn, G. J., Rapport, F., & Kinnersley, P. (1998). Primary health care teams re-engineered. *Journal of Interprofessional Care, 12*(2), 189-198.

Franklin, C., & Streeter, C. L. (1995). School reform: Linking public schools with human services. *Social Work, 40*(6), 773-782.

Gibelman, M. (1999). The search for identity: Defining social work—past, present, future. *Social Work, 44*(4), 298-310.

Gutierrez, L. M., DeLois, K. A., & GlenMaye, L. (1995). Understanding empowerment practice: Building on practitioner based knowledge. *Families in Society: The Journal of Contemporary Human Services, 76*(9), 534-542.

Gutierrez, L. M., GlenMaye, L. F., & DeLois, K. A. (1995). The organizational context of empowerment practice: Implications for social work administration. *Social Work, 40*(2), 249-258.

Gutierrez, L. M., & Lewis, E. A. (1999). *Empowering women of color.* New York: Columbia University Press.

Haynes, K. S. (1998). The one hundred-year debate: Social reform versus individual treatment. *Social Work 43*(6), 501-511.

Heineman Pieper, J., Tyson, K., & Heineman Pieper, M. (2002). Doing good science without sacrificing good values: Why the heuristic paradigm is the best choice for social work. *Families in Society: The Journal of Contemporary Human Services, 83*(1), 15-28.

Hirsch, E. D. (1987). *Cultural literacy: What every American needs to know.* Boston: Houghton Mifflin.

Kinder, G. L. & Cashman, S. B. (1998). Community oriented definition of the health workforce and core competencies. *Journal of Interprofessional Care, 12*(2), 141-155.

Lewandowski, C. A., & GlenMaye, L. F. (2002). Teams in child welfare settings: Interprofessional and collaborative processes. *Families in Society: The Journal of Contemporary Human Services, 83*(3), 245-256.

Lewin, R. (1992). *Complexity: Life at the edge of chaos.* New York: Macmillan.

Marett, K. M., Gibbons, W. E., Memmott, R. J., Bott, R. L., & Duke, L. (1998). The organizational role of clinical practice models in interdisciplinary collaborative practice. *Clinical Social Work Journal, 26*(2), 217-225.

Mitchell, L., Harvey, T., & Rolls, L. (1998). Interprofessional standards for the care sector: History and challenges. *Journal of Interprofessional Care, 12*(2), 157-168.

National Association of Social Workers (1999). Code of Ethics of the National Association of Social Workers. Washington, DC: Author.

O'Brien, K. A. (1998). Interagency collaboration and coordination: Implications for professional development. In S. J. Jones & J. L. Zlotnik (Eds.), *Preparing helping professionals to meet community needs* (pp. 111-125). Alexandria, VA: Council on Social Work Education.

Payne, M. (1997). *Modern social work theory* (2nd ed.). Chicago: Lyceum Press.

Pelton, L. H. (2001). Social justice and social work. *Journal of Social Work Education, 37*(3), 433-444.

Pohl, H. (1998). Rural health care: A challenge for academic medical centers. In S. J. Jones & J. L. Zlotnik (Eds.), *Preparing helping professionals to meet community needs* (pp. 35-44). Alexandria, VA: Council on Social Work Education.

Schneider, R. L., & Netting, F. N. (1999). Influencing social policy in a time of devolution: Upholding social work's great tradition. *Social Work, 44*(4), 349-358.

Smith, A. J., & Stowitschek, J. J. (1998). School-based interprofessional case management: A literature-based rationale and a practitioner-molded model. *Preventing School Failure, 42*(2), 61-65.

Specht, H., & Courtney, M. (1994). *Unfaithful angels: How social work has abandoned its mission*. New York: The Free Press.

Stuart, P. H. (1999). Linking clients and policy: Social work's distinctive contribution. *Social Work, 44*(4), 335-348.

Sue, D. W., Carter, R. T., Casas, M. J., Fouad, N. A., Allen, E. I., Jensen, M., et al. (1998). *Multicultural counseling competencies: Individual and organizational development*. Thousand Oaks, CA: Sage.

Swenson, C. R. (1998). Clinical social work's contribution to a social justice perspective. *Social Work, 43*(6), 527-538.

Towle, C. (1957). *Common human needs*. New York: National Association of Social Workers.

Witkin, S. L. (1998). Is social work an adjective? *Social Work, 43*(6), 483-487.

Witkin, S. L. (1999). Identities and contexts. *Social Work, 44*(4), 293-297.

Chapter 6

Model Six: Monmouth University

INFUSING INTERNATIONAL CONTENT
INTO ADVANCED GENERALIST PRACTICE

Mark E. Rodgers and Robin S. Mama
Monmouth University

> "Social work education...has failed to make serious strides to learn or teach about the rest of the world." (Ramanathan & Link, 1999, p. xi)

It is becoming increasingly difficult for social workers to operate today without a larger picture: that of the global environment. "Forces beyond national economics and politics have a direct impact on local well-being as the economy becomes increasingly transnationalized and the global actors such as the World Bank and the International Monetary Fund increasingly influence social policy within countries" (Hokenstad & Midgley, 1997, p. 2). "International content in social work curricula is not a new phenomenon" (Ramanathan & Link, 1999, p. 14). Concern for international or global issues was present in the beginning of the profession. "Social work and educators were working on international causes before World War I, most notably that of world peace" (Ramanathan & Link, 1999, p. 15). Not only is there history of development work in the profession, but recent publications indicate it is timely and appropriate in the new millennium to take a fresh look at international development (Stoesz, Guzzetta, & Lusk, 1999, p. ix). Initial work in the settlement house movement of the late 1800s was with immigrant-related issues. "From its inception, the United States has been a land of immigrants. Likewise, the field of social work has a long history of working with immigrants and refugees" (Balgopal, 2000, p. ix). Therefore, since the emergence of social work as a profession, social workers have had to concern themselves with matters related to international practice. After the first International Conference of Social Work, held in Paris in 1928, the International Committee of Schools of Social Work was formed with more than 40 member schools in 10 different countries (Kendall, 1967). Since the early beginnings of social work as a profession there has been concern among social work educators about internationally related problems and the development of some internationally related curriculum. For the most part, however, this has resulted in one or two courses, usually at the master's advanced or doctoral level, focusing on international social work.

As the profession continued to emerge, and at times follow a medical model (perhaps in reaction to the Flexner Report), international concerns have at times waxed and waned. The strongest support for international perspectives in social work education occurred through the adoption of the 1962 Curriculum Policy Statement (CPS) developed by the Council on Social Work Education (CSWE). As Lynn Healy, in Ramanathan & Link (1999) indicates, global events had a great impact upon this CPS. She indicates that the 1962 CPS was formulated during years of considerable international activity. It was revised several times during the 1960s, 1970s, and 1980s, but it was not until 1992 that the CPS took an additional step in the area of recognizing the importance of including international concepts and principles in social work curricula. The statement of most significance stresses that "social work programs should recognize the interdependence of nations and the importance of worldwide cooperation" (Ramanathan & Link, p. 20).

In addition to the CPS and its various revisions, the establishment of an International Commission (IC) as part of the CSWE commission structure was a step toward recognizing the importance of global interdependence and the need for social work curricula to include an international perspective or emphasis. As a group the IC has worked tirelessly to influence the profession and future versions of the CPS to reflect the growing interest, literature base, and practice examples of international social work.

ADVANCED GENERALIST CONNECTION

Where does international social work content fit within the advanced generalist curriculum? First, describing the advanced generalist practice continuum has been a difficult and often daunting task in social work academia. It is assumed that the advanced generalist continuum works well with the BSW curriculum, since it provides beginning practitioners with a broad range of skills, allowing them to practice in a variety of contexts (Gibbs & Locke, 1990; Schatz & Jenkins, 1990). When considering the MSW curriculum, many programs have opted to design specializations or concentrations that reflect the environmental conditions that surround the program. However, graduate programs that have opted to provide an advanced generalist practice specialization have defined this more by the "expectations of greater depth and breadth of performance...and the capacity of independent practice" (Gibbs & Locke, 1990, p. 234).

Several authors have noted that the generalist practice method has two elements: it is problem-solving centered, and it uses the person-in-environment model for assessment and intervention (Miley, O'Melia, & DuBois, 2001; Gibbs & Locke, 1990; Martinez-Brawley, 1987; Sheafor & Landon, 1987). These elements allow "the social worker to respond not only to an immediate problem of the individual, such as job training, but also to the conditions in the community and society that present barriers..." (Gibbs & Locke, p. 234). It is exactly these two features that provide the basis for infusing international content within the advanced generalist curriculum. They are foundational elements in the curricular model discussed in this chapter.

Building upon the earlier versions of the CPS, the work of the International Commission, the roots of the profession, and the interest of faculty, Monmouth University developed, piloted, and had accredited the first advanced concentration in international and community development. The remainder of this chapter will focus on the development of this concentration and its effective use in the advanced generalist curriculum.

SCHOOL MODEL

Framework

In 1998 the Department of Social Work at Monmouth University established a unique concentration within its MSW program, called International and Community Development (ICD). The ICD concentration clearly and proactively addresses international social and economic justice issues and prepares students for careers in international and domestic community development, and therefore can be utilized by MSW programs with an advanced generalist practice focus. The ICD program shares its foundation MSW courses with the other program concentration in Practice with Families and Children, which likewise emphasizes the concept of families within a global context. The department has continued to expand its faculty to include international social work specialists, thus broadening its capacity to effectively support the ICD specialization.

ICD applies macro social work skills such as social policy development and implementation, community organizing, social planning and program development and evaluation to the international context. More specifically, the curriculum focuses on sustainable economic development, community and social development, micro credit lending, capacity building, program planning, needs assessment, direct equity, equality and social justice issues, legislative organizing, grass-roots advocacy, and community organizing. Students completing this program have the option to complete an eight-week field placement working abroad in international community development and related focused projects.

Curriculum Design

The curriculum in the MSW program at Monmouth University emphasizes three themes: the strengths perspective, an empowerment approach, and a focus on families in a global context. These themes strongly support an advanced generalist framework based on the two foundations mentioned earlier: using a problem-solving approach and a person-in-environment perspective for assessment and intervention.

The ICD concentration primarily uses community development theory and practice to address Third World social and economic justice, inequality, oppression, and discrimination issues in First and Third World environments. Culturally competent community development as practiced respects the integrity and worth of individuals and communities with diverse backgrounds. The ICD concentration focuses the practice of social work at mezzo and macro levels with agencies and client populations within a context of global interdependence of social problems. Courses stress the knowledge, values, skills, and ethics of practice at the mezzo and macro levels, with specific content on the ethics of the International Federation of Social Workers and the declarations of the United Nations. Skill development in the program specifically focuses on mezzo and macro techniques that can be used in any situation or country students may finds themselves in. This is an essential element of the advanced generalist practice concept: that a practitioner will have the depth and breath of knowledge and skills necessary to allow them to work in any setting, on any social problem, and with any client population.

Field assignments occur at the local and international levels with organizations that have community development as a part of their social work mandate. Additional information about field application is provided in a later section of this chapter. Students integrate classroom learning with field experiences in their application of knowledge, skills, values, and ethics to community development practice. This concentration also offers students the ability to practice social work in field internships overseas, as well as to become members of the international social work arena, submitting abstracts and attending international conferences.

The objectives for the ICD curriculum are as follows:

1. Develop and systematically apply the professional social work knowledge, values, and skills of advanced international and community development practice.
2. Demonstrate the ability to empower groups and communities in working toward a just and equitable society.
3. Develop, articulate, analyze, implement, and evaluate an international and community development practice paradigm that emerges from a human rights and social justice perspective.
4. Demonstrate an ability to apply, analyze, and evaluate knowledge about the impact of oppression and discrimination in the assessment and intervention of groups and communities.
5. Conceptualize, implement, and evaluate social development strategies to empower groups and communities within appropriate cultural forms.
6. Demonstrate an ability to synthesize international and community development theories emphasizing the strengths-based empowerment perspective.
7. Conduct research to evaluate international and community development practice, and to determine outcomes using both qualitative and quantitative methods.
8. Produce scholarship that promotes the knowledge, values, and skills of international and community development practice emphasizing the strengths perspective, an empowerment approach within a global context.
9. Develop skill in initiating and maintaining collaborative relationships with international and community development practitioners, agencies, and other regional organizations.
10. Analyze and evaluate the knowledge and skills of advanced social work practice within an international and community development context.

Course Descriptions

Brief course descriptions of the core ICD classes are provided below, along with highlights of the types of work completed in these courses.

SW 608—Social Planning. This course is an introduction to social planning and is the first course in the ICD concentration. Working within a social systems context, the course surveys different approaches to planning, offers a generic rational planning model, and develops a number of specific planning methods and techniques. Planning as a process of making public choices between equally appealing alternatives is experienced.

Students working in a group of three or four will complete a needs assessment project for their field practicum agencies. These agencies are basically the community development agencies-an advanced setting for the student of international concentration.

SW 615—International and Community Development. This course is designed to introduce the student to global arenas for social work activities. Different perspectives on, and realities of, development and underdevelopment; policies and practices of international aid and humanitarian agencies; and the role of social work in addressing human rights and needs of such groups as the displaced, unwanted refugees, victims of terror, the impoverished, and children are critically examined. The relationship and tensions between First and Third World development are explored using social and economic development policy concepts such as Appropriate Technology (AT), Center Periphery Phenomenon (CPP), and other analytical constructs.

Students are assigned to do their research paper in an advanced application of field of practice to international and community development. Students demonstrate advanced social work practice in an identifiable concentration through their assigned presentation during the seminar. Examples of areas include community development and international social work-related fields such as health, education, human rights, social justice, domestic violence, international security, and peace.

SW 655—Seminar in Advanced International and Community Development. This seminar is designed for students interested in advanced international social work and community development. It is designed to prepare students for international social welfare practice abroad and/or for transnational work in the United States with immigrants, foreign students, international adoption, etc. This seminar is also relevant for international social work students who wish to apply social work principles to practice in their own countries.

Students are assigned to do their presentation and research paper in an advanced application of field of practice to international and community development. Each student will make two presentations and lead the subsequent discussion. The first presentation will be based on the examination of an income maintenance program in a selected country. The second will analyze a field of social services provision in either the same or a different country.

Field Seminar Classes

Students enrolled in the field internship are required to attend a weekly seminar class throughout the semester. These classes focus on specific themes that are relevant to the ICD concentration and that support the advanced generalist perspective. For example, in SW 630-B, students work in groups to complete a project on an advocacy issue for their field agency. Students show the ability to understand, analyze, and evaluate how local, regional, or national problems are interrelated to other nations within a global environment for social provision.

In SW 640-B, a field seminar class, students complete a paper on agency diversity, using a cultural competency framework on an issue in their field agency. The proposal is developed in consultation with their field supervisors and/or clients for including cultural content in something not currently present in the field agency.

International and Community Development Concentration

The courses that constitute the entire ICD concentration are as follows:

SW 608: Social Planning
SW 615: Seminar in International and Community Development
SW 626-B: Program Evaluation Research
SW 627: Implications for Diversity in Practice (required for all MSWs)
SW 630-B: Field III-Methods of Advocacy
SW 640-B: Field IV-Cultural Competency in Organizations
SW 655: Seminar in Advanced International and Community Development
SW 669: Integrative Research Seminar (required for all MSWs)

Students choose two electives, one in the fall semester of the concentration year and one in the spring semester of the concentration year. Elective courses that augment the concentration include the following: Grant Writing, Social Work Administration, Social Work Supervision, Issues in International Health Care, Social Work and the Law, Environmental and Occupational Health, International Women's Issues, Civil Society and NGOs, and Sustainable Development.

FIELD APPLICATION

Monmouth University's Department of Social Work establishes its international field placements in a variety of global settings by building relationships with various agencies in countries that face a wide range of social service challenges. Once again, the ability of advanced generalist practice to influence the field internship is evident in the program. Students are prepared with advanced skills that allow them to practice in any country, any setting, and with any client population. This ability is critical to the success of the Monmouth program. While we have established internships in several countries, other opportunities for internship occur every year, and we continually are expanding our field agency base overseas. Each country has unique needs for community or social development, and our students must be able to accommodate those needs immediately.

Connections are established with organizations well grounded in the local community development context (both local and international, and nongovernmental and governmental agencies) as well as with universities that have existing programs in social work and fields related to community development. This coordinated support strategy provides the student with the operating base, logistical backup, and supervisory insight to be able to contribute in a meaningful, culturally sensitive way to current community development challenges. Past field assignments have involved students in assessing the needs of the immigrant (overstayer) work force population in Singapore, conducting research related to long-term antipoverty planning and homelessness of children in Latvia, and implementing literacy and schooling services for child laborers in Bangladesh. Upon return students share their experiences with the university community and future student interns, highlighting both their work and their increased commitment to the profession as a result of this transformative experience.

Academic Preparation and Program Design

Students electing the field abroad option perform their first 375 hours locally while preparing to do their last 125 hours in an international placement. Field abroad typically begins the first work day of March and ends the last work day of April, an eight-week experience. When a student identifies a country as their field placement of choice, their concentration course work and assignments immediately focus on building an in-depth knowledge of that country. While the program and student fully recognize that acculturation is possible only through immersion, this focused academic strategy prepares the student intern to enter the country and begin the assignment having thoroughly researched the culture, social service system, government, economics, and other critical contextual factors. This is considered crucial, given that the placement period is relatively brief and students typically arrive only a day or two prior to the start of the field placement. Student interns typically work on their assignments three days a week during the eight-week period. The remainder of their time is spent on concluding their degree course work using the Internet to access distance learning software (WebCT).

Field abroad students have the same access to their peers and professors as do domestic field students, albeit electronically. While the classes still meet for students who stay locally, those locally placed students are required to participate in the distance learning component of the courses, as are the professors. Additionally, field abroad students have the same access as local students to the Guggenheim Library's electronic resources, including electronic reserves. When field abroad students return to Monmouth, they are required to present their international work and experience to the university community.

Where possible, the department encourages paired placements. Now in its fourth year of operation, this international placement design has proven to provide both a successful learning experience for the student intern and a meaningful contribution to the supporting institution(s).

Exposure to the realities of international work is critically needed for students pursuing international careers. This applies not only to the quality of their educational experience as ICD social work students, but also equally (if not on a grander scale) to their ability to secure international jobs. Many potential employers require graduates to have some international experience to be considered for jobs involving international work or international travel. Indeed, the field abroad experience has even been a major asset to alumni applying for jobs focused on domestic community development. The field abroad model Monmouth has developed and utilized is designed to provide the academic and field knowledge needed to be a competent community development practitioner. The model allows a student to be exposed to international work settings while allowing them to continue in their regular academic courses. The field abroad approach creates a placement experience that assures the greatest degree of comparability possible while affording students the opportunity to gain firsthand experience in international social work and development. In fact, the program is designed so that the 375/125 hours placement split is the only difference between ICD domestic and ICD field abroad student experiences.

Internships play a vital and fundamental role in social work education. International internships play a vital and fundamental role in international and community development education in social work. The field abroad model is a progressive approach to meeting the need for international experience while meeting the need to produce quality social work professionals with the academic preparation necessary to play a critical role in social work and the helping professions in the developing world.

Types of Projects

Student interns carry out a mutually identified and appropriate project related to community development that can be accomplished within an eight-week period. Field interns do not engage in direct provision of counseling or social services to individuals, but maintain a more appropriate focus on community-level initiatives, research, or policy support. Some illustrative examples of appropriate projects would be the following:

> - Needs assessments
> - Research activities
> - Program development
> - Program coordination
> - Program evaluation
> - Proposal writing
> - Policy analysis
> - Training activities
> - Social mobilization efforts
> - Documentation support

TRIALS AND TRIBULATIONS

Developing a new MSW program is inherently prone to a number of trials and tribulations. However, developing a program that contains a full concentration devoted to international and community development has a few more pitfalls. From the very beginning of its conceptualization, this concentration has required all of us—faculty, administration, and students—to think outside the box. The typical configuration of courses and field work do not apply in the traditional sense for this concentration. The fact that a great deal of content and field work can be completed in a foreign country required a new model of teaching and learning to be developed and implemented.

We are very fortunate that our university has been supportive of this concentration almost from the inception of the program. We say almost because it demanded a great deal of effort to convince administration that the concentration was doable, that we had a model for overseas field internships, that students would be able to complete the program on time, that we would actually have students register for this program, and that we could get it accredited by the CSWE. We knew that of the two concentrations, the ICD concentration would be less attractive (at first) to the students entering our MSW program. We knew from our needs assessment that most students were coming to Monmouth to earn an MSW for the purpose of obtaining a clinical license. So the second hurdle (after getting administration on board) was numbers. The program began with only 4 students, challenging the administration to again think outside the box: most classes at Monmouth require 10 or more students for the class to run.

This led to another slight hurdle for our social work faculty. Our clinical concentration, Practice with Families and Children, routinely has 40 to 50 students per year, which means that faculty who teach these classes have anywhere from 15 students (field seminar classes) to 30 students (advanced practice classes) per class. A great deal of open discussion was required with the faculty so that resentments would not occur between faculty who were teaching 25 students in a class versus those teaching only 4 students.

Preparing students for an intense international experience takes a great deal of planning, which begins in the fall semester of the concentration year. The field seminar class (SW 630-B) is the anchor for their preparation, requiring the students early on to declare what country they will be studying in, the type of work they are interested in pursuing, and whether they have the financial means to see their overseas stay through.

One of the major lessons we have learned is that students need to be carefully guided about the nature of their trip and their responsibilities. From the time they declare their country of interest, students must meet biweekly with an ICD professor for extensive student briefings and to review all details of their trip. They must complete extensive research into the country and culture (much of which is carried out in SW 615, Seminar in International and Community Development). Students must also be socially educated about the nuances of the culture they will be encountering. Additionally, since our students must provide their own funding for their trip, a fair amount of time must be spent on financial planning, including housing, meals, transportation in country, airfare, and tourism.

Concurrently, students must also be in contact with their housing arrangements and agency supervisors long before they leave the United States. It is essential that this communication occur (usually through email and by phone) to allow both parties an opportunity to get to know each other better. This enhances the student's ability to begin working in their overseas agency and to become oriented more quickly. It also helps them narrow down and focus on the projects they will be completing overseas.

Whenever possible, our department has attempted to send students overseas in pairs. We have found that students who have a partner (or partners) fare much better than those who go to a country alone (although this has not always been the case). Generally, students working together can keep each other in check, both for their field requirements and for completing their remaining assignments for the spring semester-all of which are completed over the Internet. Students abroad need to be mentored and monitored by the field instructor using the phone, email, and fax when necessary. This offers the student support and improves the integrity of the experience.

OUTCOME ASSESSMENT

At this point, we have three years of graduates to assess. The ICD concentration is a much smaller concentration than our Practice with Families and Children concentration. Total ICD graduates to date number 23. One outcome measure we are examining is how long after graduation it takes our students to find employment and where they are employed. To date, all graduates found employment within one month of graduation and all are employed in macro social work practice in a variety of settings. None of our graduates is employed in international settings; the majority are employed in community development organizations.

Our second outcome assessment piece is a competency exam that is administered to all MSW graduates just prior to graduation. We employ one exam for our clinical students and one for our ICD students.

THE FUTURE OF ADVANCED GENERALIST PRACTICE UTILIZING INTERNATIONAL CONTENT

Utilizing the two elements of advanced generalist practice discussed above—centering the material in the problem-solving model and using the person-in-environment model for assessment and intervention—social work curriculum can easily accommodate and infuse international content. We recommend the inclusion of a macro community development course in the foundation year as a beginning introduction for global content. Many links can be made between community practice domestically and community development internationally. "The standard definitions of community development consider the process of group formation, need identification, resource development and then action" (Clarke, 2000, p. 17). These same processes are found in international community development and therefore become the springboards from which content can be infused into other social work courses, such as policy, research, and practice.

We also recommend that existing foundation courses reach beyond consideration of the domestic picture and include the rest of the world. Policy courses should consider including international policy-making bodies as well as international policy documents as standard parts of the course content. This also means, therefore, that students should also be well-versed in social economics and international economic policies. Research courses should include program evaluation research as well as other types of research that is conducted for international organizations. Practice courses should at the least include the International Code of Ethics of the International Federation of Social Workers. Unlike in years past, when community organization content was placed or "tacked on" to the end of practice curriculum, we are advocating that international content be infused throughout the curriculum rather than winding up as the 14th week's lecture for the semester.

PRACTICE AND RESEARCH IMPLICATIONS

Today, in the fourth class of ICD students, we have noted three distinct areas that any program developing international curricula or considering international placements should consider: the student, the curriculum, and the implementation of the program.

APPENDIX

OVERVIEW OF INTERNATIONAL PLACEMENT OBSTACLES

The overview is broken into three distinct sections: the intern/student, course work, and administration and implementation of the placement process.

Intern/Student

1. General student readiness. The need for extensive student briefings was anticipated from the beginning of the process. However, the degree to which the information in these briefing sessions is understood by the student was found to vary greatly. In the case of student briefings, more is better than less.

2. Maturity. The international experience requires a high degree of independence and maturity. It is a quality that does not appear correlated with age.

3. Ambassadorship. It must be stressed to students early in the process that they are ambassadors of our program. Students clearly need to understand the importance of maintaining good relationships with our field sites. We strive to maintain quality relationships while ensuring quality internship experiences. Those who go before set the tone for those who follow.

4. Finances. It must be stressed to students the importance of assessing their financial capabilities for completing their internship abroad. Students continue to pay tuition to the home institutions while additionally incurring the cost of airfare, housing, food, and incidental expenses while overseas.

5. Cultural competency. Cultural competency is infused throughout our undergraduate and graduate curriculum. Every opportunity to discuss cultural competency is explored with the students. We have realized that rudimentary language training as well as description of cultural nuances specific to that society must be part of the orientation prior to the student's in-country experience.

6. Focus. Students are far away and must posses a certain degree of self-discipline and focus to be successful. This applies equally to course work and field work.

7. Physical health and vigor. Social work in general often requires a vigorous constitution, and this is codified in the MSW Student Handbook. A student wishing to complete an internship abroad must exceed the general requirement of health and vigor, as the experience is often physically demanding and at times exhausting.

8. Flexibility. A hallmark of a successful international internship is the student's ability to be flexible.

9. Vacation. Students must understand this is not a vacation. In many cases while in country they will experience cultural programs and be taken to historic sites, but they need to realize that their overseas internship is not a vacation.

Course Work

1. Students are ardently briefed on the strenuous nature of keeping up with their course work while in an international placement. Students must be reminded that they will be completing their course work over the internet through WebCT. This requires social work faculty to be active participants in the development and implementation of their courses electronically. To this end, several of the ICD classes are web-enhanced in the fall semester in preparation for the student's total electronic course work.

2. Electives. It is important that all faculty understand and be involved in the information loop as to how courses are being electronically processed.

3. Core classes such as SW 627 and SW 669 need to be taught by a faculty member who is aware of the requirements of the program and is willing to participate electronically.

4. Library. Electronic resources are generally adequate to meet most of the student's needs. Students still need to plan well in advance of leaving the country and carry additional materials needed to complete projects. Advance planning is critical.

5. Faculty in the ICD concentration need to meet regularly during the fall and spring semesters, both in preparation for and placement of the students overseas. Troubleshooting and student concerns can be raised, accountability regarding assignments can be discussed, and curricular planning occurs so that not all projects are due at the same time.

Administration and Implementation

1. Advance preparation is critical for all overseas internships. In some cases international placements were developed from preexisting faculty relationships with professionals in other countries. Even in these known cases, the turnaround time for paperwork can be daunting.

2. Forms. Every form or document that requires a signature must be reviewed by an attorney. Additional forms have been developed each year the program has been implemented.

3. Support. Obtaining approval for this activity requires a real commitment from central administration at the university and a real commitment of finances as well. Teamwork is crucial among university administrators, social work faculty, and students.

4. Waivers of liability are a reality. It is not possible to obtain approval from central administration for this activity without a waiver covering liability.

5. Insurance. Although medical coverage is not a university requirement, we have found it beneficial and suggested that students purchase such coverage.

6. Personal and professional liability. Our university liability policy covers the students worldwide. This should be explored in all other programs planning international field internships.

7. Travel physician. Some international locations present significant health and immunological hazards. Students are advised strongly to seek the assistance of a travel physician and receive their travel immunizations months prior to departure. In some cases, countries will not allow entry without documentation of immunization records.

8. Hazards. To the best of our ability, we must make students aware of the conditions they are agreeing to be in for eight weeks. Students must be offered the opportunity to think this over for a few days before signing that they have been informed of the conditions or specific hazards. The worst possible event would be to have an incident in which a student is endangered, injured, or missing. Field teachers and the coordinator of field periodically survey U.S. State Department warning bulletins and World Health Organization reports to determine the suitability of placements.

9. Emergency information. Students must have emergency contact information and phone numbers. A formal raised seal letter explaining who the student is and why they are in country is an excellent idea.

10. Supervision. The details of supervision must be worked out prior to the student's departure. In some cases, alternate models need to be explored, particularly when there is an absence of a high number of professionals with an MSW degree. In all cases students, with their limited vocational consistency, must be counseled to develop an ability to maintain a professional identity while in a foreign land and new culture.

11. Debriefing. It is critical to have several debriefing sessions for students upon their return and as they start back in their classes. Reentry should not occur in the final week of the semester. Students need a place to bring issues about reentry and present feelings, emotions, and knowledge acquired while abroad.

12. Housing. One of the most critical elements of the placement process is where the student intern will live. Students need to be acquainted with the fact that

standards for housing vary greatly from country to country. We have found it advisable for the country supervisor to send photographs of the planned housing. Safety, of course, is a primary concern.

This process has been exciting and invigorating for our entire department. However, the energy and costs have been at times been overwhelming and exhausting. As much as flexibility has been required of our students, so too has it been required of our faculty and administration.

REFERENCES

Balgopal, P. R. (Ed.). (2000). *Social work practice with immigrants and refugees.* New York: Columbia University Press.

Clarke, S. (2000). *Social work as community development.* London: Athenaeum Press.

Gibbs, P., & Locke, B. (1990). Paradigm for the generalist-advanced generalist continuum. *Journal of Social Work Education, 26*(3), 232-241.

Hokenstad, M. C., & Midgley, J. (1997). *Issues in international social work.* Washington, DC: NASW Press.

Kendall, K. A. (1967). Highlights of the new CSWE program of international cooperation in social work education. *Social Work Education Reporter, 15*(2), 20-23, 37, 42.

Martinez-Brawley, E. E. (1987). Rural social work. In A. Minahan et al. (Eds.) *Encyclopedia of social work* (18th ed.), (pp. 521-537). Silver Spring, MD: National Association of Social Workers.

Miley, K., O'Melia, M., & DuBois, B. (2001). *Generalist social work practice: An empowering approach* (3rd ed.). Boston: Allyn & Bacon.

Ramanathan, S., & Link, R. J. (1999). *All our futures: Principles and resources for social work practice in a global era.* Boston: Brooks Cole.

Schatz, M. F., & Jenkins, L. E. (1990). Milford redefined: A model of initial and advanced generalist social work. *Journal of Social Work Education 26*(3), 217-232.

Sheafor, B. W., & Landon, P. S. (1987). Generalist perspective. In A. Minahan et al. (Eds.) *Encyclopedia of social work* (18th ed., pp. 660-669). Silver Spring, MD: National Association of Social Workers.

Stoesz, D., Guzzetta, C., & Lusk. M. (1999). *International development.* Boston: Allyn & Bacon.

SECTION 2: A THEORETICAL PERSPECTIVE

Chapter 7

DEFINING COMPLEXITY:
THE THEORETICAL BASIS OF ADVANCED
GENERALIST PRACTICE

Linnea F. GlenMaye, Cathleen A. Lewandowski, and Brien L. Bolin
Wichita State University

INTRODUCTION

Advanced generalist practice is an evolving concept in social work education. Some social work scholars have suggested that the advanced generalist model can serve as a framework for the entire graduate curriculum (Gibbs, Locke, & Lohmann, 1990; Hernandez, Jorgensen, Judd, Gould, & Parsons, 1985). Others have suggested that advanced generalist practice is most appropriate for rural (Campbell & Shepard, 1990; Mason & Lusk, 1992) or international settings (McMahon, 1994). The process of defining advanced generalist practice is in part driven by the Council on Social Work Education's (CSWE, 1994) requirement that MSW programs provide foundation content and advanced curricula having specialized knowledge and practice skills in an area of concentration. The specialized knowledge and skills of the concentration are said to be necessary in order to effectively intervene in complex client situations (Gross, 1992).

Previous descriptions of advanced generalist practice state that advanced generalist practitioners address direct and indirect practice situations where there is "extensive system dysfunction and sustained complexity" (Schatz, Jenkins, &

Sheafor, 1990, p. 226). The concept of complexity as applied to practice situations has not been fully defined, however, which contributes to the difficulty programs have in describing an advanced generalist curriculum that prepares students for a "specialization."

The purpose of this chapter is to contribute to our understanding of complex advanced generalist practice by defining the concept of complexity within chaos and complexity theories. We will draw on chaos/complexity theory to provide a perspective on advanced generalist practice. By providing a perspective that addresses complexity, advanced generalist practice can be further distinguished from the MSW foundation and baccalaureate practice.

In this chapter we will review current thinking on advanced generalist practice, describe the principal components of chaos/complexity theory, and synthesize these components with the core values of social work. Finally, some practice principles for advanced generalist social work practice based on the concept of complexity, from a multidimensional perspective, will be proposed.

ADVANCED GENERALIST PRACTICE

Although there is some agreement on common characteristics, there is still no consensus on the definition of generalist practice at either the baccalaureate or graduate level of social work education (Landon, 1995). There does appear to be some agreement that multi-method and multilevel approaches are central to generalist practice and that it is, or should be, applicable to the public and private service sector and attuned to considerations of social justice (Landon, 1995). Derezotes (2000) describes advanced generalist practice as multidimensional and more in-depth. Raymond, Teare, and Atherton (1996) found that the advanced generalist model is congruent with the actual tasks performed by MSW workers across fields of practice. Some descriptions of advanced generalist curricula focus on certain dimensions or settings of multilevel practice, such as group work, administration, health, and rural or international settings (Campbell & Shepard, 1990; McMahon, 1994; Rittner & Albers, 1999; Pardeck, Yuen, Daley, & Hawkins, 1998; Thompson, Menefee, & Marley, 1999). The Raymond, Teare, and Atherton study, however, found that there were no meaningful differences in tasks performed by MSWs employed in different fields of practice. Likewise, Holliman, Dziegielewski, and Datta (2001) found that, in terms of core tasks, discharge planners perform tasks typically resembling those of generalist social workers. In other words, in the real world of practice, social workers are incorporating an advanced generalist perspective, but without specification of a model.

Although the definition of advanced generalist practice has evolved, its use as a specialized body of knowledge and skills remains attenuated until its theoretical bases and practice competencies are more fully described. Despite almost two decades of development, the approach needs further development in ways that clarify the knowledge and theoretical base of the advanced generalist paradigm (Schatz, Jenkins, & Sheafor, 1990). The conundrum of advanced generalist practice consists precisely in its definitional intractability: How can one be a specialist and a generalist at the same time? The puzzle is not without a solution, however. The concepts of multidimensional practice and complexity provide a basis for an advanced generalist practice, as will be seen in the following sections.

MULTILEVEL, MULTISYSTEM, AND MULTIDIMENSIONAL PRACTICE

Multilevel or multisystem practice models can be found in several fields of practice. These fields of practice include work with families and children in poverty (Vosler & Nair, 1993); work with the elderly (Argüelles & von Simson, 1999); family preservation (Cimmarusti, 1992); mental illness in African American families (Boyd-Franklin & Shenouda, 1990); family therapy with African American and Latino families (Boyd-Franklin & Bry, 2000); group work (Rose, Duby, Olenick, & Weston, 1996); and work with transsexuals (Ma, 1999). Many of the models draw heavily on systems or ecological theory for their framework. The primary characteristic of a multisystem or multilevel practice model is that workers are encouraged to see the client as part of ever larger systems and to take this context or environment into account, especially during the assessment phase. Multisystem models encourage intervention at more than one level, or in more than one system, and suggest that social workers must have a depth of understanding of many mezzo and macro systems (Vosler & Nair, 1993). Although these models speak to the interrelationships of systems and problems, there are several limitations to multisystem or multimethod practice models.

First, the models do not fully acknowledge or demonstrate the complexity of social work practice, nor the complexity of human interactions in their rather simplified descriptions of multisystem work. The models tend to use static depictions of nested systems. Thus, the ebb and flow of communication, interaction, action, and reaction are not fully modeled, nor *could* they be and still be intelligible and simple models.

Second, the models tend to emphasize assessment with individual clients within a multisystem framework rather than intervention at the mezzo or macro levels. Macro-oriented interventions are not clearly linked to individual assessment, and so it is not clear how the social worker might use this perspective with individual clients experiencing multiple problems in multiple systems. Practice still tends to be dichotomized into micro and macro practice, and work with larger systems may appear less important, less crucial, or so monumental as to seem impossible.

Third, although the models often describe the interdependence of the numerous and complex levels or systems, they still tend to look for "cause and effect" explanations for client dysfunction and difficulties, seeking simple and linear explanations for the complex interactions that often defy description.

Finally, the models tend to reify social systems as things in themselves (Chubb, 1990), when in fact it is the interactions that define system boundaries, just as "ecosystem" refers to the reciprocal relationships between organisms and their environments (Chubb, 1990; Robbins, Chatterjee, & Canda, 1998). Such reification may contribute to workers' reluctance to intervene at larger system levels, since those systems are viewed as structures rather than as dynamic systems defined by their transactions, interactions, and qualities of communication between individuals.

MULTIDIMENSIONAL PERSPECTIVE

In contrast to the multisystem or multilevel approach, the multidimensional framework draws upon chaos and complexity theory to develop a practice model that may more accurately reflect the dynamic complexity of social work practice. The terms multisystem and multilevel express key aspects of systems. In our view, the term *multidimensional* captures the multiple dimensionality of systems, especially human systems, which have complex, rich relationships having length, breadth, and depth, and which interact within the dimensions of both space and time. The dimension of time is crucial to a multidimensional framework because it allows one to view systems of all sizes as process rather than as structure (Chubb, 1990; Ellenberger, 1958).

Understanding systems as process (which necessarily involves change) can facilitate intervention at multiple levels, so that macro interventions are equal to micro interventions, because it helps to identify where, how, and when one actually intervenes. Change, from a multidimensional framework, is normalized, being a quality of all systems. In contrast to the sequential nature of levels, a multidimensional perspective allows for the possibility of simultaneous interactions across dimensions.

The simultaneity of the multidimensional perspective has been used in other theoretical contexts such as communication theory, in which communication is seen as occurring at many levels simultaneously (Watzlawick, Beavin, & Jackson, 1962). Human beings send and receive communications at many levels all at once, but are often unaware of this multiplicity of communication. Social work has long recognized that when change occurs, it is multisystemic in its effects: change in one system both effects and affects change in others (Lewin, 1992). In working with individuals and families, one is constantly dealing with flux and change, both healthy and unhealthy. The changes seen in individuals and families are to some extent mirrored in the fluidity of the context of practice today, which is marked by changes in the number and types of agencies operating in a community at any given time, and the ongoing evolution of agency mission and goals as policies and funding change. New agencies are constantly emerging, while other agencies may close their doors. A multidimensional perspective increases the complexity of assessment and evaluation by acknowledging the multifaceted web of systemic relationships and environments that are the substance of human interaction, which, as Bolland and Atherton (1999) suggest, implies that it is not possible to know everything about the present, nor can the future be predicted with certainty.

Systems theory and ecological theory have attempted to unravel the nature of systemic relationships in order to understand and predict behavior (that is, predict change). Change is the heart of practice and, as Butz (1997) suggests, "Change is the process that ferries people from one stable period to the next in their lives" (p. 3). However, the complexity of human relationships is such that a new theory of relationship and change is needed, one that takes into account the essential nonlinearity of change in the human system. Chaos/complexity theory has much potential for understanding the rapid, sudden, and unpredictable change that marks much of social work practice and the human condition. In the following sections, the basic components of chaos/complexity theory will be presented and its implications for advanced generalist practice discussed.

COMPLEXITY AND CHAOS CONCEPTS

Traditional paradigms such as systems theory and ecological theory have been an integral part of social work practice for decades and are well known to social workers. One of the basic tenets of systems theory is that the world-indeed, the universe-can be viewed as systems within systems (Germain & Gitterman, 1980; Hearn, 1958; Laszlo, 1972; Meyer, 1983). Some suggest that a strict adherence to systems theory promotes a functionalist perspective of the world that discourages critical thinking and action for social change, and that the emphasis on equilibrium and stability fosters a conservative view of society and social change (Berger, 1986; Gould, 1987; Martindale, 1988; Turner, 1986).

The ecological perspective (Germain & Gitterman, 1980) is often presented as a more holistic alternative to systems theory (Robbins, Chatterjee, & Canda, 1998). This variation on systems theory, along with systems theory itself, tends to emphasize adaptation and goodness of fit, with an emphasis on the stability of systems. Though ecological theory is a more dynamic model of living systems and its authors have tried to de-emphasize stability, it still tends to see systems as orderly and rational (Warren, Franklin, & Streeter, 1998). See Figure 7.1 for a comparison of traditional systems theory and complexity theory.

In recent years, systems theory has been enriched by the infusion of chaos and complexity theory, lending more depth and breadth to the understanding of the processes of system growth and change (Byrne, 1998; Butz, 1997; Perna & Masterpasqua, 1997). The theories of chaos and complexity are related to systems theory and draw on that theory's concepts to some extent. In contrast to systems theory, however, chaos and complexity theory seek to understand systems that change in nonlinear ways. Thus, at the outset, these theoretical perspectives should resonate with social workers, who tend to agree that human development, change, and interactions are inherently complex, nonlinear, and stubbornly resistant to predictability (Bolland & Atherton, 1999).

Chaos theory is perhaps better known than complexity theory, but complexity theory is the more general term and chaos may be thought of as a component of complexity theory (Butz, 1997). Bolland and Atherton (1999) point out that chaos theory is not a theory in the accepted meaning of sets of interrelated propositions. They suggest that chaos/complexity theory is a way of thinking about complex phenomena. The definitions of both chaos and complexity, in fact, vary between theorists, with little agreement on exact definitions of each concept (Butz). It is beyond the scope of this chapter to present a full discussion of the theoretical intricacies of chaos and complexity. (See Gleick, 1987 and Mandlebrot, 1993, for an introduction to the mathematical details of the theory.) In the following section, some of the most salient concepts of chaos and complexity will be described.

Characteristic	Linear Model Focus on Individual System	Nonlinear Model Complexity/chaos focus
Social System	Organic (family system) Reified Structures	Nonorganic System as Process
Subsystems	Systems in a system	Nested Complexity Interdynamic Process
Micro Mezzo Macro	Either/Or Embedded	Holistic, change in one affects change in another. Change in context changes individual. Macro as important as micro.
Behavior of Social Systems	Action/Reaction	Structural Coupling Iterative Discontinuous Recursive
Change	Linear Predictive Systematic	Nonlinear Unpredictable Dynamic Discontinuous Humans are altered by every experience
Process	Beginning/End	"Flow"
Stability	Homeostasis	Nonlinear systems tend to settle down over time and to develop certain patterns.
Growth	Linear & Systematic Equifinality	Sensitive Dependence on Initial Conditions. If two sets of conditions differ by any amount at the outset, the specific solutions will diverge dramatically over the long range.
Role of Social Worker	Act on the system	Becomes part of the system
Role of Research	Cross-Sectional Quantitative	Longitudinal Qualitative
Power	Social workers have "power" Clients "resist"	Structurally coupled systems "perturb each other." Can't make anybody do anything.
Problems/Dysfunction	Define "Normal/Not Normal"	Problems are socially defined. Human relationships are process–not function.
Self Organization		Structure emerges in an open system without specifications from outside environment. It has both spatial and temporal organization, which contribute to speed of change and the organization of the space around the system.

Figure 7.1 Comparison of systems and complexity perspectives

CHAOS AND ORDER

Chaos is commonly understood to be random, hence lawless, behavior. Chaos many look chaotic, but within the randomness there is order or an emerging order (Butz, 1997). Chaos, however, is not the absence of order; rather, it is extremely complex information (Byrne, 1998). Chaos has been defined as "stochastic behavior occurring in a deterministic system" (Masterpasqua & Perna, 1997, p. 304). As pointed out by Masterpasqua and Perna, there is a paradox within the definition of chaos since it is lawless behavior (stochastic) that is nevertheless governed by law, so that "systems in chaos are determined, but not by linear methods" (p. 9).

Complexity theory focuses on understanding the universal processes that occur as a result of the dynamic interaction of system elements and on how order appears "out of the apparent randomness of chaos" (Perna & Masterpasqua, 1997, p. 11). Masterpasqua (1997) states that order evolves out of spontaneous transactions of complex adaptive systems that "swim against the currents" (p. 31) of the law of entropy (all processes moving toward disorder). These complex adaptive systems, which include the human system, "adaptively and dynamically roam between stability and chaos" (Masterpasqua, 1997, p. 31). Systems in chaos, as Masterpasqua points out, are most capable of reorganization and novel activity. Of great importance in complexity theory is the notion that the change that occurs is nonpredictable, but with an underlying order. Complex adaptive systems organize and reorganize toward more complex and integrated structures, and without chaos, new organization and increased complexity would be impossible (Masterpasqua, 1997).

Extremely ordered systems are not able to innovate in ways important to development and survival (Butz, 1997; Warren, Franklin, & Streeter, 1998). As Peters (1987) states, "change means disruption" (p. 335). Chaotic systems are on the other extreme and are characterized more by change than by order. Complex structures arise in a region on the edge of order where they can take advantage of the possibility of sudden change inherent in nonlinear dynamics while maintaining the order necessary for continuity (Waldrop, 1992). Some complexity theorists have described this situation as "the edge of chaos" (Kauffman, 1991; Lewin, 1992).

NONLINEARITY

Linear change refers to straightforward cause and effect change that is proportional, additive, and predictable, and where the response of the system is proportionate to the inputs (Masterpasqua & Perna, 1997). Nonlinearity in systems refers to relationships that are open-ended, not strictly proportional, and essentially nonpredictable (Bolland & Atherton, 1999). These systems show qualitative, not quantitative, change across time, with small changes leading to unpredictable and large changes later in development (Masterpasqua & Perna).

One of the assumptions of complexity theory is that very simple nonlinear models can lead to behavior that is quite complex (Gleick, 1987). As Gleick explains, Lorenz (1963) demonstrated this with a simple experiment using a water wheel and a steady stream of water. If the system were linear, one could predict a stable state, with the water wheel steadily turning in one direction, or in a predictable alternating of direction. Lorenz found, instead, that the system was nonlinear and chaotic, with the system displaying infinite complexity, never repeating itself, but yet staying within certain bounds. Changes are rapid in any nonlinear process that builds on itself (Warren, Franklin, & Streeter, 1998). Chaos/complexity theory does not view change in terms of an isolated event. Rather, change is understood in the context of a series of events in a process called *iteration* (Warren, Franklin, & Streeter).

Iteration is a mathematical model of a feedback loop. For example, one could estimate the growth in population through an iterative model, with each year's population figure fed into subsequent years to predict growth. Mathematical iterations demonstrate that change happens with enormous speed in such a system, and that a small difference in the initial input value will quickly turn into a large difference in output. In linear systems, the feedback loop can be modeled and outcome predicted. In nonlinear systems, however, the change can occur even more rapidly, and may be huge (Warren, Franklin, & Streeter, 1998). Though the iterations vary vastly from the original event, there are some limits to the range of possible iterations. These limits or boundaries of potential change are inherent within the characteristics of the dynamic system and environment.

The unpredictability of nonlinear systems comes from a major feature of chaotic systems, which is their *sensitive dependence on initial conditions*: If two systems differ by even the smallest amount at their onsets, they eventually diverge from each other exponentially....[A]lthough patterns of behavior may appear, within those patterns chaotic systems always are irregular and unpredictable" (Masterpasqua & Perna, 1997, p. 307).

Sensitive dependence on initial conditions was what came to be called, only half-jokingly, the Butterfly Effect (Butz, 1997): A butterfly fluttering its wings in one part of the world causing massive weather change in another. This concept stands in contrast to *equifinality*, a concept developed by von Bertalanffy (1968, p. 40), that refers to the property of systems in which systems can start at different states but end up in similar end states.

BIFURCATION AND PERTURBATION

Systems go through phases of stability and instability over time. Butz (1997) explains that instability means that change is occurring or about to occur, and stability indicates that change has occurred or is somewhere off in the future. A dynamical system has three possible states: stable, bifurcation, and chaos. Between stable periods and chaos, Butz states, are *bifurcation* points:

> A point at which there are two distinct choices open to a system; similar to a fork at which a path divides into two. Beyond this critical point the properties of a system can change abruptly (Coveney & Highfield, 1990, as cited in Butz, 1997, p. 11).

Ice melting into water is an example of bifurcation, and so too is a stream that divides as its channel is no longer able to contain the volume of water (Butz, 1997). Bifurcation is an indication of instability resulting from an internal or external stressful influence (Butz, 1997) or *perturbation* (Warren, Franklin, & Streeter, 1998). The system is now moving toward a less ordered state, and as it moves and becomes more unstable it bifurcates further and instability becomes substantial. The more unstable the system becomes, the harder it is to return to its previous stability. Eventually, given the continued movement toward disorder, the system will move into chaos (Butz). During a chaotic period, as Butz explains, "predictability is no longer a viable possibility, since the dynamics of the system have become so complex and sensitive" (p. 10).

Attractors, as described by Lewin (1992), are "states to which the system eventually settles, depending on the properties of the system" (p. 20), or, simply stated, "something that attracts this or that" (Butz, 1997). Butz further explains, "A system's movement through chaos happens as a result of the tension or stress a system experiences in moving from one attractor toward another attractor" (p. 12). Three types of attractors are described in the chaos/complexity literature: fixed point attractor, limit-cycle attractor, and strange attractor, all describing the system's movement over time (Butz). The strange attractor is of most interest in chaos/complexity research because it is nonlinear, with objects in its attraction moving about within parameters, but within those parameters the behavior is unpredictable. The strange attractor is, according to Butz, "the equivalent of chaos in attraction dynamics" (p.13).

SELF-ORGANIZATION

Strangely enough, as Butz (1997) states, "out of chaos a new stability forms....a more complex and adaptive form of order" (p. 15). Self-organization refers to the spontaneous emergence of order after a chaotic period (Barton, 1994; Butz, 1997; Prigogine, 1989) and is "matter's incessant attempts to organize itself into ever more complex structures, even in the face of the incessant forces of dissolution (Waldrop, 1992, cited in Butz, 1997). Self-organization is a change and becomes a perturbation of the environment. As Warren, Franklin, and Streeter (1998) state, "systems and environments perturb each other and are therefore constantly changing" (p. 361). A change in the system will lead to a change in the environment that will force a further change in the living system. Systems, then, are autonomous and self-organizing, having the ability to push themselves to higher forms of organization, and respond to the environment according to their own development and internal organization (Warren, Franklin, & Streeter, 1998).

Complexity theory offers a new way of thinking about dynamic, hence complex, systems. To be sure, this chapter has only skimmed the surface of the theoretical richness of this perspective. The theory, as Bolland and Atherton (1999) point out, provides an alternative to linear, deterministic models—an alternative that more closely approximates the natural workings of dynamic systems. As these authors suggest, chaos/complexity is a way of understanding and making sense of uncertainty, but without oversimplifying the concept. Chaos/complexity has some major implications for social work and for an advanced generalist paradigm, which are discussed in the following section.

COMPLEXITY AND ADVANCED GENERALIST PRACTICE

Chaos and complexity theory contribute to the definition of advanced generalist practice and its requirement for advanced and complex practice knowledge. Schatz, Jenkins, and Sheafor (1990) suggest that advanced practice skills are those that address complex direct and indirect practice situations, including competencies for treating multiple problem, chronic, and chaotic client systems, and that encompass the full spectrum of direct and indirect services. The concepts of chaos and complexity suggest that timing is an extremely important part of system change. As Warren, Franklin, and Streeter (1998) suggest, different interventions are needed in different stages of the change process. A number of advanced generalist practice principles can be derived from the theory:

- In terms of multidimensional practice, this theory suggests that intervention on the macro level is as important and as effective in contributing to individual change as direct intervention with individuals.

- Assessment and intervention are process oriented rather than fact based in advanced generalist practice. The skills and knowledge brought to the intervention are themselves process based, meaning that the expertise of workers is found more in their being "present" with the client, to discover patterns of behavior and new ways of coping (Warren, Franklin, & Streeter, 1998).

- Intervention is guided by the self-organizing capacity of the client system; change, when it occurs is rapid and transformative. Advanced generalist practice, then, tends to be time limited, appropriate to the change state of the client system, and empowerment oriented.

- The process of assessment is ongoing, and takes into account both time and space. Assessing the phase of system change is crucial to intervention planning. Using the concepts of complexity theory, the client can be described as being between stability and chaos. Clients are often in situations that are too linear, with rigid and narrow choices, or too chaotic, with no order or structure that facilitates healthy choices. A wide repertoire of skills helps the advanced generalist know when and how to intervene in multidimensional contexts.

- The goal of advanced generalist practice is not to understand the complexity of the client system, but rather to understand the natural movement of systems through stable, bifurcated, and chaotic states and to help promote self-organization, or, if the system is in chaos, to provide the resources (perturbations) needed to move the client back toward the edge of chaos. Treatment is focused on increasing the complexity in the client system, wherein the client system interacts in new ways within itself or with its environment, thus moving the client system toward self-organization (Butz, 1997). Adding complexity to a complex, adaptive system (in the form of relationship) is necessary to survival. Change and growth and survival are essentially synonymous.

- The principle of sensitive dependence on initial conditions suggests that it is important to pay attention to small changes, as even small changes can contribute to bigger changes down the road.

- Advanced generalists make use of the dynamic interaction of systems through the use of a holistic perspective integrated with the value stance of empowerment, social justice, and cultural competency.

- Advanced generalists look for complexity in relationships and behavior, and order in seeming disorder. The concept of strange attractors is helpful in understanding clients who appear to be caught in a loop of healthy and unhealthy behaviors and erratic behavior.

SYNTHESIS OF THEORY AND CORE VALUES FOR ADVANCED GENERALIST PRACTICE

Because of its focus on unpredictability, complexity theory may sometimes be viewed as a value-free perspective. From the perspective of social work, this would be a serious limitation. Any theory that attempts to inform and guide practice must be seen within a values context. In our conceptualization of advanced generalist practice, we have chosen to integrate the values of social justice, empowerment, and cultural competency with chaos/complexity. (See Figure 7.2 for integration of values with complexity theory.) Chaos/complexity concepts place process and relationship at the heart of its theory of change. Social justice, empowerment, and cultural competency are goals as well as processes. However, they are primarily about process, since the outcome of these efforts is contiguous with the expression of the values in pursuit of the goal. Social justice, cultural competency, and empowerment are unique yet interrelated values. From a chaos/complexity perspective, addressing any of these values through action will impact the others. (See O'Melia & Miley (2002) for readings in practice perspectives that emphasize social justice, empowerment, cultural competency, and multilevel practice.)

	Social Justice	Empowerment	Cultural Competency
Change Process (Complexity Theory)	-a life-long process -present in every social work situation -social justice in one context can contribute to the creation of an injustice in another arena	-process and goal -the end in the means	-committed to an ongoing process of assessment, of self and surrounding cultural environments
Relationships/ Communication	-cannot *not* communicate about social justice in any given situation -justice evolves through dialogue	-cannot *not* communicate about power within the helping relationship -process must be about both client and worker empowerment	-cannot *not* communicate about culture, race, etc. of client, and of self
Context of Practice (Phenomenology)	-justice and fairness defined in terms of meanings of clients	-client's world is one of complexity–of having/ finding power and of being disempowered -empowerment linked to small changes	-enter into the culture of individuals, families -functioning on the edge of chaos

Figure 7.2 Integrating values and complexity

Social Justice

Based on an understanding of perturbation, achieving social justice in one context can contribute to the creation of justice in another arena. Similarly, positive change in one system will create instability in another. For example, the closing of a chemical plant or corporate hog farm that pollutes groundwater contributes to layoffs and unemployment. How the changed system responds will depend on the attractors and energy available to the system. In order for self-organization to occur, however, the systems must be in communication with each other (Butz, 1997). Therefore, maximum social justice can be achieved through maximum participation in the ongoing pursuit of justice and by individuals and groups pursuing their vision of social justice. These systems are coevolving, and they "act in concert as a result of the dynamics of the system; [and] they do so as a result of individuals within the community myopically optimizing their own ends and not as collective agreement toward a common goal" (Lewin, 1992, p. 188).

Cultural Competency

As a process, cultural competency is not about acquiring facts about diverse cultures as it is impossible to acquire the complex "facts" of every culture to be competent. The concept of systems existing on the edge of chaos is helpful in understanding diverse individuals, families, groups, and organizations. By being on the edge of chaos, a system is "poised to respond, nudged into creative activity by simple perturbations" (Lewin, 1992, p. 166). Although systems can and do navigate through chaos to a new stability, living on the edge of chaos allows the system to avoid the tremendous expenditure of energy needed to create new order, but allows the system to innovate and respond efficiently to the ever-present changing environment. This concept has particular application for at-risk communities required to respond to an ongoing onslaught of external perturbations. Individuals, families, and communities faced with chronic stress are in constant bifurcation (forced down pathways that cut off options for stability), thus in danger of total disorganization and chaos. Living on the edge means making "just good enough" adaptation (Butz, 1997), which suggests exactly the kind of change and innovation that families in crisis and stress can handle.

Empowerment

The concept of self-organization resonates with the primary goal of empowerment to increase personal, interpersonal, and political power in individuals and groups (Gutierrez, GlenMaye, & DeLois, 1995). Empowerment seeks to create a context for self-empowerment, i.e., giving people the tools they need to act on their own behalf (Byrne, 1998). Drawing on the dynamic interdependence of systems in complexity theory, it is clear that pursuing empowerment within the helping relationship will affect the client-worker relationship, as well as systems and relationships far removed from the intervention setting. Thus, practitioners are in a simultaneous process of empowerment: as clients are empowered, workers are "perturbed," and must deal with the change that occurs as clients move toward self-organization and change.

CONCLUSION

The advanced generalist practice model seeks to encompass complexity while not being overwhelmed by that very complexity. To think of relationships as dynamic process, to view clients and ourselves holistically, and to promote multidimensional, transformative change that is empowering, socially just, and culturally competent offers much potential for revitalizing social work practice.

This chapter is based on a paper previously presented at the Annual Program Meeting of the Council on Social Work Education, Dallas, Texas, March 2001.

REFERENCES

Argüelles, S., & von Simson, A. (1999). Innovative family and technological interventions for encouraging leisure activities in caregivers of persons with Alzheimer's disease. *Activities, Adaptation, and Aging, 24*(2), 83-97.

Barton, S. (1994). Chaos, self-organization, and psychology. *American Psychologist, 49*, 5-14.

Berger, R. M. (1986). Social work practice models: A better recipe. *Social Casework, 67*(1), 45-54.

Bolland, K. A., & Atherton, C. R. (1999). Chaos theory: An alternative approach to social work practice and research. *The Journal of Contemporary Human Services, 80*(4), 367-374.

Boyd-Franklin, N., & Bry, B. H. (2000). *Reaching out in family therapy: Home-based, school, and community interventions.* New York: The Guilford Press.

Boyd-Franklin, N., & Shenouda, N. T. (1990). A multisystems approach to the treatment of a black, inner-city family with a schizophrenic mother. *The American Journal of Orthopsychiatry, 60*(2), 186-195.

Butz, M. R. (1997). *Chaos and complexity: Implications for psychological theory and practice.* Washington, DC: Taylor & Francis.

Byrne, D. (1998). *Complexity theory and the social sciences: An introduction.* New York: Routledge.

Campbell, J. A., & Shepard, M. (1990). Social work education for rural practice: The advanced generalist. *Human Services in the Rural Environment, 14*(1), 21-24.

Chubb, H. (1990). Looking at systems as process. *Family Process, 29*, 169-175.

Cimmarusti, R. A. (1992). Family preservation practice based upon a multisystems approach. *Child Welfare, 71*(3), 241-256.

Council on Social Work Education (1994). Handbook of accreditation standards and procedures (4th ed.). Alexandria, VA: Author.

Derezotes, D. S. (2000). *Advanced generalist social work practice.* Thousand Oaks, CA: Sage.

Ellenberger, H. F. (1958). A clinical introduction to psychiatric phenomenology, in R. May, E. Angel, & H. F. Ellenberger (Eds.) *Existence: A new dimension in psychiatry and psychology*. New York: Touchstone Books.

Germain, C., & Gitterman, A. (1980). *The life model of social work practice*. New York: Columbia University Press.

Gibbs, P., Locke, B., & Lohman, R. (1990). Paradigm for the generalist-advanced generalist continuum. *Journal of Education for Social Work 26*(3), 217-233.

Gleick, J. (1987). *Chaos: Making a new science*. New York: Penguin Books.

Gould, K. H. (1987). Life model versus conflict model: A feminist perspective. *Social Work, 32*(4), 346-351.

Gross, G. M. (1992). A defining moment: The social work continuum revisited. *Journal of Social Work Education, 28*(1), 110-118.

Gutierrez, L. M., GlenMaye, L. F., & DeLois, K. A. (1995). The organizational context of empowerment practice: Implications for social work administration. *Social Work, 40*(2), 249-258.

Hearn, G. (1958). *Theory building in social work*. Toronto, Ontario: University of Toronto Press.

Hernandez, S. H., Jorgensen, J. D., Judd, P., Gould, M. S., & Parsons, R. J. (1985). Integrated practice: An advanced generalist curriculum to prepare social problem specialists. *Journal of Social Work Education, 21*(3), 28-35.

Holliman, D. C., Dziegielewski, S. F., & Datta, P. (2001). Discharge planning and social work practice. *Social Work in Health Care, 32*(3), 1-19.

Kauffman, S. (1991). Antichaos and adaptation. *Scientific American, 264*(8), 78-84.

Landon, P. S. (1995). Generalist and advanced generalist practice. In R. L. Edwards & J. G. Hopps (Eds.), *Encyclopedia of social work* (19th ed.). Washington, DC: NASW Press.

Laszlo, E. (1972). *The systems view of the world*. New York: George Braziller.

Lewin, R. (1992). Complexity: Life at the edge of chaos. New York: Macmillan.

Lorenz, E. N. (1963). Deterministic nonperiodic flow. *Journal of Atmospheric Sciences, 20*, 130-141.

Ma, J. L. C. (1999). Social work practice with transsexuals in Hong Kong who apply for sex reassignment surgery. *Social Work in Health Care, 29*(2), 85-103.

Mandlebrot, B. (1993). Fractals. In J. Holte (Ed.), *Chaos: The new science* (pp. 1-33). Lanham, MD: University Press of America.

Martindale, D. (1988). *The nature and types of sociological theory* (2nd ed.). Prospect Heights, IL: Waveland Press.

Mason, D. T., & Lusk, M. W. (1992). Development theory for advanced generalist practice: Implications for intervention and education. *Human Services in the Rural Environment, 16*(2), 12-17.

Masterpasqua, F. (1997). Self-organization in developmental processes. In F. Masterpasqua and P. A. Perna (Eds.)., *The psychological meaning of chaos* (pp. 23-40). Washington DC: American Psychological Association.

Masterpasqua, F., & Perna, P. A. (Eds.) (1997). *The psychological meaning of chaos.* Washington DC: American Psychological Association.

McMahon, M. (1994). Advanced generalist practice: An international approach. Englewood Cliffs, NJ: Prentice Hall.

Meyer, C. (1983). *Clinical social work in the eco-systems perspective.* New York: Columbia University Press.

O'Melia, M., & Miley, K. K. (Eds.). (2002). *Pathways to power: Readings in contextual social work practice.* Boston: Allyn & Bacon.

Pardeck, J. T., Yuen, F. K., Daley, J. G., & Hawkins, C. L. (1998). Social work assessment and intervention through family health practice. *Family Therapy, 25*(1), 25-39.

Perna, P. A., & Masterpasqua, F. (1997). Introduction: The history, meaning, and implications of chaos and complexity, in F. Masterpasqua & P. A. Perna (Eds.), *The psychological meaning of chaos.* Washington, DC: American Psychological Association.

Peters, T. (1987). *Thriving on chaos: Handbook for a management revolution.* NY: Harper/Collins.

Prigogine, I. (1989). *Order out of chaos: Man's new dialogue with nature.* Toronto, Ontario: Bantam.

Raymond, G. T., Teare, R. J., & Atherton, C. R. (1996). Is "field of practice" a relevant organizing principle for the MSW curriculum? *Journal of Social Work Education, 32*(1), 19-30.

Rittner, B., & Albers, E. (1999). Developing a group work sequence: Bringing the community into group work. *Journal of Teaching in Social Work, 18*(1/2), 113-131.

Robbins, S. P., Chatterjee, P., & Canda, E. R. (1998). *Contemporary human behavior theory: A critical perspective for social work.* Needham Heights, MA: Allyn & Bacon.

Rose, S. D., Duby, P., Olenick, C., & Weston, T. (1996). Integrating family, group, and residential treatment: A cognitive-behavioral approach. *Social Work with Groups, 19*(2), 35-48.

Schatz, M., Jenkins, L., & Sheafor, B. (1990). Milford redefined: A model of initial and advanced generalist social work. *Journal of Education for Social Work, 26*(3), 217-231.

Thompson, J., Menefee, D., & Marley, M. (1999). A comparative analysis of social workers' macro practice activities: Identifying functions common to direct practice and administration. *Journal of Social Work Education, 35*(1), 115-124.

Turner, J. H. (1986). *The structure of sociological theory* (4th ed.). Chicago: Dorsey.

Von Bertalanffy, L. (1968). *General systems theory*. New York: George Braziller.

Vosler, N. R., & Nair, S. (1993). Families, children, poverty: Education for social work practice at multiple systems levels. *International Social Work, 36*(2), 159-172.

Waldrop, M. M. (1992). *Complexity: The emerging science at the edge of chaos*. New York: Simon & Schuster.

Warren, K., Franklin, C., & Streeter, C. L. (1998). New directions in systems theory: Chaos and complexity. *Social Work, 43*(4), 357-372.

Watzlawick, P., Beavin, J. H., & Jackson, D. D. (1962). *The pragmatics of human communication: A study of interactional patterns, pathologies, and paradoxes*. New York: W. W. Norton.

SECTION 3: THE CHALLENGE OF FIELD EDUCATION

Chapter 8

PROVING GROUND: FIELD EDUCATION AND ADVANCED GENERALIST PRACTICE

William T. Fisher, Jr.
Springfield College
and
Mary P. Byrne
Salem State College

THE EVOLVING CONTEXT

Field education is a crucial element in the education of graduate social work students (Bogo & Globerman, 1999; Schneck, Grossman, & Glassman, 1991; George, 1982; Council on Social Work Education (CSWE), 1962). The field component provides the setting in which students explore social work values and theories and execute social work skills and interventions as a prelude to professional practice. Challenges frequently identified in field education are ongoing. They include student-agency fit, supervisory styles, student learning needs, curricular integration, and the importance of developing working relationships among school, field, and student. Advanced generalist field education programs must address these challenges and more. The authors of this chapter propose that the advanced generalist approach, while bringing special challenges to field education, is also uniquely equipped to produce novel, creative, and far-reaching responses and solutions to social work practice today and in the future.

The advanced generalist approach helps us realize Smalley's 1967 contention that social work releases (a) human power in individuals that allows them to reach their full potential and contribute to society *and* (b) social power to bring about changes in society, social institutions, and social policy that affects opportunities for individuals and groups. But, as a profession, are we victims of social change or makers of social change? And how can we, as educators, best serve students, clients or consumers, our profession, and society? Field education from an advanced generalist perspective has much to offer in answering these questions.

Field education, once in the background of social work curriculums, has taken center stage in the contemporary environment. As schools become more globally connected there has emerged a more universal consensus that field education is the "crucial component" of social work education (Noble, 1999). Field placements, when integrated with community practice, are increasingly viewed as the "cornerstone" of graduate social work experience (Jennings, 2001) and as a truly integrative force in the curriculum.

Landmark articles by Jarmon-Rohde, McFall, Kolar, and Strom (1997) and Reisch and Jarmon-Rohde (2000) have challenged social work education, and field education in particular, to respond to the massive environmental forces pulling, pushing, and shaping society. Social work and field education must develop creative responses to economic globalization, the shifting political climate, the growing use of technology, and demographic shifts affecting cities and rural communities. These forces also generate changes in social service agencies and higher education. Far-reaching and potentially devastating effects on social service agencies are occurring because of reductions in federal funding, the creation of block grants to the states ("devolution"), cost-containment mandates, and managed care. Individually and interactively, these forces directly affect the ability of agencies to provide educational experiences to social work interns.

In the following pages, the authors identify the environmental influences affecting social work field education and emphasize the value of the advanced generalist approach in addressing them. Both challenges and opportunities are identified. Models of field education and curricular integration utilizing an advanced generalist perspective are also provided.

NEEDS AND DEMANDS OF THE ENVIRONMENT

Global Forces

As human beings in a social environment, we are bound to time and context. While human beings both construct and adapt to extant social environments, what may be different in this era is the rapidity of change to which we are required to adapt. Significant, ongoing, and intensifying changes in economic and social forces necessitate changes in all areas of life and social endeavor. Social work practice, social work education, and social work field education are not exceptions. The massive global social changes affecting contemporary life may be conceptualized as: (a) information and technology, (b) economic variability, and (c) diversity.

Information and technology. All citizens will require the skills to continually adapt to a rapidly shifting environment that demands the abilities to absorb, sort, manipulate, and effectively use information in greater and greater quantities. Reich (2002) has noted that in the future there will be a bifurcation of the workforce between the information manipulator and non-manipulator. In this formulation, information manipulators who are technologically literate will compose the middle and upper classes; those who are not information manipulators will be left behind and compose the poor, isolated, and socially marginalized. The well-documented widening divide between the well-off and the poor will result in more complex needs among clients and client groups. Groups left behind by the information explosion and periodic economic booms will be affected most severely. Social work will be called upon to address the needs of these groups, and advocacy and social change efforts will become increasingly important.

   The information explosion has affected all areas of social work practice. Demands for greater accountability to funding sources and consumer groups, needs for practice skill in wider varieties of treatment and intervention approaches, and efforts to develop community-based organizations and services are among the results brought about by greater access to information by all stakeholders in society. Accountability requires the development of tracking systems and outcome indicators, as well as the involvement of consumers. The variety of research-based, proposed, and newly emerging treatment approaches requires ongoing education of practitioners. Community-based clients and programs require an expansion of social work skills in the areas of case management, referral, and advocacy, as well as in administration, program development, and program evaluation. Information has become the lifeblood not only of the marketplace, but also of practice in all the social services. Students must have opportunities to work effectively with information and to develop related relevant skills that address client systems needs.

Economic variability. The periodic rises and falls of Western and global economies are forces with ramifications for social work and social work education. While the dismantling of social programs has been several years in the making, it must unfortunately be said that fighting the war on terrorism further decreases resources and diverts public will for social programs. In the wake of welfare reform (the Personal Responsibility and Work Opportunity Reconciliation Act of 1996) and as responsibilities for social programs continue to be turned back to states and localities—which may have competing agendas and constituencies—the least able to be heard suffer the effects the most. Despite society's need for social workers, recruitment and retention of social workers in community-based settings has been difficult (O'Neill, 2002; Reeser & Epstein, 1987). However, field education experiences in an advanced generalist program reinforce community practice that is holistic, problem-solving, and change-oriented.

While licensure has provided economic benefits and professional recognition, the requirements of licensure communicate a limited scope for social work practice. As health care costs come under greater scrutiny, third-party reimbursements using a medical model pay for only the "billable" hours, effectively restricting time devoted to outreach, program development, community collaboration, or advocacy with health and governmental systems. The result? Social service organizations that seek survival need licensed providers, including social workers, for the revenue they provide. This marketized model of social work practice will be changed through advanced generalist practice and a vanguard of practitioners.

Diversity. The recognition of diversity, in all its forms, is a social force with vast implications for social work practice and education. As the world shrinks and as more and more previously excluded and disenfranchised groups become part of the fabric of daily life, human helping services must be provided in culturally sensitive and appropriate ways. If ever social workers sought a universal way to work with individuals, families, groups, or communities, that effort is surely now behind us. Joined with becoming culturally literate, the best social work tool now is systems theory, a concept given greater utility by the ecological, person-in-environment approach (Germain & Gitterman, 1987). But do forces from continual information expansion and economic necessity undermine the promise of the systems-ecological approach? Can vast amounts of information enervate rather than motivate? Does knowing more translate into action at levels where it needs to make a difference? Do economic forces hold the sole power to define the practice of social work? Given the current social context, is it more manageable to focus on the "problem individual" or "problem family" than to address the social situations that create individual, family, community, and social ills? New models of social work practice are needed, and advanced generalist field educational programs are providing them.

Changes in Social Service Agency Environments

Social service agencies, where students first practice, have been required to conduct business differently as a result of rapid changes in practice environments, brought about by socioeconomics, the explosion of technology, and the need for management of change itself. Moving from categorical and publicly provided or faith-affiliated social service institutions, the business of agencies is described largely in terms of community network affiliations and managed care systems. Contracts use product-oriented terminology and establish performance-based targets to determine program sustainability. Even publicly contracted agencies, providing what in the past were considered the institutionalized and categorical services of the state, must manage capitations, federally monitored block grants, cost containments, and productivity in order to provide services.

Consequently, field educators and academic partners must prepare students to understand and manage the environment with sophisticated collaboration skills, while simultaneously mastering the skills of relationship-building, assessment, and creative intervention. This is the dual challenge of knowledge building coupled with the "doing" of the profession (CSWE, 2001; Schneck & CSWE, 1997). Unlike students in earlier eras, today's students witness agencies threatened with extinction or merger, affiliating with and becoming network partners to assure economic and service survival, or competing as entrepreneurs and network leaders. Education in economics and business ethics become as essential as the theoretical bases and social work ethics of care. "Ecosurvival" is a necessity.

As noted, a second wave of social change affecting agencies is the use of and interface with technology. Although technology currently is chiefly an adjunct and support to traditional educational methods in most social work programs (Reisch & Jarmon-Rohde, 2000), students are increasingly encountering technology in field settings, including its use as a primary means of communication. In 1997, Krueger predicted that the development of "hypertechnologies" would make intervention skills obsolete. Some of his predictions have been realized, e.g., a shift from the family as a locus of intervention to age- and gender-specific, market-driven populations has occurred, and a "borderless" business world has emerged (Krueger). However, while the substitution of headphones and speakers for voices of need has not yet taken place completely, perhaps technology can be used to make voices more widely and loudly heard. This is one possible role of the advanced generalist social worker in the cyber-environment.

Increased knowledge sharing among the social work advocacy, research, and practice communities is a means by which technology serves the advanced generalist conception of practice. In addition to the use of technologies for distance learning (Reisch & Jarmon-Rohde, 2000) in social work programs and in post-graduate continuing education, there has been an increase in the use of satellite conferencing, bringing new developments in the field to a wider audience. Novel uses of the Internet for information sharing, data dissemination, policy development, and legislative action have also occurred, creating an upsurge in the use of "listservs" to create virtual and global practice communities, some spanning both practice and national boundaries. One example is a listserv (Geraty, 2002) that emerged after September 11, 2001 that united international social workers and humanitarian aid workers who provided micro and macro services to affected populations.

Field education provides a context in which social work students can begin to master and use technology to enhance communication, build connections and intervention bridges, and survey the field of practice more quickly for models already being used with changing populations and for changing needs. Instead of hampering connection to and awareness of the voices of the vulnerable, technology creates opportunities to assure that those voices are heard. The advanced generalist approach, with its emphasis on cross-systems interfacing, is suited to this era. The following list demonstrates just a few ways in which agency business and education are transacted differently as a result of the information age and technological resources:

- Use of public media and marketing to demonstrate competency and effectiveness, convey the value of the organization, and secure funding and public support.

- Increased school and agency collaboration on needs assessments, service improvements, and performance outcome analyses.

- Development of field education projects that inform and provide agency direction, make compelling arguments to legislators, and advocate for and with consumer groups.

Another agency-centered change has been the need for "boundary spanning," and agency representatives who can move across methods and disciplines and interact effectively with diverse spheres of service and funding. These individuals must possess the skills to bring about what Senge (1990) has termed "learning cultures," oriented to learning and evolving rather than controlling. Building learning cultures and organizations requires advanced generalist professionals who can create as well as critique visions, and who can balance inquiry with advocacy. As true systems thinkers who see interrelationships and move beyond blame to possibilities, these individuals focus on opportunities for success and creative change. Field education models may be created where "circles of learning" or "learning teams" are composed of stakeholders at all levels, including consumers and representatives of natural resources in the community, thus embodying the resources and skills valued in advanced generalist practice.

Client System Changes

Almost since the advent of systems theory, the human helping professions have been seeking to adopt the concept for use in practice. Systems theory compels us to seek out and recognize the myriad influences that affect human beings, families, groups, communities, organizations, societies, and the human family and natural environment across the globe. The development of the ecological model of social work practice and person-in-environment as methods for identifying and analyzing influences in the lives of individuals provided a new language and tools to address both micro and macro needs. Despite the tremendous contributions of these approaches, the following questions may still be asked: Has social work as a profession gone far enough in addressing the needs of individuals, families, groups, organizations, and society by providing the impetus and leadership to create and sustain health within and among these entities? Because of the economic pressures of managed care and the need for the survival of social service agencies, has the ecological model at times been reduced to another micro-level approach that continues to make the victim central rather than the cause?

To fulfill the promise and vision of systems theory, the ecological model, and person-in-environment, social workers must be prepared to intervene at many levels of human functioning, including the intra-organizational, the inter-organizational, and the political. These are the critical basic tenets of advanced generalist practice. These ideas radically alter conceptions of client systems and require practitioners to be adept at carefully considering, moving among, and manipulating elements within micro, mezzo, and macro levels of human social functioning and understanding. Challenges inherent in accepting a systems vision are: integrating into a coherent whole the enormity of relevant information about clients and communities (however defined or delimited); determining when, where, and how to act most effectively; and maintaining awareness of and a commitment to social change. Awareness is but a precursor to action; description alone does not provide prescription. Thus, the boundaries we choose to draw around the "client" must be elastic and inclusive. And the actions we are prepared to take with and on behalf of clients must be informed, value-driven, and broad in scope. Field education experiences must reflect these enlarged conceptions of client systems.

The vital role for advanced generalists who are informed, guided by values, and able to grasp contextual breadth is illustrated by the development of community-based services for empowered consumers, who in earlier eras were removed from the mainstream of society. While cost containment was clearly a factor in moving consumers into the community, ongoing "naturalization" of services has, over time, resulted in the increased inclusion of service recipients in treatment planning and program development, unique partnerships with and greater communication among providers, and an awareness of the wider environment as the context for creating and sustaining health. Though the mobility and anonymity possible in modern life may threaten shared senses of community, with the assistance of advanced generalists, students, and seasoned professionals, many locales are building collaborations that improve the quality of life of residents who formerly would not have been part of the life of the community.

Student Changes

The demographic profiles of graduate social work students have changed and will continue to change. Increases in the enrollment of older and nontraditional students with careers in progress, families with needs, and financial responsibilities have added to the challenges of graduate education, field education, and the influences of the service environment. While social work students have never been completely removed from the "real world" even in the earliest days of social work education (George, 1982), today's students are less able and willing to submit to the dictates of an educational program that may have been undertaken to advance one's career, not divert it. Multiple obligations and layers of influences, interacting in novel and often unexpected ways, are the norms of contemporary life, as the ecological model has elegantly identified. Field education must be responsive to the needs of students and forward-looking in developing educational experiences that reflect sensitivity to the systems in which students find themselves.

Graduate students today are adult learners who have extremely practical goals for their education, including career progression. Among this group of students may be individuals of color, older students, military veterans, and career changers. Individuals with careers in the social services already begun are attracted to the financial remuneration, as well as the prestige, that accompanies postgraduate professional designation and licensure. Students with these goals are less content with passive learning and with having controlled structures that dictate educational experiences and controlled outcomes. This is particularly true of the field component of their education. Engaging with students in determining individualized learning and career goals, developing means for them to achieve these goals, and providing flexible monitoring and evaluation indicators are necessary. The life experiences mature students bring to the educational process make them ideal candidates for advanced generalist practice.

THE ADVANCED GENERALIST IMPERATIVE

Advanced generalist practice has emerged in the past two decades as a viable practice orientation and educational approach that provides practitioners and students with the skills and competencies to respond effectively to a complex and chaotic environment. In a national sample of 2,500 social workers, the advanced generalist model was considered the "organizing principle for the advanced social work curriculum" (Raymond, Teare, and Atherton, 1996). Gibbs, Locke, and Lohmann (1990) laud the holistic qualities of a generalist approach that is "problem-solving centered, rather than methods-driven," and that prepares practitioners for a range of possible settings and circumstances.

> The ethical base of social work commits to a stance that people should have equal access to resources, services, and opportunities for the accomplishment of life tasks and goals....The crux of generalist practice...involves not only the way a generalist views a situation (the gestalt of the person-situation-environment) but also how the situation is responded to (intervention at potentially several different levels while assuming any number of roles). (p. 235)

Gibbs, Locke, and Lohmann (1990) provide a useful elucidation of generalist roles that may operate concurrently or as subsets, depending on the needs of any given situation. It is among the challenges of an advanced generalist curriculum, including the field component, to promote and reinforce skills that support these roles: broker, advocate, evaluator, outreach worker, teacher, behavior changer, consultant, caregiver, data manager, administrator, enabler, mediator, and community planner. Through actions of increasingly greater nuance and sophistication, practitioners with graduate-level preparation are expected to perform these roles with greater "depth and breadth."

In fact, a relatively early study found that graduates of advanced generalist programs do use macro skills more frequently than do micro-prepared practitioners, despite little difference between the practice settings and populations served by the two groups (Teigiser, 1983). Generalists more frequently included organizations, administrators of other agencies, and communities in their practice approach and considered it their role to initiate and develop new ideas.

Hernandez, Jorgensen, and Judd (1985) pointed out the need for a "new kind of helper": one who can work not only with the "victims of social problems," but with the social problems as well. They provide a useful history of an effort to build an "integrated practice" curriculum that "views the problems of individuals as fundamentally nested in broader social contexts that are legitimate targets for intervention" (p. 30). This group also identified professional roles advanced generalists should assume across the client systems of individual, family, small group, organization, and community (including society as a whole). These are: conferee (or the primary source of assistance to the consumer or client in problem-solving), enabler, broker, mediator, advocate, and guardian. The field practicum is central to developing skills for these roles. In addition to direct work with individuals, families, and groups, field experiences in this curricular model include administration, community organization, and political intervention activities. "Generalists will need to guide and engineer the problem definition and means of solution, as well as the development and management of community resources for mutual problem solving" (Parsons, Hernandez, and Jorgensen, 1988, p. 417).

Further explicating skills defining an advanced generalist practitioner, Schatz, Jenkins, and Sheafor (1990) contend that despite limited agreement in a 1987 Delphi study among social work "experts" there nevertheless exists a unique generalist methodology. Generalist practice must be "theoretically and methodologically open" in order to respond to the unique needs of any situation and set of environmental factors. The advanced generalist has skills to address "complex direct practice situations" and "more complex indirect practice situations at the bureaucratic, organizational, and community levels," as well as the abilities "to conduct disciplined and systematic eclectic practice" and "to engage in theoretical and practice research and evaluation" (Schatz, Jenkins, and Sheafor, p. 226). Advanced generalist field experiences must provide learning opportunities for students to develop the full range of social work skills relevant for use now and into the foreseeable future.

Field educators certainly recognize results of the forces creating change in current social work practice environments. The 1997 survey of field educators, sponsored by the CSWE's Commission on Field Education, asked "What particular challenges or difficulties are you facing currently in the delivery or teaching of the field experience?" The number one category of concern was "social service system turmoil." Environmental turmoil was seen as leaving little time for student supervision. According to these educators, the primary means of addressing environmental change and flux should be through networking—within the educational setting, the larger educational institution, and the community—to bring about programmatic changes and curriculum "revisioning, refining, and expansion," as well as greater outreach and collaboration (Schneck and CSWE, 1997).

ENVIRONMENTAL CHANGES AND EDUCATIONAL AND PRACTICE NEEDS

What are the educational and practical effects of sweeping and far-reaching social change? Continued conflict over resources within all levels of society and the service community is inevitable, and ethical and practice principles have been and will be affected:

> Field education will need to be reconceptualized as part of a broader effort to develop new practice frameworks and methods that focus less on accommodating to new practice realities and that rely more on community-based approaches to transform those realities. Under this redefinition, the traditional distinctions between micro and macro practice, social and economic development, individual and community change, will no longer be valid. (Reisch & Jarmon-Rohde, 2000, p. 208)

Social work education and the field experience in advanced generalist programs must provide students with opportunities to acquire adaptable skills in service coordination and integration; develop a greater understanding of economic forces affecting individuals, families, and communities; and practice increased collaboration with agencies and communities to develop innovative responses to social needs. Springfield College and Salem State College, both in Massachusetts, are two schools that have embraced the advanced generalist model for their curriculums and have instituted field education programs reflecting expanded conceptions of social work practice.

Advanced generalist programs seek to reflect the realities and needs of the service environment and provide opportunities for students to learn theories and develop skills with utility in the current practice environment—including the skills to change the current practice environment. Toward that end, research has assessed the presence of and need for advanced generalist skills among practitioners. For example, a persuasive argument can be made that the skills necessary for social work administration are also necessary for effective direct practice when the skills are broadly conceptualized rather than discretely and specifically compartmentalized (Thompson, Menafee, and Marley, 1999). Boundary spanning, futuring, facilitating, managing resources, teaming, evaluating, supervising, advocating, leveraging, and policy practice are all areas in which both direct and indirect social work practitioners must engage. Other research has suggested that generalist skills are critical to a variety of practice areas, including work with homeless individuals with mental health needs (Cohen, 1990) and discharge planning for patients leaving the hospital (Holliman, Dziegielewski and Datta, 2001). O'Conner (1988) presented a three-tiered model of case management and advanced generalist practice skills, and contended that social work should view case management as an essential social work function in which the most complex level is executed by managers and administrators.

INTEGRATION OF THE CURRICULUM AND FIELD EDUCATION

Field educators have for some time shared a degree of agreement on the need for advanced generalist practice skills to be part of students' educational experiences. Reprising and extending a Delphi study of 1983, Raskin (1994) found "strong consensus" among field educators on two statements with important implications for advanced generalist field education. Agreement that "despite the generic or multi-method objectives many schools have for their students in the field, the casework method remains the most highly conceptualized form of practice by most field instructors," indicates the perception that more can be done to concretize what an advanced generalist field experience should be. Agreement that "field education programs should make use of the total agency for teaching, not just a single mentor-apprenticeship relationship," begins to move the agenda forward. For advanced generalist field education to be effective, it requires the following:

- An expansion of concepts related to what field education can or should provide.
- Ongoing integration of field education with the curriculum, including creative assignments within the field experience.
- Increased acclimation of field supervisors or instructors to the advanced generalist perspective.
- A concerted commitment to organizational development, community organization, and social change.

Effective advanced generalist programs have integrated curriculums with the educational goal of coordination among sequences of courses and intensifying levels of learning sophistication as students proceed. This means moving from a concurrent, parallel model of methods and concentrations to a model that provides an interrelated, comprehensive approach. Examples of this are cross-concentration and cross-course initiatives, including (and at times driven by) data from the field. Other possibilities are development of cross-discipline academic and field curriculums with other educational programs in the helping professions, such as education, nursing, criminal justice, psychology, and law. Community initiatives built on partnerships to bring about child and elderly kinship care, a full-service school, or to enhance services to residents of a low-income housing project of diverse ethnicity are just a few of the possibilities in this curricular model and illustrate programs in place or in planning at Salem State College's School of Social Work.

Using Reisch and Jarmon-Rohde's vision (2000), the components of an integrated advanced generalist curriculum include the following:

- A systems and transactional framework, recognizing ecological and ecocultural elements.
- A contextual approach with a client-centered systems emphasis on problems and possibilities.
- Analysis and actions to address the local and macro affects of globalization, political climate, and demographic changes.
- The use of technology in the classroom and in field sites.
- Demonstration of flexibility in practice and skills for the future.

Further, heeding a call for "sustained and multifaceted outreach," advanced generalist programs partner with field supervisors or instructors, their agencies, other agencies, other disciplines, and additional stakeholders to develop a critical mass of collaborators for creative initiatives.

The opportunities inherent in providing an effective field experience in an advanced generalist curriculum include the following:

- Ongoing development of a fully integrated curriculum.
- Increased collaboration with agencies that value the advanced generalist approach.
- Maintenance of flexibility in field-related assignments and requirements, and exploration of new ways that assignments may be completed.
- Increasing outreach efforts and partnerships with many stakeholders.
- Development of initiatives that address the needs of communities and multiple systems.

THE UNIQUENESS OF ADVANCED GENERALIST FIELD EDUCATION

The advanced generalist approach provides "a perspective focusing on the interface between systems" (Schatz, Jenkins, and Sheafor, 1990, p. 223), on the interpersonal in transactions, and on an openness to possibilities as well as problems. Field experiences in advanced generalist education may be conceptualized as reflecting three unique descriptive constructs. First, generalist field education is the academic application of the *wrap-around model* frequently applied in social work practice today. That is, the field education experience takes on a context and shape that is totally immersed in the population and possibility and/or problem the community context provides. There is, therefore, no precise script for what experiences a student will have in the field, even with predictable curricular assignments. Instead, there needs to be the guarantee that the experience will be client-centered, will be involved with systems of all sizes, will assess assets and resources as well as vulnerabilities and deficits, and will address the contemporary transactional challenges present, including the cultural and socioeconomic contexts.

The second construct unique to advanced generalist field education is similar to Schon's (1987) conception of the *reflective learning experience*. The philosophical core of the advanced generalist experience, with a player acting at many potential levels of intervention, does not simply require self-reflection on a one-to-one, personal level of experience, but requires something more inclusive and larger. Field experiences must become a stimulus for critical reflection on political contexts, social action, and social justice. Through this process, students come to see themselves not only as knowers, but also as doers and change agents (Crawford, Dickinson, and Leitmann, 2002). The reflective learning concept integrates the "critical consciousness" skills promoted by Freire (1973) where understanding of social situations reaches a depth of interpretation encompassing true systemic analysis. The field education experience, with multiple players, layers, and possibilities, using "people's knowledge," becomes a "culture circle" (Friere, 1970, 1973), or what Senge (1990) would term a "learning culture," and employs what advanced generalist educators and practitioners call grass-roots, community knowledge.

While all field education can be described as "participatory learning," advanced generalist field education integrates participatory learning with community practice (i.e., practice that recognizes and seeks to address or modify contextual systems)—however "community" or the "client system" may be defined (Castelloe & Watson, 1999). The student is challenged to develop critical skills in assessing and understanding how systems interface at a variety of levels of interaction, in order to locate barriers and generate possibilities for change. In a strategically designed generalist field practicum, the student will struggle with the *interaction of action and reflection*, and develop a "critical consciousness" (the third construct) that has an impact on the student as well as on field supervisors or instructors, colleagues, clients or consumers, and the contextual community. These must be combined with recognition of reciprocal autonomy among players and an understanding and demonstration of cross-discipline and cross-hierarchical interdependence (Robb, 2000). As both Robb and Senge (1990) suggest, it is the adaptive skills that allow the student to align forces that often are oppositional and work with the resources at hand, thereby building professional resiliency as well as concrete adaptive skill sets. These learning challenges incorporate participatory practice with critical and reflective analysis (Castelloe & Watson), thereby building awareness of one's ability to address and create change in both larger contexts and micro-level personal situations.

BUILDING AND USING ADVANCED GENERALIST FIELD EDUCATION MODELS

Advanced generalist curriculums require field education to develop learning experiences that reflect and shape current and future practice environments. Because "traditional models of field education do not fit with the trend toward community-based, integrative services," Reisch and Jarmon-Rohde (2000) see important opportunities for social work education and field education to respond to multilayered and systemic forces in innovative and productive ways. They recommend that educational programs be creative with supervision, agency liaison efforts, and field site development, especially in seeking opportunities to partner in mutually beneficial ways with agencies, including those in the public sector. Social services agencies and educational institutions are confronted with the need to use media for marketing and networking, and both must become increasingly adept at developing means to evaluate the effectiveness of educational and practice outcomes. Creative partnerships assist both kinds of organizations with meeting missions and addressing constituencies. Opportunities abound for schools to initiate agency collaborations for practice and population-based research, program evaluation, and program development. Social activism and political action, "focus[ing] on 'common human needs' more strategically to influence national priorities," are also needed in the current context (Reisch & Jarmon-Rohde, 2000, citing Krueger, 1997).

Changes in agency contexts and student lifestyles, along with the reality of the dynamic needs of clients and communities, must all be taken into account to develop new field education models that are workable and effective at a variety of levels. In addition, agency-based field educators have less time to develop their "educator role" and need to be provided with convenient ways to link with educational programs and resources to strengthen that function. Technology may be one means for this to occur.

Field education models that develop effective advanced generalist social work professionals have the following components:

- A fully integrated curriculum linking course work and field experiences through flexible assignments and projects with demonstrable learning outcomes.
- Innovative use of information and communication technologies that model and promote systemic intervention at multiple levels.

- Creatively designed experiences for both students and field supervisors or instructors to develop advanced generalist skills, which are undertaken along with other agency supervisors, other agency employees, and faculty.
- An emphasis on collaboration between educational institutions and agencies, providing incentives for agencies to become and remain field learning centers that demonstrate effective advanced generalist practice and provide models for future practice.
- Outcomes relevant not only to student learning and professional development, but also to the enhancement of agency and community effectiveness.
- Practice models that provide for competency demonstration and measurement, and which allow tracking of curricular integration and effectiveness of diverse field education models.
- Collaboration models for practice-based research and curricular innovation that provide dynamic feedback among agencies and school-based faculty (including but not limited to grants, formal research, agency evaluation, curriculum evaluation research, and program innovation).
- Ongoing opportunities to assess curricular and field integration and learning outcomes as part of sustained feedback efforts intended to enhance and improve the advanced generalist educational experience.

While outreach and community partnerships are not new approaches to informing the curriculum (Regensburg, 1966; Libassi, 1983), current field education efforts reflect a renewed commitment to agency providers and the community (Reisch & Jarmon-Rohde, 2000; Hendricks & Rudich, 2000). For example, the schools of social work at both Case Western Reserve and the University of Maryland recently launched special programs and related curricular innovations that seek community input and information resulting in the development of new and novel field placements that address community needs from an advanced generalist perspective. The Springfield College School of Social Work is engaged in similar efforts with several community and state agencies: the regional sheriff's department and its women's incarceration unit; an urban-based multiservice community center serving primarily people of color; two local housing programs collaborating with the YMCA and a mental health agency primarily serving individuals and families of color; a multiservice mental health agency's program for homeless victims of violence; and a state agency providing child welfare and protection services.

Indeed, both well-established and experimental models exist in most advanced generalist programs. Models that reflect current efforts to create effective advanced generalist field experiences are described below.

Internationally Focused and Community Immersion Models

Bolea and McFall (1999) conducted a study on the impact of exposure to international field education opportunities at two Michigan universities. As a result, students began to think more critically and practice more globally, two desired outcomes of an advanced generalist curriculum. While not all programs offer international placements, there are other ways of building a more global focus into field education in advanced generalist programs. Through community immersion or engagement in cross-national networking, students gain global perspectives on how problems are addressed and managed. This is Ife's concept of "globalization from below" (Bolea & McFall). Technologies such as interactive television, desktop videoconferencing, and other Internet connections provide students with direct exposure and even participation in global approaches to community and systems challenges similar to those they experience in their field placement. Inclusion in cross-national committees and conferences as part of field education mentorship by the professional community can also open new possibilities for student learning and professional development as advanced generalist practitioners.

The Field Unit and Integrated Seminar Model

Field units, first pioneered in the 1960s to assist underserved populations and communities, and in which school faculty play an integral role, have reemerged in new forms to address the advanced generalist imperative for integrated and systemic practice. Although a large investment of faculty and staff time and energy must be anticipated, curriculum development, practice innovation, effective responses to a rapidly changing environment, and opportunities for research are all possible positive outcomes reflecting the advanced generalist model of practice. Ideally, separate funding for units is acquired that may also include student stipends (Selber, Mulvaney, and Lauderdale, 1998).

At Salem State College and Springfield College, field units are groupings of students in one agency or across agency sites serving common vulnerable populations. Students may be employed within the agency or newly placed in the agency. In this model, the field faculty liaison plays a key role, providing oversight and leadership for the unit, and providing support and instruction as needed to field supervisors or instructors who provide direct student supervision. The on-site faculty liaison may be an agency employee or play a resource role for the agency. Whatever the relationship with the agency, this individual is responsible for relationship-building among both students and field supervisors or instructors in order to facilitate student learning (Fogel & Benson, 2000).

The advanced field integrative seminar becomes a capstone experience, a vehicle for providing depth and focus through the integration of information from advanced core courses, and can often result in novel interventions. For example, at Salem State College, students placed in public child welfare units were grouped into an integrated field seminar with a field faculty leader knowledgeable in public child welfare practice. The school and the student group partnered with the public child welfare region to collect data on current area practices related to kinship families in order to inform recommendations for systemic change and best practices. Students used this focus in the advanced policy class, the year-long research laboratory, and their administrative practice class, as well as in their field placement. The result was a public forum attended by regional supervisors and administrators from the state's Department of Social Services, as well as by faculty members from all academic and practice areas who addressed anticipated outcomes. Several of the papers presented included data and policy recommendations helpful to another school's Gerontology Institute, which had been looking for current information about kinship patterns in the state. At the request of the state legislature, the Gerontology Institute prepared a report to the state Committee on Human Services.

Student-Agency Partnership Model

Another example from Salem State College is a grouping of students employed and placed for their field experience in agencies serving older adults. These students formed a peer cohort and shared an integrative field education seminar. Each student's employer made a commitment to subsidize tuition, allow class and field education time, and develop one field education placement within the agency. Students and employers then developed prototype designs of model systems of care for elders, with specific attention given to diverse cultural needs and preferences, thereby reflecting an advanced generalist approach to social work practice with this often invisible population. Students developed assignments for second-semester advanced courses such as practice, policy, and research around these placements, resulting in new knowledge and recommendations to agencies and to the school curriculum committee. One student group in the cohort developed a proposal for a quantitative study of the specific supports elders need to maintain maximal levels of independence in the community. Funding was pursued to conduct this research. Another group conducted a qualitative study with elder care community agencies, a domestic violence agency, and a group of elder battered and abuse survivors. The result was not only the launch of support groups for elder survivors of abuse, but also the creation of stronger prevention links among agencies and community stakeholders and a published research article.

The AmeriCorps program at Springfield College provides another example of a community partnership that provides financial resources to students in addition to educational opportunities. Working in collaboration with the Springfield Public Schools, students are placed in alternative and mainstream programs to assist school social workers and students in school adjustment services. In return for committing to the requisite number of hours, interns receive a stipend and an educational award at the conclusion of the program. Funds for the program, administered through Springfield College, are received from a grant provided by the state, which receives federal funds for AmeriCorps programs. Groups of social work interns are teamed to allow for peer support. Teams are also able to undertake more extensive programmatic, outreach, and administrative projects, resulting in greater gains to the placement school and its students. Group supervision also provides a sense of community and shared purpose.

General Partnership Agency Model

This model requires partnership with larger, multisite agencies interested in accepting students in a variety of program settings and population specializations. Students are matched with an agency employee at the supervisory level who serves as field education liaison. Students placed in the agency meet in an integrated seminar, thereby gaining exposure to richly diverse settings and populations. They may choose to work together on agency-wide macro initiatives or on evaluative projects that require advanced generalist social work skills.

Community-Based Models

This model uses a variety of placement sites within an academic year for a select group of students, and pairs faculty members with agency supervisors from diverse practice settings within a community—defined either as geographic or population-based. This requires skill in coordination and collaboration in conducting an integrative seminar. Rotating students across agencies and settings reinforces cross-discipline learning and collaboration. Social change projects developed by groups of students address significant community issues, reinforcing a range of advanced generalist skills. Recently one such group at Salem State College comprised students in the following settings: community hospital emergency services, school-based settings, a family support program with a Head Start component, a visiting nurses association with a hospice component, a police station, a housing advocacy program, an employee assistance program within the community, and a community health clinic serving a diverse population. Despite the diversity in settings (which participants eventually grew to appreciate), students identified cross-population community issues that stimulated social change projects and prompted active reflection on personal social work practices and agencies' community effectiveness.

Agency-Community Research Initiatives

In this model, agency partnerships bring about student and faculty projects that take place in the field setting. At Salem State College, partnerships stimulate student projects that satisfy the required year-long research laboratory project in the concentration year. A history of partnering has built stronger connections between the research and field education faculty and participant agencies. Partnering successes have led to the Center for Research and Practice, initiated by the schools of social work at Boston College and Simmons College in collaboration with Boston University and Salem State College colleagues. The center serves as a technical and educational resource for agencies engaged in practice-based research in their community or across agency settings. A research center integrated with agency partners affords a range of learning possibilities for master's and doctoral students. It also results in tangible benefits to the community, illustrating the positive results of advanced generalist social work practice.

Teaching Centers in Community Organizations

Teaching centers may take many forms. At the least, they are organizations with which a formal agreement for field experiences is established and some kind of "educational coordinator" is assigned. Such centers are typically more involved in exchanges of resources and information with the educational institution (Bogo & Globerman, 1995) than typical field placement agencies. The relationship brings greater collaboration and reciprocity, as well as field supervisor or instructor involvement in curricular matters, continuing education, and research initiatives. "Such partnerships enhance the university's connection to the current and emerging needs of the community, and provide the university with the opportunity to collaborate to promote social change" (Bogo & Globerman, 1999, p. 272).

Social Services Coalitions and Community Service Centers

School partnerships with a broad constituency of agencies or with existing community and provider networks can be used to identify needs and develop comprehensive services for specific populations or communities (Hendricks & Rudich, 2000); to develop a social services center to meet unmet needs in the community (Skolnik & Papell, 1994); or to focus on environmental community concerns such as toxic hazards (Rogge, 1993). These coalitions and centers model inclusive partnering and comprehensive approaches to social needs that are critical elements of the advanced generalist perspective.

How can advanced generalist educators meet the demands of the current practice and educational environments, and begin to develop measures and mechanisms for a transformation of social work that will enlarge the practice framework and reflect social work's commitment to social change and to assisting those disenfranchised by the sociopolitical system? The most effective means of teaching, illustrating, and acquiring the skills related to advanced generalist practice appear to be (a) concerted outreach, (b) inclusive collaboration, and (c) comprehensive planning and implementation. If we seek to teach advanced generalist skills that empower, connect, and meet needs at multisystemic levels, we must engage students, clients, consumers, practitioners of other disciplines, and community members and leaders in dialogue and mutual action to address the range of social conditions that affect individuals, families, groups, organizations, communities, and society. Field education can be the bridge to and catalyst for dialogue, action, and curricular and practice innovation.

CONCLUSION

Three interrelated and multisystemic forces compel us to prepare social work leaders of the future in ways that bring about comprehensive skills and vision: changes in global society (Reisch & Jarmon-Rohde, 2000); changes in organizational need, including productivity, adaptability, and survival (Robb, 2000); and changes in the career trajectories of social workers, who may find themselves quickly in leadership positions requiring macro skill sets (Thompson, Menafee, & Kryder-Coe, 1998). How have social work education and social work field education responded to the massive changes taking place in society and affecting students and social work practice? Part-time programs help to address the needs of mature students or students with careers in progress. Programs that allow work-based placements that meet CSWE strictures and standards (including those that require only one internship with extended hours) address some of the multiple demands of modern life. Providing multiple opportunities for students to present interests and learning goals is a way to address diversity in student populations. Allowing multiple site interviews is another.

The process of becoming an advanced generalist professional can be reflected in the educational experience, including recognition of interrelated systems, consumer empowerment, environmental fit, and global forces. If we wish graduates of advanced generalist programs to practice from an advanced generalist perspective, then the educational process will reflect the values that make up the advanced generalist perspective. Ideally, both content and process will be brought to the practice settings in which students and graduates find themselves. What better way to teach power sharing and the importance of addressing the systems that individuals and groups are part of than by modeling interest in these as elements of students' engagement in education, and by responding in relevant, systemic ways—ways that reinforce educational rigor and standards and move the profession forward?

In addition to the challenges field education has long sought to address, such as supervision and student-agency fit, current and emerging challenges for programs with advanced generalist curriculums include the following:

- Development of effective and educationally appropriate responses to student needs.
- Institutionalization of ongoing efforts to integrate field experiences with the curriculum.
- Development of effective responses to the changing service and social contexts.
- Renewed commitment to CSWE and Social Work Code of Ethics provisions to address the needs of underserved and marginalized populations.
- Development of opportunities for students to attain multisystemic understanding and skills, including social change.
- Increased engagement with stakeholders, constituencies, and communities.
- A commitment to prepare social workers capable of acting to influence current and future practice and social environments.
- Development of relevant student learning outcomes and means of evaluation.

Given the vast and sweeping changes occurring in social services, society, and the world, and if we agree that social workers should be acting to bring about social change for greater equality and social justice, it seems clear that the advanced generalist approach can prepare well-equipped and adaptable social workers for the future. Adherence to traditional models of social work field education is no longer possible. Experiences are needed that enlarge the scope of vision to include larger social goods.

> Instead of producing future generations of functionaries to serve organizations that neither share nor respect social work values, schools of social work need to reassert the community-based origins of the profession....Innovative models of field instruction—including new sites, new patterns of supervision and new structural requirements—are needed. (Reisch & Jarmon-Rohde, 2000, p. 210)

Will there be an "end of social work" where communities are destroyed because of insidious economic imperatives; social groups are marginalized and stripped of political power; supportive institutions such as religious and educational centers are marketized; and the family seen only as a consumer and producer of goods and services (Krueger, 1997)? Social work education can, and should, provide the means to reshape the agenda. Field education has a critical role to play in preparing new professionals for harsh realities and equipping them with the skills and tools to direct and redirect the course of the future.

How will social work move forward in the 21st century? Who will be the social work leaders? Who will be able to step forward and use information about human needs and engage in dialogue with all stakeholders in society, including economic and governmental leaders, for the good of individuals, families, groups, communities, organizations, and society itself? The advanced generalist practitioner is most suited to these efforts. Field education provides the first proving ground where these skills are developed and where advanced generalist results come about.

REFERENCES

Bogo, M., & Globerman, J. (1995). Creating effective university field partnerships: An analysis of two inter-organization models of field education. In G. Rogers (Ed.), *Social work field education: Views and visions* (pp. 17-29). Dubuque, IA: Kendall/Hunt.

Bogo, M., & Globerman, J. (1999). Interorganizational relationships between schools of social work and field agencies: Testing a framework for analysis. *Journal of Social Work Education, 35*(2), 265-274.

Bolea, P. S., & McFall, J. (1999). *International field education: A study of student reflection and program innovation.* Conference Proceedings of the Joint International Conference on the International Federation of Social Work and the International Association of Schools of Social Work. Retrieved November 18, 2002 from http://www.arcaf.net/social_work_proceedings/ftp_files6/StowBolea.pdf.

Castelloe, P., & Watson, T. (1999). Participatory education as a community practice method: A case example from a comprehensive Head Start program. *Journal of Community Practice, 6(1),* 71-89.

Cohen, M. B. (1990). Practice with homeless, mentally ill clients: A challenge for field education. *Journal of Teaching in Social Work, 4*(2), 3-18.

Council on Social Work Education. (1962). *Official statement of curriculum policy for the master's degree program in graduate professional schools of social work* (p. 7). New York: Author.

Council on Social Work Education. (2001*). Educational policies and standards.* New York: Author.

Crawford, F., Dickinson, J., & Leitmann, S. (2002). Mirroring meaning making. *Qualitative Social Work, 1*(2)*,* 170-190.

Fogel, S. & Benson, M. (2000). Clarifying student competence in the agency setting: A model of practice for field liaisons. *Arete 24*(2), 14-29.

Fook, J., Ryan, M., & Hawkins, L. (1997). Towards a theory of social work expertise. *British Journal of Social Work, 27*, 399-441.

Friere, P. (1970). *Cultural action for freedom.* Cambridge, MA: Harvard Educational Review Press.

Friere, P. (1973). *Education for critical consciousness.* New York: Seabury Press.

George, A. (1982). A history of social work field instruction. In B. Sheafor & L. Jenkins (Eds.), *Quality field instruction in social work: Program development and maintenance.* 37-59. New York: Longman.

Geraty, E. (2002). Global social work: An internet-based international social work community (listserv). http://www.hometown.aol.com/egeratylsw/globalsw.html.

Germain, C. B., & Gitterman, A. (1987). Ecological perspective. In A. Minahan (Ed.), *Encyclopedia of social work* (18th ed., Vol. 1, pp. 488-499). Silver Spring, MD: National Association of Social Workers.

Gibbs, P., Locke, B. L., & Lohmann, R. (1990). Paradigm for the generalist-advanced generalist continuum. *Journal of Social Work Education, 26*(3), 232-243.

Hendricks, C. O., & Rudich, G. (2000). A community building perspective in social work education. *Journal of Community Practice, 8*(3), 21-36.

Hernandez, S., Jorgensen, M., & Judd, P. (1985). Integrated practice: An advanced generalist curriculum to prepare social problem specialists. *Journal of Social Work Education, 21*(3), 28-35.

Holliman, D. C., Dziegielewski, S. F., & Datta, P. (2001). Discharge planning and social work practice. *Social Work in Health Care, 32*(3), 1-19.

Jarman-Rohde, L., McFall, J., Kolar, P., & Strom, G. (1997). The changing context of social work practice: Implications and recommendations for social work educators. *Journal of Social Work Education, 33*(1), 29-46.

Jennings, M. (2001). Community practice: A training ground for social work students. *The Qualitative Report, 6*(1), 1-15.

Krueger, L. W. (1997). The end of social work. *Journal of Social Work Education, 33*, 19-27.

Libassi, M. (1983). An integrative approach to primary prevention in the field. In J. Bowker (Ed.), *Education for primary prevention in social work.* New York: Council on Social Work Education.

Noble, C. (1999). The essential yet elusive project of developing field education as a legitimate area of social work inquiry. *Issues in Social Work Education, 19*(1), 2-16.

O'Connor, G. G. (1988). Case management: System and practice. *Human Services in the Rural Environment, 14*(1), 21-24.

O'Neill, J. (2002, January). Private agency turnover high. *NASW News.*

Parsons, R. J., Hernandez, S. H., & Jorgensen, J. (1988). Integrated practice: A framework for problem-solving. *Social Work, 33*, 417-421.

Personal Responsibility and Work Opportunity Reconciliation Act of 1996, Pub. L. No. 104-193 (1996).

Raskin, M. (1994). The Delphi study in field instruction revisited: Expert consensus on issues and research priorities. *Journal of Social Work Education, 30*(1), 75-89.

Raymond, G. T., Teare, P. J., & Atherton, C. R. (1996). Is "field practice" a relevant organizing principle for the MSW curriculum? *Journal of Social Work Education, 32*(1), 9-30.

Reeser, L. C., & Epstein, I. (1987, December). Social workers' attitudes toward poverty and social action: 1968-1984. *Social Service Review.*

Regensburg, J. (1966). Report of an exploratory project in field instruction. *Field instruction in graduate social work education: Old problems and new proposals.* New York: Council on Social Work Education.

Reich, R. B. (2001). *The future of success: Working and living in the new economy.* New York: Alfred A. Knopf.

Reisch, M., & Jarman-Rohde, L. (2000). The future of social work in the United States: Implications for field educators. *Journal of Social Work Education, 36*(2), 201-216.

Risler, E. A. (1999). Student practice portfolios: Integrating diversity and learning in the field experience. *Arete, 23*(1), 89-96.

Robb, D. (2000). Resilient organizations. *OD Practicioner, 32*(3), 27-32.

Rogge, M. E. (1993). Social work, disenfranchised communities, and the natural environment: Field education opportunities. *Journal of Social Work Education, 29*(1), 111-120.

Rosenblum, A. (1997). Developing partnerships between social work programs and the professional community: An exploratory study of field advisory groups. *Journal of Teaching in Social Work, 14*(1/2), 111-125.

Schatz, M. S., Jenkins, L. E., & Sheafor, B. W. (1990). Milford redefined: A model of initial and advanced generalist social work. *Journal of Social Work Education, 3*, 217-231.

Schneck, D., and Council on Social Work Education, Commission on Field Education (1997).*Survey of field educators and directors on standards and guidelines for field education and resources.* New York: Council on Social Work Education.

Schneck, D., Grossman, B., & Glassman, U. (1991). *Field education in social work: Contemporary issues and trends.* Dubuque, IA: Kendall/Hunt.

Schon, D. (1987). *Educating the reflective practitioner.* San Francisco: Jossey-Bass.

Selber, K., Mulvaney, M., & Lauderdale, M. (1998). A field education model for developing quality agency partnerships. *Journal of Teaching in Social Work, 17*(1/2), 121-136.

Senge, P. (1990). *The fifth discipline: The art and practice of the learning organization.* New York: Doubleday.

Skolnik, L., & Papell, C. P. (1994). Holistic designs for field instruction in the contemporary social work curriculum. *Journal of Social Work Education, 30*(1), 90-96.

Smalley, R. (1967). *Theory for social work practice.* New York: Columbia University Press.

Teigiser, K. S. (1983). Evolution of education for generalist practice. *Journal of Education for Social Work, 19*(1), 79-85.

Thompson, J., Menafee, D., & Kryder-Coe, J. (1998). Meeting the continuing education needs of social work managers. *Professional Development: International Journal of Continuing Social Work Education, 1*(3), 53-60.

Thompson, J., Menafee, D., & Marley, M. (1999). A comparative analysis of social workers' macro practice activities: Identifying functions common to direct practice and administration. *Journal of Social Work Education, 35*(1),115-124.

Tourse, R., McIniss-Dittrich, K., & Platt, S. (1999). The road to autonomous practice: A practice competency teaching approach for supervision. *Journal of Teaching in Social Work, 19*(1/2), 3-19.

SECTION 4: ESSAYS AND READINGS

Chapter 9

MENTAL HEALTH
AND MANAGED HEALTH CARE

Katherine Walsh-Burke
Springfield College

ADVANCED GENERALIST SOCIAL WORK PRACTICE AND MANAGED MENTAL HEALTH CARE

According to the National Association of Social Workers (NASW, 2002) social workers are the dominant profession in the provision of mental health care in the U.S. There are more than 200,000 trained social workers in this country, more than those trained in any other mental health profession (Austrian, 2000). At the same time, the need for mental health intervention has increased. This is due, in part, to the recognition of the impact of trauma resulting from 9/11 and other critical events that have affected whole communities through multiple stressors, reduced income, and loss. As there continue to be shortages of other mental health professionals, such as psychiatrists and psychologists, particularly in urban and rural areas serving vulnerable populations, there will be an increased need for social workers in the mental health arena.

Practitioners in this field must be trained to provide a wide range of interventions to address the complex problems experienced by people coping with mental disorders in challenging, often oppressive, environments. Knowledge of biological, psychological, social, cultural, economic, and spiritual influences are essential in accurate assessment and comprehensive treatment planning for individuals presenting with mental health issues. These are all areas emphasized in advanced generalist social work training.

This chapter reviews how and why advanced generalist social workers are uniquely prepared to provide services to clients with mental health problems. The issues and tensions identified by advanced generalists practicing in contemporary managed health care systems also will be analyzed. Despite these issues and challenges, advanced generalists are finding ways to provide effective services. The theories and skills they use to deliver these services will be identified and curriculum implications will be addressed.

ADVANCED GENERALIST SOCIAL WORKERS ARE WELL PREPARED TO ASSIST CLIENTS WITH MENTAL HEALTH ISSUES

Advanced generalist training best prepares social workers to work with the multi-faceted problems presented by clients in the mental health system. This is because clients with mental health conditions, especially those with severe and persistent mental disorders, present with complex biological, psychological, and social problems that require breadth of knowledge and depth of skill by practitioners. Despite the tremendous increase in knowledge about the etiology of many mental disorders such as bipolar disorder, borderline personality disorder, and generalized anxiety disorder, there continues to be much debate about the efficacy of individual treatment approaches. While evidence-based practice is always recommended, there is still much evidence to be gathered about what types and combinations of treatment approaches offer the best outcomes over time.

For example, major depression is a serious and common problem for which many seek help. At any given time, 11 million Americans suffer from depression (Gitterman, 2001, p. 163). "The etiology of Major Depressive Disorder is controversial, and partisans of an entirely biological or entirely psychological or entirely social causation can be found. However, the consensus of most experts is that it is biopsychosocial" (Gitterman, p. 164). Complex problems such as depression, which have biological, psychological, and social causes and effects, require comprehensive treatment plans that address each of these contributing factors. Treatment planning and implementation is further complicated by the current mental health system. The provision of mental health services has undergone rapid and continuing change over the past decade as the reflexive goal of cost containment has had influence that is equal to, if not greater than, the transitive goal of improved mental health of clients. Managed care "generally refers to a system where the financial and clinical aspects of a client's care are examined and controlled through a variety of measures with the ultimate goal of containing costs while maximizing quality" (Strom-Gottfried, 1997, p. 8).

The current mental health care system is composed of a complex and fragmented web of subsystems that include for-profit insurers, government agencies, pharmaceutical companies, and myriad service providers such as hospital corporations, outpatient clinics, and private practitioners—all competing for survival. More than ever before, practitioners providing care to individuals with mental health needs must able to:

- navigate this complex and fragmented system themselves as providers;
- assist clients in navigating the system;
- select and carry out interventions from a wide array for an increasingly diverse population; and
- advocate for policies and services that adequately address client needs in an increasingly restrictive economic environment.

Thus, breadth of knowledge and depth of skill are essential for effective micro, mezzo, and macro system assessment and intervention.

ISSUES AND TENSIONS

The current model of managed care presents many challenges to all social workers, but particularly to the advanced generalist social worker. Several factors contribute to the dilemmas advanced generalists experience in attempting to provide effective and comprehensive services to clients with mental health difficulties.

- Reimbursement is based on a pathology-oriented, micro system-focused medical model that conflicts with the person-in-environment, multi-systems framework of advanced generalist social work.

While social work practitioners are trained to complete a comprehensive psychosocial assessment, often the only information required by third-party payers in a managed mental health care system is a diagnosis based on the Diagnostic and Statistical Manual of Mental Disorders (DSM-IV) Multiaxial Assessment. This tool, as noted by Kirk and Kutchins (1995), contradicts many of the basic tenets of social work.

However, because a primary reflexive goal of practitioners and organizations providing mental health services is reimbursement, the DSM-IV diagnosis is usually considered most important. Reimbursement is then paid only for direct services that address Axis I and (less often) Axis II diagnoses. No reimbursement is paid for services addressing problems recorded on Axis IV, Psychosocial and Environmental Problems, which include the following: problems with primary support group; problems related to the social environment; educational problems; occupational problems; housing problems; economic problems; and problems with access to health care services (DSM-IV-TR, p. 32).

These reimbursement policies create dilemmas for the advanced generalist practitioner. Take for example, the practitioner completing an assessment and intervention plan for a non-English-speaking older woman who, according to her family, has been less engaged with her family and has given up most recreational activities. Her family worries that these behaviors, along with other changes in affect, indicate depression. The worker believes that a culturally competent neuropsychiatric evaluation is needed to help make an accurate differential diagnosis and to rule out a medical condition that might account for the changes. However, the worker identifies the lack of access to health care services as a problem on Axis IV. This is both because the client lacks health insurance and because the providers in their geographic area are not equipped to provide culturally competent assessment in the client's own language. While part of the advanced generalist treatment plan calls for research into resources and advocacy within the health care system to address this problem, the worker's agency can receive no reimbursement for these interventions. Reimbursement is paid only for psychological or biological intervention aimed at addressing the diagnosis recorded on Axis I or Axis II.

Clinicians trying to work within behavioral managed care are finding that DSM-IV is used as a management tool rather than as a clinical tool, as its categories are the key factor in determining the type and length of intervention in the name of cost-effectiveness. The alliance between DSM-IV and behavioral managed care with its emphasis on "medical necessity" has led to a return to a more linear, medical model of assessment and intervention. Thus, clients who were formerly seen for marital, family, work, or social relationship problems now *must* be given an Axis I diagnosis (Austrian, 2000, p. 7).

The person-in-environment assessment tool was developed by the NASW to capture important data from the psychosocial assessment, and much better reflects both the multi-systemic and strengths perspective of advanced generalist social work. Yet this tool is not used by third-party payers for reimbursement and therefore is rarely used by social work practitioners providing mental health services.

> **Decisions made within the helping systems that have evolved within managed care are most influenced by short-term financial cost-containment goals rather than goals defined mutually by the client and social worker.**

Wernet (1999) notes that managed care began with private industry's wish to contain health care expenditures. "The managed care solution has several goals. The first is constraint of the autonomous decision making of the medical practitioner....The second goal is the use of generic treatment." (p. 2). According to Corcoran and Vandiver (1996):

> Managed care programs are not a single system of mental health care but a variety of systems, although they share common factors. One is the transfer of control of clinical services from the hands of clinicians and clients to the financial ledgers of business corporations....And yet, the managed care organization may well determine if clinical services are necessary, who may provide what specific intervention and how much it should cost—or at least how much will be paid. (p. ix)

Austrian (2000) explains that "social work is a profession with its own mission, knowledge base and repertoire of skills. It serves clients who present a broad spectrum of problems...and its activities include direct service, case management, advocacy and program planning" (p. 1). In addition to utilizing a variety of activities to assist clients with health and mental health conditions, social workers are trained in a reciprocal and mutual process of treatment planning. "The client-worker roles must be carried out in a mutual, reciprocal and respectful manner and shift from those of subordinate recipient and superordinate expert to those encouraging collaboration" (Gitterman, 2001, p. 27). Every social work practice text, in fact, stresses the concept of client participation in the process of mutual contract development, based on a key social work ethical code of client self-determination. "A contract summarizes what you as a worker and your client system agree to do during the intervention process. We continue to stress involving clients during every phase of the intervention process" (Kirst-Ashman & Hull, 2001, p. 209). Yet, says Austrian (2000):

> Managed care and third-party carriers, with their emphasis on cost-cutting and accountability, seem determined to limit assessment, and thus intervention planning, to decisions made on the basis of classification systems. In addition, with very short medical, or psychiatric, inpatient stays and reimbursement for outpatient intervention for persons with mental disorders limited to very few sessions, the time needed to make a thorough biopsychosocial assessment has been greatly reduced. (p. 292)

With decision-making regarding treatment increasingly being based on rapid, unidimensional assessments and "cost-effective" interventions determined by managed care corporations, it is easy to see why so many social work practitioners find it a struggle to feel effective working within a managed care model.

THEORIES AND SKILLS TO MEET THE CHALLENGES OF CLIENTS IN A MANAGED CARE ENVIRONMENT

Derezotes (2000) describes advanced generalist practice as both *advanced* and *inclusive*:

> Inclusive social work practice is advanced generalist practice because the social worker values and uses both conventional generalist assessment *and* intervention strategies, as well as alternative strategies drawn from a variety of cultures and traditions. This inclusive strategy recognizes the diverse and ecological nature of human life, in that each person is influenced by his or her own intricate internal psychology, as well as by the complex social and natural environments in which he or she lives. The inclusive perspective embraces the many seemingly opposite positions that now polarize social workers. For example, both direct practice with individuals, couples, families and groups, as well as indirect practice with agencies, institutions, and communities are valued as interrelated processes. (p. viii)

This inclusivity also means that advanced generalist practitioners provide in-depth assessment and intervention on all three system levels encompassed within the social work framework: the micro, mezzo, and macro. Yet, while social work educators and theorists generally espouse multiple-level interventions, few training programs routinely require learning activities in internships or in integrative course assignments that prepare students to assess and intervene simultaneously on all three levels. While the generalist curriculum foundation of every social work MSW program exposes trainees to the breadth of knowledge and skills needed for multi-system assessment and intervention, only advanced generalist training prepares social workers with the depth of knowledge and skills for each of these system levels. In traditional clinical or case work-oriented programs, for example, students special-izing in the fields of mental health or child and family services gain depth in micro system assessment and intervention. However, their required course work and field assignments do not equip them with equal depth of knowledge and skills for com-munity organizing, organizational and social policy development, or research de-sign and implementation.

The need for depth as well as breadth in knowledge and skill of those working in mental health is highlighted by experts who treat survivors of trauma, whose subsequent problems are evidenced in a variety of serious mental health disorders including post-traumatic stress disorder (PTSD), dissociative identity disorder, sub-stance abuse, and borderline personality disorder. These problems account for a significant percentage of mental health visits in the U.S. While managed care com-panies often ask only for the primary mental disorder diagnoses when determining what type and amount of treatment will be reimbursed for a person presenting with a mental health problem, clients with histories of trauma rarely present with a single clearly defined problem that can be rapidly assessed or treated. This is because, as van der Kolk, McFarlane, & Weisaeth (1996) note:

> Naïve one-to-one notions about the causal relationships between trauma and these disorders would oversimplify the very complex interrelationships among specific traumas, secondary adversities, environmental chaos and neglect, nature of preexisting and subsequent attachment patterns, tempera-ment, special competencies and other contributions to the genesis of these problems. (p. 183)

Because trauma-related problems are often caused or exacerbated by environmental factors such as poverty and oppression, treatment requires intervention aimed at the mezzo and macro systems contributing to these as well as the individual's behavior. Herman (1997) further underscores the need for both assessing and intervening on the mezzo and macro system levels:

> Traumatized people are frequently misdiagnosed and mistreated in the mental health system. Because of the number and complexity of their symptoms, their treatment is often fragmented and incomplete. Because of their characteristic difficulties with close relationships, they are vulnerable to become re-victimized by caregivers. They may become engaged in ongoing, destructive interactions, in which the medical...system replicates the behavior of the abusive family. (p. 123)

Advanced generalist social work practitioners are well prepared to identify the environmental influences that contribute to the difficulties that clients such as trauma survivors and those with other health and mental health conditions experience in interactions with mezzo and macro systems. They are trained to intervene at the organizational as well as at the state and federal government levels to effect system change on behalf of clients. These skills become especially important when clients experience oppression within the very system that is supposed to be designed to help ameliorate their difficulties.

> **Advanced generalist social workers assess and intervene from a strengths perspective that not only supports the individual dignity and worth of every person, but also focuses on competence and capacity building with the ultimate outcome of client system empowerment.**

The foundation of all effective social work intervention, including that of the advanced generalist practitioner, is the comprehensive psychosocial assessment. This includes consideration of the biological, psychological, social, cultural, and spiritual factors influencing the difficulties an individual is experiencing, as well as the strengths the individual has shown.

> The most effective evaluation process is client centered, strength oriented, and individualized...[but] in many practice settings social workers are required to use particular DSM-IV diagnoses in assessment summaries. The effective social worker realizes that although such diagnoses may be useful in communicating about mental disorders, they are quite limited in describing client strengths and successes. (Derezotes, p. 50)

The multidimensional assessment that includes the strengths of clients and their social environments serves as the basis for a treatment plan. With strengths identified in the assessment, the treatment plan, in turn, includes activities and interventions designed to maximize client strengths and community network supports. A unidimensional intervention (such as a series of brief treatment sessions with a cognitive-behaviorally focused psychotherapist or a trial of a medication) increases the risk that the intervention will fail if family and neighborhood support of client capacities are left out of the equation.

Yet many social workers who specialize in "clinical" social work or "case work" receive more in-depth training in diagnosis and micro system intervention methods, particularly in the second year of an MSW program, than in family or network therapy, program development and administration, and social change/social policy. Many of these social workers, like psychiatrists and psychologists, take required courses in "psychopathology" that not only emphasize micro system approaches, but also are antithetical to both the strengths and ecological perspectives, without the concomitant advanced required courses in social policy, social change, and qualitative research methods that are coherent with these perspectives.

The grass-roots advocacy efforts of AIDS and cancer survivors are good examples of the maximization of client capacities that fit with an advanced generalist approach. Rather than exclusively attending to their emotional or behavioral needs, participants in the community organizing efforts of the survivorship movements in both these fields have focused on macro system change. In doing so, they have effectively influenced policy and funding directed at ameliorating or eliminating the social problems that contribute to the development of these medical conditions or that create barriers to service access. By capitalizing on the strengths of these survivors and utilizing their expertise and motivation, these advocacy groups have also been effective in coalition-building to pool resources directed at social change. While micro system-focused clinicians and case workers might focus on increased individual well-being, participants in the community organizing efforts of the survivorship movements in both these fields have made significant contributions to increasing the well-being of all survivors. Not only have they effectively influenced policy and funding, they have increased individual self-efficacy for themselves and others who might otherwise feel disempowered by illness and depressed or anxious in reaction to it (Leigh, 2002; Stovall and Clark, 1996).

Reamer (1994) underscores another reason that the strengths and empowerment as well as a multisystem focus are essential in social work with all clients, including those in the mental health system:

> The conditions that cause people to seek help from social workers and social services are invariably consequences of oppression and injustice....While not all social and emotional difficulties that bring people to social services would immediately vanish were oppression and injustice eliminated, many certainly would. (Reamer, 1994, p. 257)

Austrian (2000) also underscores the shortcomings of the micro system focus of providers, contemporary managed care, and third-party carriers in our mental health system. Referring to the DSM-IV diagnosis of writing disorder, for which insurers will provide treatment reimbursement, she writes:

> Poor writing skills might be a symptom of a mental disorder, but they are more likely to be found, on assessment, to be the result of a range of social problems, including family, English as a second language; lack of space and other conditions conducive to writing, poor schooling; physical problems; or simple lack of ability. [*sic*] (p. 291)

Advanced generalist social workers are trained to facilitate larger system changes to address these kinds of problems, along with addressing the changes that might be needed in the individual presenting with symptoms of a mental disorder.

> **Practice with cultural competence that acknowledges and addresses differences in the manifestation and management of distress by members of different cultural groups.**

Cultural competence is a construct that is still evolving in social work education. Green (1999) describes some dimensions of cultural competence outlined by Pinderhughes (1995) that include the following:

> the capacity to perceive others through their own cultural lens; knowledge of specific beliefs and values in the clients' community; personal comfort with those differences; a willingness to change previous ideas; the ability to be flexible and adapt one's thinking and behavior in novel settings; and the skill of sorting through diverse information about a community to understand how it might apply to particular individuals. (p. 74)

The concept of diversity that is promoted in advanced generalist social work implies that each client and client system is unique and requires careful, sensitive, and differential assessment (Derezotes, 2000, p. xiv). Cervantes and Arroyo (1994) articulate how contextual variables and cultural bias influence DSM-IV diagnoses of Hispanic children and adolescents. This is evidence of how crucial culturally competent practice is in the mental health field. Yet, without the added depth and integration of theories and skills related to person-in-environment that is provided in advanced generalist training, it is possible for social workers and other mental health practitioners to err in making a diagnosis, resulting in an ineffective treatment plan.

As noted above, the attention paid in advanced generalist social work practice to person-in-environment requires that the practitioner assess the strengths of the client's environment as well as those of the client. Green (1999) underscores the importance of respecting indigenous strategies in culturally competent practice, noting:

> The point to be emphasized is that in virtually all communities, including highly urbanized ones that are well-supplied with professional healers and therapists, there are many alternative sources of help...in pluralistic societies such as our own, one of the critical problems in providing social services is the relationship of the dominant provider system to indigenous alternatives. (p. 64)

Advanced generalist training does not eliminate the potential problems that result from cultural differences and lack of cultural awareness. It does, however, prepare mental health practitioners who are acutely aware of the influence of culture on the client as well as on the practitioner-client relationship, and provides a framework for attending to this in both assessment and treatment planning for an increasingly diverse population.

PRACTICE IMPLICATIONS

Despite the challenges they face in managed care environments, advanced generalist social workers do succeed in carrying out effective and comprehensive assessments and treatment plans. The depth and breadth of advanced generalist training means that practitioners are able to identify and offer to clients a wide range of intervention methods to address the complex and multifaceted problems that influence their mental health. The difference between an advanced generalist practitioner and a clinical social worker is most evident in the treatment plan. Advanced generalists include in their focus the mezzo and macro systems that influence the client, and intervention is offered beyond the micro system. Thus, in addition to the combination of cognitive behavioral therapy and medication (micro system interventions) often prescribed for depression, mezzo and macro system interventions that emerge from the comprehensive psychosocial assessment are also a part of the advanced generalist practitioner's treatment plan.

One example of an organization level (mezzo) intervention by an advanced generalist social worker is the development of a voice mail system for homeless veterans. Many of the veterans who are part of this vulnerable population and served by social workers in the Veteran's Administration (VA) system are diagnosed with PTSD and depression. Many are also unemployed. Unemployment can be both cause and effect: the symptoms of these disorders may interfere with successful employment, and unemployment can contribute to, or exacerbate, anxiety and depressed mood. Even if the symptoms are reduced through psychotherapy and/or medication, the veteran is still at risk because, once homeless, it is difficult to find employment with no residential telephone number to provide to potential employers. The voice mail system improved veterans' chances for employment, which, in turn, influenced overall well-being.

An example of a macro system intervention conducted by an advanced generalist social worker is the development of a statewide coalition that includes grassroots, veteran-run advocacy groups and traditional social service agencies in addition to workers within the VA system. This coalition developed a strategic plan to advocate on the local, state, and federal levels for increased services to homeless veterans, many of whom, again, suffer with PTSD and other diagnoses. These advocacy efforts are vital to improving both the health and mental health of individual veterans, since their needs cannot be met simply with the biological (e.g., medication) and psychological services provided within a managed mental health care system. Other problems that must be addressed include lack of housing caused by both discrimination and limited affordable units in certain communities, and social problems such as lack of gender-specific services for women veterans.

Some might argue, in keeping with traditional social work training, that these mezzo and macro system interventions be carried out by administrators or community organizers rather than by advanced generalist social workers. However, it is precisely the combination of direct practice skill and mezzo- and macro-level skills that are required to assist clients with complex problems. It is the direct practice skills of assessment and development of an effective therapeutic alliance that enables the advanced generalist to establish sufficient trust and rapport with clients and colleagues to effectively identify the need for and carry out these multisystem interventions. This is especially true in coalition-building when participants include those struggling with the symptoms of a serious mental disorder, whose level of trust in those with authority may be very limited.

Individual social workers, along with clients, can influence improved provision of care through mezzo and macro system interventions such as administration, supervision, program development, research, community organization, and political advocacy to shape mental health care policy. Yet it is a challenge to find the time and resources to do so in a managed care environment. Advanced generalist social workers, as a subgroup of the social work profession, must maintain our holistic, person-in-environment perspective despite the restrictions of managed care reimbursement policies. Strom-Gottfried (1997) reminds us that:

> Many clients have complex and long-standing difficulties that are intricately related to environmental conditions, oppression, and poverty. Regardless of the worker's skills, resources, and motivation, some problems will prove difficult and time-consuming to remediate. She asks, how can we promote efficiency and effectiveness, yet also assure that workers and clients are not set up for failure by trying to meet unrealistic performance standards with insufficient time and resources? (p. 14)

We can do this precisely through the use of our advanced generalist skills: actively conducting and utilizing research to demonstrate the efficacy of multisystemic intervention, and using community organizing skills to mobilize clients and practitioners to advocate for policies such as those in the proposed mental health parity legislation. "Ultimately, social workers must advocate for structural change and for a health care funding mechanism that is more humane, effective, and reflective of the profession's values and more inclusive of all who need service" (Strom, 1992, p. 402). Meanwhile, social workers must use administration and program planning skills within both managed care organizations and mental health provider organizations to find ways to foster effective care that is consistent with social work values and principles.

These skills are evidenced when social workers share information with each other and with clients about how to effectively navigate managed care systems, and when funding from managed care companies and provider organizations is obtained for activities such as advocacy training. As a recent graduate of our advanced generalist MSW program wrote, "We must learn to deal ethically with the system as it exists, but also challenge the system by trying to make changes that will make services more accessible to clients and practice less conflictual for clinicians" (Kelly, 1997, p. 7).

CURRICULUM IMPLICATIONS

Advanced generalist social work training programs have a major contribution to make in the following areas:

- expanding the role and influence of social work in mental health care;
- expanding the understanding of policy makers, organizations, and persons affected by mental health issues of the biopsychosocial and multisystemic influences that must be addressed to effectively assist individuals and communities affected by mental health issues; and
- effecting change in the current model of mental health care.

Part of the challenge for both field instructors and faculty in advanced generalist training programs is to assist students as they struggle with the conflicts they experience when they practice within a managed care model. One of the tensions described above is the conflict experienced by advanced generalist practitioners pressured to produce rapid, unidimensional assessments in the managed care environment. While many seasoned practitioners also experience this tension, social work students are particularly vulnerable. Before entering social work training, contemporary students may not have been exposed to models that effectively provide care based on the comprehensive psychosocial assessment completed autonomously by a social worker, without the influence of managed care. In many contemporary settings, emphasis is placed primarily on the DSM-IV Multiaxial Assessment and diagnosis for reimbursement, and both students and workers are often required to assign at least a provisional diagnosis on intake.

Advanced generalist faculty and practitioners are understandably concerned by this. In a rapid assessment environment, an incorrect diagnosis may be assigned to a client based on insufficient information. As noted, an inaccurate or incomplete assessment is likely to result in an ineffective treatment plan. Seasoned practitioners also are often aware of the potential problems clients will experience once a stigmatizing diagnosis is made. Thus they want to be certain of both the diagnosis and the adequacy of the treatment plan that is dependent on the assessment process.

However, because of their subordinate status, students in training may feel pressured to put emphasis on the perceived need to meet immediate reflexive goals of securing reimbursement in a managed care setting, rather than on the generative goals of working toward social justice, social change, and human rights for those affected by mental illness. Students routinely report experiencing dilemmas in practicum settings because rapid assessments are required for reimbursement. One student recounted an interaction he witnessed in a practicum in which the assessing clinician was describing a complex situation a client had presented on intake to a managed care case manager. The worker was told by the case manager, "I need a number," referring to a diagnosis on Axis I of the DSM-IV. Aware that (a) it is important to complete a comprehensive psychosocial assessment, and (b) it is difficult, in many situations, to rapidly assign a single accurate diagnosis, the student acknowledged being unsure about what the social worker should do at that point.

This is a particular concern in Massachusetts and states like it that allow field practicum agencies to bill insurers for the services provided by second-year social work interns. Students often express concern about carrying this responsibility and participating in the managed care system before they have acquired either experience or sufficient status to feel empowered to advocate for clients or their own treatment recommendations. This can be a challenge for students with either a managed care company's case manager or within a capitated reimbursement system in an agency.

As Strom-Gottfried (1997) notes, there are many ways to educate students about managed care: in field seminars, HBSE, and practice classes. The challenge for faculty in advanced generalist programs is to help students apply what they are learning effectively in the field. Faculty must collaborate effectively and creatively with clinical field instructors who may be more focused on, and more comfortable with, supervising students in direct service (micro-level) activities. Advanced generalist faculty must help to educate field instructors and agencies about advanced generalist practice. This can be accomplished only partially through traditional vehicles such as dissemination of syllabi, continuing education seminars, and courses for field instructors. What is also required is a continuous facilitative process that encourages the following:

- active sharing of examples with students and field instructors of effective advanced generalist practice;
- collaborative research that generates empirical evidence of effective advanced generalist practice; and
- dissemination of these in the mainstream professional literature consumed by practitioners who serve as field instructors.

If we succeed in doing this, we will be helping to facilitate the use of inclusive theories and skills by our students and professional colleagues, *and* we will be demonstrating the efficacy of these through our own education and practice strategies.

REFERENCES

Austrian, S. (2000). *Mental disorders, medications and clinical social work* (2nd ed.). New York: Columbia University Press.

Cervantes, R. C., & Arroyo, W. (1994). DSM-IV: Implications for Hispanic children and adolescents. *Hispanic Journal of Behavioral Sciences, 16*(1), 8-20.

Corcoran, K., & Vandiver, V. (1996*). Maneuvering the maze of managed care: Skills for mental health practitioners*. New York: The Free Press.

Derezotes, D. (2000). *Advanced generalist social work practice*. Thousand Oaks, CA: Sage.

Gitterman, A. (2001*). Handbook of social work practice with vulnerable and resilient populations*. New York: Columbia University Press.

Green, J. (1999*). Cultural awareness in the human services: A multi-ethnic approach*. Boston: Allyn & Bacon.

Herman, J. (1997). *Trauma and recovery*. New York: Basic Books.

Kelly, B. (1997). *Treatment dilemmas for social workers: Increasing restrictions in a managed care era*. Exemplar paper. Springfield, MA: Springfield College School of Social Work.

Kirk, S., & Kutchins, H. (1995). Should DSM be the basis for teaching social work practice in mental health? "No!" *Journal of Social Work Education, 31*(2), 148-168.

Kirst-Ashman, K., & Hull, G. (2001). *Understanding generalist practice*. New York: Wadsworth.

Leigh, S. (2002). Veteran survivor: From victim to activist. *CURE, 1*(2), 64-66.

NASW (2002). Social Workers Support Full Mental Health Parity! http://www.socialworkers.org/pressroom/2002/053102.asp

Pinderhughes, E. (1995). Empowering diverse populations: Family practice in the 21st century. *Families in Society, 76*, 131-140.

Reamer, F. G. (1997). Managing ethics under managed care. *Families in Society, 78*(1), 96-101.

Stovall, E., & Clark, E. J. (1996). Survivors as advocates. In B. Hoffman (Ed.), *A cancer survivor's almanac: Charting your journey*. Minneapolis, MN: Chronimed.

Strom, K. (1992). Reimbursement demands and treatment decisions: A growing dilemma for social workers. *Social Work, 37*(5), 398-402.

Strom-Gottfried, K. (1997). The implications of managed care for social work education. *Journal of Social Work Education, 33*(1), 7-17.

Van der Kolk, B. A., McFarlane, A. C., & Weisaeth, L. (Eds.) (1996). *Traumatic stress: The effects of overwhelming experience on mind, body, and society* (pp. 182-213). New York: Guilford Press.

Wernet, S. (1999). An introduction to managed care in human services. In S. Wernet (Ed.), *Managed care in human services*. Chicago: Lyceum Books.

Chapter 10

ADVANCED GENERALIST SOCIAL WORK
PRACTICE WITH CHILDREN

James M. Canning and Walter J. Mullin
Springfield College

Advanced generalist practice is "a model of assessment, theoretical perspectives and intervention using central themes of social justice, human rights and social change" (Vecchiolla et al., 2001). The three themes above, of social justice, human rights, and social change, ground our conception of advanced generalist practice with children. Although practitioners strive to apply these three themes at every level of practice and among all populations of persons at risk, applying them to children is sometimes easier said than done, since children in our society, particularly children who are poor and at risk, are hidden from view (Ehrenreich, 1985; Sidel, 1986, 1996). Even practitioners who are highly motivated and educationally prepared to address the needs of these children cannot be adequately attuned to them when children are absent from their field of vision. In this chapter we shall examine ways that social work advanced generalist practitioners increase the visibility of children at risk and more dependably protect their human rights, insure social justice, and promote social change.

One form of the invisibility of children in social work occurs when practitioners see the lives of children only partially. A practitioner may attend to the person of an individual child but may fail to examine the child's environment, or a practitioner's attention to the child's environment may distract her from attention to the child's individual needs. An example of the former might be when a clinician prescribes medication for a child's school behavior problem without adequately assessing his situation at home. An example of the latter might be the situation where a social worker in a family support program, assisting a mother in finding work and housing, fails to note that her toddler is seriously developmentally delayed.

In this chapter, we shall introduce an advanced generalist practice frame that reflects the holistic, multilevel, multi-theoretical preparation of an advanced generalist social work education. This perspective takes in both the developing child and the environment and reduces the risk of invisibility in important aspects of children's lives. As such it encompasses two realms: one relating to the environment, or child well-being; and the other to the life of the individual child, or development. Both of these elements are essential, are joined in reality and in spirit, and reflect the overarching goal that we conceptualize as "making way for children."

WHAT DO WE MEAN BY CHILD WELL-BEING?

How is the concept of *child well-being* related to advanced generalist practice with children? A child's well-being is derived from a balance of environmental factors that describe the landscape in which the child lives. Positive well-being contributes to the child feeling safe, emotionally secure, physically healthy, and competent. When things go well, and there are enough financial resources for the child's basic needs, the child is able to concentrate on schoolwork, and is able to make age-appropriate friendships. Well-being is a provision for the child that falls within the domains of the child's family, school, culture, and community. Since neither the domains nor the child's development are static, well-being is constantly changing.

In social work, the concept of child well-being has not been adequately developed. Seaberg (1990) examined the usefulness of standardized, concrete measures of child well-being in child welfare practice. These standards take the form of lists of specific provisions that children need. Seaberg identified several problems in conceptualizing child well-being categorically, because this does not permit the social worker to understand the broad child perspective. In addition, he claimed that most definitions of child well-being reflect values that are not universally accepted. For example, it is difficult to reach agreement about realistic expectations for the life of the individual child. Should well-being be thought of only as meeting basic child needs such as having food, clothing, and shelter? Would each of the domains of child well-being have the same importance in determining the adequacy of child well-being? Seaberg cautions that a standardized, categorical definition of child well-being is not useful as a decision-making tool.

However, when considered within the context of advanced generalist practice with children, the definition of child well-being overcomes the problems raised by Seaberg, since it does not identify concrete, value-laden elements, but instead opens a field of categories relating to resources that are useful to a child. It is drawn from the conceptualization of the hierarchy of human needs developed by Abraham Maslow (1968), who established that basic needs such as physiological needs, safety needs, and belongingness needs must be addressed before higher-level needs, including esteem needs, self-actualization needs, and self-transcendence needs.

Thinking hierarchically and holistically, as Maslow did, provides direction to the advanced generalist practitioner and opens the way for a creative exploration of the child's well-being. Assessment that considers a simple and expandable list of needs is fundamental to determining holistic practice intervention. Starting with the most basic needs, using Maslow's hierarchy of needs, and including some of the domains suggested by Seaberg, this list includes the following: (a) physical safety and sustenance; (b) attachment; (c) emotional security; (d) medical and mental health care; (e) rites of passage; (f) space for privacy and play; (g) socialization; (h) education; (i) creativity, music, art, and literature; and (j) cultural and spiritual stimulation.

The following case shows a social worker's creative assessment of child well-being and reflects the advanced generalist perspective:

John, age five years, began living with his mother following his parent's separation. John's mother suffers from depression compounded by substance abuse. John's father lives with his parents. John's father and his paternal grandparents have been positively involved in John's life. John is attached to his mother and to his father. John's father initiated the services of a social worker to help him explore the option of his gaining custody of John. After assessing the situation, the social worker determined that, while John's mother's was providing adequately for his well-being at basic levels such as attachment, food, shelter, and clothing, she was unable to engage him emotionally, to play, or to support his social and school activities. The social worker found that John's father and grandparents were able to meet John's basic needs as well as his higher-level needs for play, friends, and learning. With the social worker's help, the parents decided that John's father would assume custody. They agreed that he could maintain attachment to his mother through regularly planned visits and live with his father and grandparents, who could better provide for him financially, emotionally, and socially. Although this was a difficult decision for the mother, with the social worker's support she was able to recognize her limitations, to collaborate with John's father, and to maintain visitation and involvement in John's life.

In this case the worker's assessment included individual assessment meetings with John and with all family members. It also included visits to John's school and to the homes of his mother and father. In assessing John's well-being, she considered domains at individual, family, and community levels. She made visible for John's mother, father, and grandparents John's greater need for emotional security, for play, and for socialization. Before John moved to his grandparent's home, his mother and father, together, prepared him for the transition and for future visits, thereby preserving his emotional security.

Environment or Child Well-Being

The term *child well-being* (as opposed to *environment* or *context*) better captures the changeability and "aliveness" of the child's world, in the here and now. The meaning of well-being implies a steady state of affairs. Child well-being is always moving and changing, since the things and persons in it are alive and interacting. The advanced generalist practitioner is an active catalyst in the child's world and makes way for the child to emerge into that world and assume a place.

Applying the advanced generalist themes of social justice, human rights, and social change (Vecchiolla et al., 2001) as they relate to children, suggests a humanity that involves the active participation of caring adults, including parents, teachers, social workers, and others. The child has the right to proceed, developmentally, and, at the same time, adults are obliged to "make way." Making way for a child involves a "spirit" that brings to mind Jane Addams, Marian Wright Edelman, and others who advocated passionately, and often successfully, on behalf of children at individual, family, community, and policy levels. This spirit of making way at multiple levels places developing children in view and enables social workers and parents to know better what children require at the time of the child's need. It reflects the principle that child development proceeds more fully when basic needs are met. The benefit of such a view is that it allows the social worker to note environmental factors that affect the individual child and to make known specific environmental strengths and weaknesses. When explored during assessment and intervention with the child, child well-being promotes holistic (as opposed to mechanical) understanding, and as such is consistent an advanced generalist perspective.

Positive and Negative Child Well-Being

At-risk children face daily challenges to well-being, including future uncertainties such as where they will live, who will parent them, how safe they will be, where they will go to school, where they will play, how they will make friends, and what materials will be provided them for daily living. A child's well-being is positive when the child can be certain of the future and when development can proceed without interference. A child's well-being is negative when the child feels uncertain about the future or when obstacles block the child's way to normal development.

The child's secure attachment to parents or caregivers is primary to child well-being. A child whose attachment to his or her parent is insecure or who is forced to worry excessively about the availability of that parent may have less curiosity and enthusiasm in school than a child whose well-being is secure. Many of the situations that require social work interventions on behalf of children are the result of adults' unawareness of a child's need for secure attachment. For example, John's mother was placed in foster care when she was three years old, leaving her without her own sense of secure attachment to John. When a sense of secure attachment is absent in the parent, he or she inadvertently may fail to "make way" for the child. The advanced generalist social work practitioner is prepared for orientation to the child's world, to assess the child's well-being, to facilitate change and to make way for the child, during their interventions.

WEIGHING RISK AND PROTECTIVE FACTORS

The advanced generalist social worker is aware of well-known areas of risk that affect a child's life. Risk factors include poverty, discrimination and racism (institutional and individual), drug abuse, child abuse, violence, illiteracy, restricted health care access, parental mental illness, parental marital or relationship troubles, and divorce. When a child is facing such risks at multiple levels his or her development and well-being are cumulatively affected. The social worker identifies various risks, large and small, at all levels, including the level of child's and parent's coping, and recommends changes at any level that will lead to positive well-being and ongoing development.

There is a challenge, however, to understanding how risk factors affect child well-being. Risk factors, by themselves, may not undermine a child's well-being if they are sufficiently offset by protective and mediating factors at multiple levels. Thus identifying and preserving existing protective factors at all levels, and creating new ones where possible, is as important to well-being as eliminating or reducing risk factors. Formulating an optimal holistic mix of protective factors and recognizing and protecting those that are critical to well-being provides a broader and more stable, dependable way in which children can proceed. Examples of such protective factors include cultural, community, and spiritual roots, the presence of a clean and safe neighborhood, access to open space for play, adequate schools, and the presence and availability of caregivers or parents.

In the case illustration of John, his parents and grandparents were able to keep John's needs in mind. His mother was able to consider options for him that were not her first choice. Her decision to do this became a protective factor for John. The added daily presence of active, willing grandparents added stability to John's well-being.

In reality, social workers may intervene with children who have positive well-being, but who face other issues. Children from stable environments also may face significant challenges to well-being. While material resources may be abundant, emotional resources may be deficient. These children and their families may be seen in child guidance clinics, mental health centers, or family service agencies. When it is clear that a child's well-being is positive, it allows the social worker to look beyond the environment for other contributing factors within the child.

WHAT IS MEANT BY DEVELOPMENT?

Soil, sunlight, and water are necessary to support all of life. However, beyond these basic requirements, every species requires other complex, less visible provisions to flourish. Flourishing means freely engaging the world across the life span. In the case of the human species, children are dependent for life supports on the adults around them, especially their parents or caregivers. They are not only dependent in terms of basics such as safety, attachment, food, clothing, and medical care, they are also dependent on parents or caregivers for a complex and widening network of well-being, including eating with pleasure, recognizing danger, playing, expressing and regulating affects, acquiring language, mastering self-care, and participating in celebrations and rituals.

Sigmund Freud's (1905) psychosexual stages of development and Anna Freud's (1963) developmental lines help practitioners to organize the dependency needs of children according to age, by depicting a gradual unfolding of the individual child both physically and psychologically. For Anna Freud and for later ego psychologists, the main axis of development is the line of object-relations, the progression from total emotional dependence in infancy to the relative emotional independence of adulthood. As useful as these early "pictures" of development are, they are incomplete, since they assume an imaginary, generic child, as well as an imaginary, unchanging, and benevolent environment. Erikson (1950) studied American Indian children who had been precipitously removed from parents and their native languages and traditions. After seeing the impacts of these losses on the children's development, Erikson elaborated a more complete, biopsychosocial theory of the child developing in a changing and sometimes chaotic family and community environment. Although other child developmental theorists have since refined Erikson's model, his eight-stage, culturally sensitive, life-cycle model continues to provide a useful, holistic picture of development suited to advanced generalist practice and child well-being.

The following example of a moment in the process of development is taken from Daniel Stern's book, *The Interpersonal World of the Infant* (1985). It illuminates both the way that development depends upon well-being and also the surprise of discovery resulting from keen observation:

> An eight-and-one-half-month-old boy reaches for a toy just beyond reach. Silently he stretches towards it, leaning and extending arms and fingers out fully. Still short of the toy, he tenses his body to squeeze out the extra inch he needs to reach it. At this moment, his mother says, "uuuuuh...uuuuuh!" with a crescendo of vocal effort, the expiration of air pushing against her tensed torso. The mother's accelerating vocal respiratory effort matches the infant's accelerating physical effort. (p. 140)

This vignette reveals a small but significant developmental event in the context of secure attachment. The child is free to explore his world when he experiences positive well-being provided by his mother.

As in the case with the term well-being, the word *development* has become so widely used that we may not adequately consider that developmental theories explain only a part on the natural unfolding of the individual lives of children. In reviewing theories of child development, Mayes (2001) considers that theorists have not recognized or appreciated that child development is both orderly and disorderly. "Rather, I suggest that order and disorder are essential twin poles in any developmental process, a constant dialectic that moves development along whether at the level of the cell or at the level of fantasy" (p. 141). The unpredictability of development calls for the spirit of making way for children that we include in our meaning of well-being. Mayes suggests that making way for the individual child means the adults' allowing for both forward and backward developmental movement. In the above example provided by Stern (1985), the mother recognized spontaneous forward movement and made way for the child to grasp the toy.

BRINGING CHILD WELL-BEING AND CHILD DEVELOPMENT TOGETHER IN ADVANCED GENERALIST PRACTICE

Making way for the developing child unites child well-being and development into a model in which the concepts are unified. Practicing with children from an advanced generalist perspective involves three practice activities: (a) close observation of children and the world that surrounds them; (b) using multiple theories to reveal what is hidden in child well-being and development; and (c) planning and taking action aimed at establishing the child's well-being and facilitating his or her development (theory, assessment, and intervention).

Close Observation of Children

In social work practice, we observe children and their environments more objectively than would a parent or a teacher. Observing closely involves the attention and acuity of the observer in Stern's (1985) story. It is noteworthy that the story comes alive because the observer is attuned to the dialectical interaction between the mother and child, to what is going on between them. Close observation also involves actively changing views from "microscopic" to "macroscopic," as if with a zoom lens. When with the child, the observer attends to minute changes in the child's facial expressions and voice, shifts in body, breathing, attention, affect, and voice. Widening the lens, the observer views longer behavioral sequences and patterns that occur in the child's day. An example of this might be the cyclical closing and distancing between the child and parent.

The advanced generalist observer first experiences the sensory impressions of the child's situation, in the here and now. Later, the observer deepens his or her understanding of the situation by examining well-being and, by using theory, assessing the developmental position of the child.

A social worker is seeing six-year-old Phillip in individual counseling, six months following the death of the boy's father. She makes a visit to his school arriving during recess. As she observes the group of first-graders on the playground and attempts to see her client, she cannot find him and imagines that out of his sadness, he may have avoided his peers during recess. However, as she looks more closely, she sees that he is there, playing a game of tag. He is so lively and involved with others in his play that

> he seems not to be the child she knows. She is struck by the joy that Phillip experiences among his peers. She had not seen this affect in his sessions and had not heard about this from his mother. The direct observation of his well-being changes the social worker's understanding of Phillip's development and of his grief.

It is noteworthy that, at first, the social worker does not think or hypothesize. She is engrossed in her observation and is moved by the child's joyful affect, his peers, the teacher who is enjoying watching, and the safe and spacious playground the school has provided. Later, in considering what she has seen, she examines the child's play in the context of a theory.

While observing the individual child in the counseling session the observer's scope is usually narrow. Observing the child's well-being reveals a more complete picture. Phillip's social worker is emotionally moved by her observation on the playground. She has witnessed the developmental unfolding of the boy. This moves her to make way for the child, to make an opening for him. It is in this spirit of making way that she facilitates changes at home and at school that will allow the boy to proceed developmentally beyond the loss of his father.

Using Theory To Reveal What Is Hidden

While observing children, one becomes engrossed in what is unfolding. It is after this, in reflecting upon the observation, that the observer employs theory. This may be described as using a theory or concept to provide a second opinion with which to compare one's understanding of observations. Observing is a primary experience; using theory is a secondary process. The theories most relevant to the child perspective are those that illuminate child development. Stern's (1985) case example is informed by the theoretical concept of *affective attunement*, the mother's matching her affect to the affect of her baby, using her voice and body. Keeping Stern's concept in mind allows us to see affective attunement, when it occurs, and to notice when it is absent in parent-child interactions.

In the example of Phillip above, the advanced generalist social worker may use two or three theories, one informing another. For example, Erikson's (1982) concept of competence during the school years may be supplemented by general systems aspects of Phillip's school and family activities. For example:

In the therapist's next session with Phillip, as she observes his play with doll house figures, she does not consider theories as she focuses upon the boy's elaborate story of a rescue by a fireman of children from a burning house. She finds herself focused on the boy's extraordinary gentleness as the fireman figure that he holds removes children from their bedrooms and takes them to safety. She feels moved by this observation and recognizes significant strengths in the boy: courage, concentration, competence "under fire," and the wish to protect others. Later, she notes that the fireman in the child's play has made way for the child. She considers that Phillip may see her as making way for him, back to well-being. Careful observation, the judicious use of theory, and the use of her own feelings have combined to provide understanding.

Planning and Taking Action

While careful observing and informing observations with the appropriate theory involves "knowing what," acting in the interests of the well-being and development of the child and his parents involves "knowing how" (Baechler, 1992). Following observation and reflective interpretation, the practitioner hypothesizes about what is going on. What does he or she do? Acting requires know-how. In the case illustration, the social worker closely observed Phillip in his sessions and closely observed his well-being at home and at school. She considered both well-being and development, together, in the spirit of making way. She informed her understanding of his world and his developmental movement using theory. She will take action, knowing that developmental movement has resumed, and that Phillip is ready to take his place among his age peers. She may recommend to his mother that his individual sessions be reduced, and that he be referred to a 12-session group for children who have lost family members to death. Before making these changes, she will prepare Phillip, reflecting with him on the progress he has made. This preparation is another way of making way.

The advanced generalist perspective in social work practice with children requires, first, that obstacles to seeing be removed. Children who are at risk need maximal visibility and have a right to social work interventions that make way for well-being and ongoing development.

INVISIBILITY OF CHILDREN COMMON IN SOCIAL WORK PRACTICE: A CLINICIAN WHO LACKS AN ADVANCED GENERALIST PERSPECTIVE

A social worker in a day hospital program has begun individual counseling with a middle-aged woman, following the woman's discharge from a three-day psychiatric hospitalization for a suicide attempt. The social worker is unaware that the woman has three dependent children who are staying with the woman's sister in another city. The client is worried that the she could lose custody of her children if the clinician became aware of them. She hides the fact that she is a parent. The social worker does not ask. Progress in the client's sessions is limited by her guilty feelings in regard to her children and by the clinician's missing important information.

While the worker above was attempting to understand her client deeply, she failed to consider if her client might be a parent. This omission compromised the client's therapy and may have inadvertently compromised the well-being of her client and the client's children. Vanharen, Laroche, Heyman, and Massabki (1993) studied the visibility of the children of adult mental health clients and found that, despite the well-known correspondence between parental mental illness and psychiatric illness in children, only a small percentage of mental health clinicians inquired as to whether their adult clients had children. The findings of Vanharen et al. (1993) support the earlier findings of social worker Selma Fraiberg (1978), who found that therapists overlooked children of adult clients with mental illness. Fraiberg (1978) identified these children as "the invisible children" and stated that a "rational approach" to a parent's treatment should include the social worker's continuous awareness of the children of mentally ill parents and asking themselves:

> Who is taking care of the baby and the older children? Where are the children? What is the quality of care provided during hospitalization? Are the children damaged? Are they in danger? Can this mother, with expert help, care for her children, or are the children endangered if they continue to live with her? If they are endangered, how can we work towards stable foster care plans? (pp. 290-291)

CHALLENGES TO INCORPORATING THE ADVANCED GENERALIST PERSPECTIVE IN PRACTICE WITH CHILDREN

In applying the advanced generalist perspective in working with children, social workers frequently encounter opposition from agencies and institutions invested in narrower approaches. These challenges present opportunities for the advanced generalist social worker to use the holistic, multilevel, multi-theoretical frame. One such challenge is created when the mission and policies of an institution or agency may not accommodate the active and holistic perspective of advanced generalist practice with children. Reasons for this may exist within and outside an agency. For example, tight budgets, precipitous reductions in funding, and reduced client entitlements may cause administrators to resist broad-based services to children. To administrators under pressure to conserve resources, the holistic approach of advanced generalist practice with children may be less attractive at first glance than services that are limited in scope and narrowly defined. In extreme cases, agencies may become stagnant, so that creativity and innovative thinking on behalf of children and caregivers stops. In order to avoid such occurrences, it is essential that agency decision makers not confuse efficiency and narrowly defined goals with organizational success and efficacy of intervention.

The advanced generalist social worker, either from within as an employee, or from outside as a consultant, represents the integrity of the holistic advanced generalist perspective. Representation of the advanced generalist perspective involves working actively with agency decision makers to keep children and their well-being in view and to make way for innovative interventions for children that both optimize efficiency and protect child well-being and child development. In one such situation, an advanced generalist practitioner successfully facilitated a collaboration between a municipal housing authority and a state department of social services to provide joint funding and planning for disabled parents who needed specialized housing to adequately care for their four young children. Before this, the agencies had not collaborated. Agency workers had been unaware of the mandated roles and resources of the other agency. This collaboration stimulated further creative collaborations between the agencies.

Second, by valuing the synergy that accompanies successful agency linkages and interdisciplinary collaborations, and by resisting the narrow specialization, segmentation, and disciplinary isolation common in the helping professions (Toulmin, 2001; Wilson, 1998), the advanced generalist social worker assumes a leadership role in collaborations aimed at better serving families and children. For example, an MSW who also was an attorney specializing in child welfare law used the advanced generalist perspective in practice with children to initiate a collaboration between the center-city child guidance agency where she practiced and the local police department. The collaboration resulted in a unique program in which officers were trained in child well-being and development, and workers shared with officers cases involving children at risk because of involvement with gangs and selling drugs. Later, by encouraging the interest of her U.S. Representative in the project, the worker enabled the agency to obtain ongoing federal financial support for the collaboration.

Third, the advanced generalist maintains a commitment to social change at higher levels and recognizes the limitations of over-focusing on one level.

> A city school superintendent was directed by the municipal school committee to raise students' performance scores on statewide standardized tests. She required school principals to make higher test scores a priority. Paul is a fourth-grade student at a crowded center-city elementary school referred to a social worker because he is disruptive and is not concentrating. The social worker has many such referrals. In meeting with Paul, she learned that his parents have just separated after a period of severe and sometimes violent conflict. Paul is worried about where he will live, frightened by his parent's anger and unsure about the future.

Here the social worker faces a choice. She could focus on the superintendent's and principal's priority of improving student test scores. This may lead her to focus on Paul's classroom behavior, hypothesizing that reducing negative behaviors will enhance the test scores of both Paul and other students. Alternatively, she could set aside the principal's priority and examine Paul's well-being and the forces that might be affecting his school performance. By taking the advanced generalist perspective in working with children, the social worker has a third choice. She may see her way to addressing Paul's needs and also promoting school policies that are more sensitive to child development and to child well-being. Addressing child well-being at multiple levels may assure that way is made for Paul's educational and social development as well as for that of other children. In terms of social justice, by successful intervention at the school level she may help Paul and also broaden the view of child well-being held by the principal, superintendent and, indeed, the community.

Fourth, theoretical orientations that do not include an advanced generalist perspective in practice with children may not address child well-being. Emotional, cognitive, or family processes should include the realm of well-being and its effects on development.

> Susan is a ten-year-old girl who lives with her mother. Her father died in an automobile crash two years prior to intake. She was referred to a child guidance clinic because of fighting in school. When Susan and her mother came to their initial meeting, the subject of Susan's fighting at school did not arise. Instead, the mother and daughter began talking about Susan's babysitter and how both Susan and her mother felt uncomfortable with the sitter. Susan then stated that the sitter had recently made sexual comments in front of Susan. Her mother and Susan quickly decided to make a change of sitters.

At the beginning of their session, the social worker faced a choice. Based on what she knew, and in the interest of staying focused on the presenting problem, she might have interrupted her clients' conversation after several minutes and directed the couple to address Susan's school behavior. By allowing her clients to continue their conversation around the decision to change Susan's sitter, the social worker supported Susan's and her mother's attention to Susan's well-being.

Finally, the advanced generalist practice perspective with children extends the worker's awareness of child well-being to include agency, community, and government policies, regulations, and laws that may influence well-being. Another example demonstrates the importance of concurrent intervention at multiple levels:

> Children who were referred to this particular mental health clinic had behavior, conduct, or attention problems that were helped with medication. The insurance policy covering services for poor clients prohibited the child being seen on the same day by the social worker and by the medication provider. As a result, the poorest clients had to come twice as often to the clinic as those who had means. This meant that some families would travel on the bus for more than an hour to go a distance that took 15 minutes by car. Social workers at this clinic advocated successfully with the insurance company to change the policy to cover two visits in one day.

In this situation, if the social workers had failed to keep insurance company policy and practices in view, they may have unthinkingly expected families to comply. This would have added considerably to the burden on the families. The stress that poor parents and their children were facing would have continued. By intervening forcefully at the insurance company level, while simultaneously providing services to those affected, social workers empowered parents and validated the importance of the parents' and their children's well-being.

PRINCIPLES AND SUMMARY

Applying the advanced generalist perspective to practice with children means entering the child's world and observing at multiple levels. To do this effectively, the social worker must employ different theories to guide various and simultaneous interventions in order to make way for children. The term *eclectic* does not capture the multiple-theory principle of advanced generalist practice, since each level of practice requires the use of whole theories relevant to problems specific to their levels and domains. The multi-theoretical principle means knowing an array of theories, selecting the ones relevant to the situation, and applying them in some depth, as opposed to a more superficial mixing and matching.

The principle of multiple systems means the social worker's holding in view a complex of interrelated systems and social realities. The zoom lens seems an appropriate metaphor for this principle that includes child's well-being and the child's development. This principle is informed by the values of social justice, human rights, and social change and requires the practitioner's promotion of awareness of oppression and discrimination that disturb child well-being.

The principle of keeping children visible and making way for development requires the worker's awareness that children do not readily have a voice in the direction of their lives, and that it is easy for adults to lose sight of children. Even professionals who are educated and trained to do so may not regularly work directly with children and may inadvertently lose sight of them. The principle of keeping children in view requires that practitioners working with adult clients are aware of the clients' parental status and consider the needs of their children. Non-holistic, pragmatic, theoretical orientations that are frequently practiced in non-social work "host" settings and that are increasingly popular with third-party payers often contribute to the invisibility of children.

Finally, the advanced generalist perspective in work with children involves flexibility and nimbleness beyond that required in working from other perspectives. This requirement is based on the developmental principle of critical periods. The developmental needs of children cannot wait. An example would be the immediate need for a hearing evaluation for a three-year-old in day care. The urgency of need in work with children is not present to the same degree in work with adults. The worker's developmental knowledge that helps to predict these needs and the skill required to articulate them must be supplemented by knowledge and skill at making way at many levels. The advanced generalist perspective for practice with children includes the social worker seeing child well-being and child development in the context of the changing and sometimes fast-moving society.

REFERENCES

Baechler, J. (1992). Virtue: Its nature, exigency, and acquisition, J. Chapman (Trans.). *Nomos, 34*, 25-48.

Ehrenreich, J. (1985). *The altruistic imagination: A history of social work and social policy in the United States*. Ithaca, NY: Cornell University Press.

Erikson, E. (1982). *The life cycle completed*. New York: W. W. Norton.

Erikson, E. (1950). *Childhood and society*. New York: W. W. Norton.

Fraiberg, S. (1978). The invisible children. In E. J. Anthony, C. Koupernik, & C. Chiland (Eds.), *The child in his family* (Vol. 4, pp. 287-291). New York: John Wiley & Sons.

Freud, A. (1963). The concept of developmental lines. *The Psychoanalytic Study of the Child, 18*, 245-265.

Freud, S. (1905). Three essays on the theory of sexuality in *The Standard Edition*, 7, 1953. London: Hogarth Press.

Maslow, A. (1968). *Toward a psychology of being*. New York: Van Nostrand.

Mayes, L. (2001). The twin poles of order and chaos: Development as a dynamic, self-ordering system. *The Psychoanalytic Study of the Child, 56*, 137-170.

Seaberg, J. (1990). Child well-being: A feasible concept? *Social Work, 35*, 267-272.

Sidel, R. (1986). *Women & children last: The plight of poor women in affluent America*. New York: Viking Penguin Books.

Sidel, R. (1996). *Keeping women and children last*. New York: Penguin Books USA.

Stern, D. (1985). *The interpersonal world of the infant*. New York: Columbia University Press.

Toulmin, S. (2001). *Return to reason*. Cambridge, MA: Harvard University Press.

Vanharen, J., Laroche, C., Heyman, M., & Massabki, A. (1993). Have the invisible children become visible? *Canadian Journal of Psychiatry, 38*, 678-680.

Vecchiolla, F., Roy, A., Lesser, J., Wronka, J., Walsh-Burke, K., Gianesin, J. et al. (2001). Advanced generalist practice: A framework for social work practice in the twenty-first century. *Journal of Teaching in Social Work, 21*(3/4), 91-104.

Wilson, E. O. (1998). *Consilience: The unity of knowledge*. New York: Alfred A. Knopf.

Chapter 11

THE ART OF SCHOOL SOCIAL WORK AND ADVANCED GENERALIST PRACTICE

Joseph R. Gianesin
Springfield College

The family and the school are the primary influences on the development of children. Despite the recent attacks on public education that speak to the inadequacies and failings of public education, schools still constitute a major socializing agent for our society. Changes in our social, religious, political, and economic environments have required public education to reexamine how schools fulfill this role with children who often enter schools not ready or not able to learn.

The practice of social work in schools in today's politically charged environment requires competent practitioners who can approach problems from an ecological perspective that views the person and environment as "a unitary, interacting system in which each constantly affects and shapes the other" (Germain, 1991, p. 27). This approach directs professional attention to the whole child and includes the school, family, and community. School social workers, who take this ecological point of view with an advanced generalist approach, position themselves to assist the child in developing social competence and educational achievement at the same time they increase the school's responsiveness to the needs and aspirations of children, parents, and community. The challenge to school social workers who practice from an advanced generalist perspective is to develop skills that assist children in their interactions with school, and also to introduce change into the organization using persuasion, bargaining, mediation, negotiation, and conflict management (Germain, p. 33).

Public education is a lightning rod for debate and criticism on many of the social issues of the moment. Economic and financial equality, segregation, civil rights, resource allocation, taxation, vulnerable populations, violence, and religious fervor have made their presence known in the public school arena. Schools are one of the last bastions of government where the general public feel they have control and input. In an age when many constituents feel disenfranchised and removed from politics, public education remains accessible for influence and involvement. School systems have retained some semblance of local governance, with local citizens elected to representative positions on school boards or councils. Participation in a democratic society at a local level creates controversy and strain on a system with many stakeholders.

The tension of influence and the degree to which schools socialize children is an ongoing debate. Families and schools differ in their expectations and aspirations regarding the child. Special interest groups and political and religious leaders debate the role of public schools, the content of the curriculum being taught, and the purpose and role of public education. Public education is the focal point for business and labor leaders who voice concern about student readiness to enter a complex work environment. Parents and students alike have concern over safety and violence issues. Despite these criticisms and attacks, the important position of the school in the lives of students and families remains a constant. Teachers, administrators, specialists, and support personnel continue to provide a composite array of services and learning environments—all the while in the spotlight of a society that is quick to judge, but reluctant to fund or participate in applying realistic solutions to complex problems.

Schools do not exist in a vacuum and cannot be held entirely responsible for the success or failure of their students. Jozefowicz-Simbeni and Allen-Meares (2002) question the recent political climate of "holding low-achieving schools (which most often are high-poverty schools) solely responsible for increasing student achievement" (p. 123), without addressing other important factors such as family poverty, the home environment, and community. Without fiscal supports to programs and services that affect achievement and school performance, increasing testing and assessment practices will not improve student achievement. In fact, recent political agendas on the conservative right call for dismantling public education, diverting public funds to religious and private schools through vouchers, and decreasing the funding level of schools while increasing performance standards.

In addition to a politically charged agenda, public education is faced with legal mandates to educate every child between the ages of 7 and 21. These include the students on the opposite ends of the spectrum of ability and achievement. Included in this diverse population are students with varying degrees of disabilities, language acquisition and mastery, cultural and ethnic differences, and mental health issues. The number of students with mental health issues has risen dramatically over the last two decades. Many students feel alienated at school, especially in urban schools, where dropouts, "pushouts," and violence tend to be the norm.

Suffice to say that public education is mandated to educate every child without regard to environmental exposure, cultural heritage, language acquisition, economic level, or ability to understand the curriculum. This presents a great challenge to educators faced with diminishing budgets, as well as politically and legally charged environments, to perform at increasingly higher levels of achievement.

CHALLENGES FOR SCHOOL SOCIAL WORK

The current educational climate and recent historical developments present a major challenge to school social workers who have long worked with educators to help students and families get the most from school by helping them cope and adjust, and by improving the environment that hinders their developmental ability. Constable (2003) writes that the purpose of school social work is to provide a diverse and flexible response to the social and developmental needs in the human learning process as it takes place. School social workers have provided a vital link between schools and communities since the early 1900s, when external social workers first intervened to address truancy problems related to the family and community (Germain, 1991).

The development of school social work has evolved over time to include a variety of tasks and functions. According to Allen-Meares (1994), social school social work tasks have dominated the literature since the conception of the field of practice. Major studies conducted by Costin (1969), Allen-Meares (1977), and Chavkin (1985) have found that the job activities performed by school social workers are composed of a continuum of direct services to individual students, work with families, liaison work, group work, consultation, policy-making, and administration and supervision. These ambitious tasks require the practitioner to demonstrate skills beyond the traditional clinical practice model. In fact, social workers who work in the schools are usually more successful if they possess vital theoretical tools and have an array of practice skills and theories they can implement at multiple levels of intervention. One of the most distinctive and powerful tools a school social worker brings to the service arena is a systems framework that facilitates the organization of services at all levels of the school (Allen-Meares, 1996; Kapp, 2000). The use of a systems framework and the multiple use of theories and levels of school social work require a knowledge and skill base consonant with an advanced generalist practice perspective.

ADVANCED GENERALIST PRACTICE IN SCHOOL SOCIAL WORK

The practice of school social work from an advanced generalist perspective is a necessity rather than an option. School social work requires the practitioner to utilize a wide range of skills to meet the challenges of working in the educational environment. Kirst-Ashman and Hull (2002) characterize generalist practice as having three major features. First, the social worker should have an eclectic knowledge base of theories and interventions appropriate to the population being served. Second, the social worker must have a planned change process that emphasizes the assessment of client strengths. Third, the social worker should demonstrate a knowledge base through which a problem can be analyzed and addressed from multiple levels of intervention that involve micro, mezzo, and macro systems of change. The ability to integrate and intervene at these multiple levels requires a complex set of skills and a philosophical foundation rooted in advanced generalist practice. For aspiring school social workers, professional training at the MSW level will be enhanced if the principles and tenets of teaching advanced generalist practice are followed. Effective intervention in the schools using an advanced generalist approach can sustain positive changes for both staff and students. Remedial assistance as well as proactive and developmental approaches can be utilized on numerous levels. Acquiring these multiple skill sets and practice philosophies requires rigorous study and experiential exposure to the school environment.

MICRO, MEZZO, AND MACRO LEVELS OF INTERVENTION IN SCHOOL SOCIAL WORK

Effective school social work practice requires the practitioner to examine the child as a whole, and then to attend to all of the child's needs so that he or she may develop and function at an optimum level. To accomplish this, social workers must be willing to work with, and for, a student on multiple levels. This requires the practitioner to work on a clinical level of assessing individual mental health and emotional needs; at the family level to assess and provide service to parents; at the school level to enable teachers and other school personnel to view the child from a holistic perspective; and at a policy level, where changes to policy and organization environments benefit children and enable them to optimize their school experience. This is often referred to as an advanced generalist approach, enabling the worker to assess each environment encountered by the student and to enact change accordingly. The Springfield College School of Social Work uses the concept of *skill sets*, which are based on tasks and/or interventions at the micro, mezzo, and macro levels of practice (Program Review, 2001).

Skill sets required to work effectively at the micro level include the ability to conduct traditional, direct service, and/or clinical interventions. The school social worker explores the critical problems of the individual, which entail both biological and psychological aspects of the student's situation. Other skill sets brought to bear in micro intervention include conducting a multidimensional assessment, psychosocial educational history, functional behavioral analysis, educational counseling with children, and parent liaison counseling.

At the mezzo level, school social workers should have a number of highly developed skill sets. For example, they must be able to conduct group work in areas such as facilitating parent-teacher conferences; conducting psycho-education, support, task, and focus groups; intervention with student peer groups; parent training and PTO interactions; and facilitating staff development exercises at the building level. School social workers also consult with teachers, administrators, parents, and outside referral sources to influence the classroom and home environment. Effective school consultation is predicated on the triadic relationship between the school social worker, the consultee (teacher, administrator, parent, other professionals), and the student (White & Mullis, 1998). Consultation is a collaborative effort between consultant and consultee, a process in which "success is going to hinge largely on communication and relationship skills" (Gutkin & Curtis, 1982, p. 822). Thus, establishing rapport and collaborative relationships between teachers, parents, and administrators is important to the success of the consultation.

At the macro level, the school social worker must be prepared to use advocacy and community organization skills on behalf of vulnerable students. Such students can easily fall through the cracks because of multiple moves, truancy, and lack of parental involvement. Schools have a tendency to under-serve multiproblem students. They may neglect or have inadequate resources to provide necessary services, use disciplinary practices to discourage difficult students from continuing in school, and set up bureaucratic barriers to school admission by promoting policies that keep these children from enrolling. Ornstein and Moses (2000) promote the idea that school social workers need to build coalitions between families, educators, and local school boards to influence policies and develop services that take into account the needs of the most vulnerable students, who are not getting the most out of their educational experience. Many school social workers intervene at the macro level when they join community boards, influence policy for both the local and state boards of education, conduct community needs surveys, and coordinate services for students involved with multiple social service agencies. All three levels of intervention are utilized throughout the process of serving a school community.

THEORIES FOR EFFECTIVE ADVANCED GENERALIST SOCIAL WORK IN SCHOOLS

Effective practice in school social work requires the practitioner to have a working knowledge base of theories and interventions appropriate to students and the school system. During the late 1960s, generic approaches to practice in school social work were no longer adequate for the complexity of problems school social workers faced. The development of literature, journals, and specialized associations led to school social work developing its own distinct identity, methodology, theory, and organization (Constable, McDonald, & Flynn, 2002, p. 15). State and national associations were formed to meet the demand for professional development and provide a forum for theory-based interventions. Since that time, school social work has become a highly organized field of practice in the United States, employing a large number of practitioners and resulting in the creation of several state and national organizations, such as the School Social Work Association of America (SSWAA). These organizations, along with the proliferation of journal articles on social work practice in schools have created a forum whereby effective theories of intervention can be disseminated among colleagues.

Theoretical frameworks for practicing school social work from an advanced generalist perspective go beyond an eclectic perspective and are therefore particularly helpful to the increasingly complex area of school social work. Effective social workers in schools employ a broad, professional knowledge base. Theoretical orientation using an advanced generalist perspective requires that the school social workers have within their disposal theories that are applicable at all three levels of intervention: micro, mezzo, and macro. One theory that helps organize the complexity of school social work is what Germain & Gitterman (1980) referred to as the *ecological perspective*. For school social workers this particular viewpoint is essential because it takes into account a multicausal perspective rather than a linear causal one. An ecological perspective provides the framework for understanding the nature of the transactions between the person and different institutions and/or systems. It helps the social worker focus on the social process of interaction and the transactions between a student and that student's environment (Allen-Meares, Washington, & Welsh, 2000). Numerous factors and institutions play important roles in the development of a child that go beyond the family and school. They might also include neighborhood, hospitals, courts, mass media, juvenile probation, peers, churches, etc. The aggregate of these influences and interactions mold the child's view and response to the environment. For example, if the child experiences domestic violence at home before entering school, the impact of that interaction may have behavioral consequences in the school setting. Without taking into account the multiple systems that are affecting the child's life, social workers and educators would be ineffective in their interventions with students and may cause more harm than good.

Human behavior and developmental theory is another vital theoretical framework for school social workers. All educators and social workers are required to take some element of child development and human behavior theory during their graduate preparation. It is essential to have this knowledge base as a guide in dealing with parents and educators. Generally, most curriculums cover the three major dimensions of human development: biophysical, psychological, and social. Each dimension plays an important role for the school social worker.

The start of school coincides with the developmental stages of middle childhood and adolescence. It is characterized by the development of important skills including coordination, physical strength, cognitive intellectual functioning, and social skills with peers. Children in school settings become more sophisticated as they grow older, developing problem-solving abilities and adaptations to peer groups. Mastery of the intellect and of social spheres become as important as the biophysical development. Without adequate knowledge of these areas, school social workers have difficulty providing adequate assessment and intervention for students.

Biophysical Dimension

The growth and development of the biophysical person plays a central role in human development. Understanding the biological processes that affect human growth and development is very important to performing the function of school social work.

The knowledge base for the biophysical realm has exploded in recent years and graduate social work education has minimally met the challenge of translating that knowledge to social work students (Ashford, LeCroy, & Lortie, 2001). Many functions performed by school social workers require knowledge of biology. These functions include student screening, referral, coordinating services with psychiatrists and pediatricians, reporting the effects of medication interventions, recognition of organic and inorganic disorders, abnormal biophysical development, and brain-behavior relationships.

Because public schools are required by law to provide a free and appropriate education for every child, school social workers will likely encounter a large continuum of biophysical issues. Knowledge of gene disorders (e.g., hemophilia), chromosome disorders (e.g., Down syndrome), neural development (e.g., fetal alcohol syndrome), and biophysical hazards is important. Any understanding of human growth and development must take into account key biophysical systems. School social workers need more than a basic understanding of the range of physical conditions that contribute to the emotional and behavioral disturbances often seen in school settings.

Psychological Dimension

The psychological dimension of human behavior is very important to the school social worker. School social workers should have a working knowledge of psychodynamic theory, Erikson's psychosocial development theory, Piaget's approach to cognition, and a basic understanding of mental measurement theories. In addition, learning theory is an obvious yet frequently overlooked theory that school social workers often employ, but don't fully comprehend in terms of the application and impact of behavioral theory on school settings. Many educators are schooled primarily in learning theory and behavioral techniques. These may include a form of operant conditioning used in the form of praise for students completing a task correctly. It is often used as an intervention in the classroom setting in the form of token economies. This behavioral intervention uses points, chips, or play money as incentives to shape and mold behaviors associated with positive school performance. Students are rewarded with some "payoff" both in the short term immediately following the desired behavior, and in the long term, e.g., points accumulated throughout the week. When school social workers act as consultants or advisors to behavioral classrooms for students, it is imperative that they have a comprehensive knowledge base in behavioral and learning theories.

Psychological processes do not influence individual perceptions and behaviors in a vacuum. All forms of human behavior take place in social settings and environments that the child comes in contact with. These may include family life, church life, community, and of course, school life.

Social Dimension

As stated previously, the use of ecological system theory (Germain, 1991) studies the relation between organisms and their environments. Thus, the school social worker must have a working knowledge of those theories that describe the interactions and dynamics that take place in those influential social systems. Examples of this might include Carter and McGoldrick's (1988) model on the stages of the family life cycle. School social workers knowledgeable about family systems theory are able to apply family therapy in their work with students and parents. They can be extremely successful in bridging the gap between the expectations of the family and the expectations of the school.

Additionally, many school social workers are called on to conduct parent-training seminars. Some utilize behavioral-oriented training programs while others use communication theories. In either case, school social workers who have a functional understanding of family dynamics, effective discipline techniques, and positive interaction patterns for families can be of great service to both the home and the school.

In addition to theories regarding family, group work theories are essential in being a competent advanced generalist practitioner. This particular knowledge base is important to school social workers because they often are required to participate in group meetings involving parents and teachers; guide staff development activities; plan and conduct treatment and support groups; mediate disputes between the family and the school; and participate in community-wide task groups to address social problems affecting students. Thus, an understanding of how groups function, roles and norms, communication patterns, and decision-making processes is essential in becoming an effective advanced generalist school social worker.

On the macro level of intervention, school social workers also should be skilled in applying theories in the context of communities, organizations, and institutions. As Heller (1990) points out, community is considered one of the most important environmental contexts for understanding human behavior and issues of personal well-being. When school social workers engage in developing, locating, linking with, and managing community resources to help students improve their social functioning and performance in school, the social worker is engaging in community practice (Hardcastle, Wenocur, & Powers, 1997). The school social workers should be schooled in recognizing the power of organizing a community toward a goal that would affect students positively. This may come in the form of helping the school or any other social institution become more responsive to its constituents. This is especially true for students who come from underprivileged households or who may be disenfranchised from the public school setting. Understanding how prejudice and discrimination of marginalized groups affects students in the public schools is vitally important to the mission of social work and the well-being of all students. Because schools encompass a large constituency of students from multiple racial and ethnic groups, knowledge about multicultural interactions and gender considerations is extremely important. In addition, discrimination in society is found at the individual and institutional levels. The ability to recognize and intervene on both levels for the benefit of students is important in school social work. In a sense, school social workers can act as the conscience of the school by advocating at multiple levels for those students and families who otherwise could not advocate for themselves. In fact, the ability to integrate and intervene for students at these various levels requires a complex set of skills and a philosophical foundation rooted in advanced generalist practice. To better understand the practicality and implementation of these skills, a case example of a school social worker is presented to highlight the effectiveness of an advanced generalist approach.

CASE EXAMPLE

School social work has long been a leader in practicing an advanced generalist philosophy. The nature of a host setting requires the competent school social worker to practice on all three levels: micro, mezzo, and macro. The target for intervention may well be an individual such as the teacher, administrator, student, or parent. On a mezzo level, the intervention may take place in a psycho-educational group of students or parents as well as in a work-based task group of teaching staff. At the macro level, many school social workers make efforts to change policies within their school districts that have negative effects on the education of children. Often, school social workers are in a unique position to call attention to oppressed and disenfranchised populations that are present in school settings. Advocacy and influential intervention at the macro level has the potential to affect a larger number of students compared with an exclusive focus at the individual, or micro level.

The following case example highlights how a typical school social worker might respond at three levels of advanced generalist practice in a school setting.

Mr. Ross is a school social worker at a suburban high school in the Southwest. The school has a population of 1,200 students in grades 9-12. The town in which this high school is located is undergoing rapid growth that has required the school district and the high school to bus in a large percentage of students from a new upper-middle class housing development across town. In years past, this high school contained neighborhood students mainly from lower-middle class working families. There is some ethnic diversity with the school composed of 12% Hispanics (mostly of Mexican-American heritage), 11% African American, 1% Native American, and 1% Asian American. The social worker has been at the high school for five years and has established a good working rapport with teachers and administrators. He is highly regarded for his crisis intervention work and ability to intervene with difficult students and families. The caseload is high, with demands outpacing the hours needed to meet the needs of this high school.

Mr. Ross recently received a referral from the assistant principal regarding a sophomore, Roberto, who has been skipping school. Roberto has failing grades and has become belligerent and defiant with some of his teachers. Roberto, a 15-year-old Hispanic male, is already talking about dropping out of school when he turns 16. He comes from a family that lives in close proximity to the high school. Mr. Ross knows Roberto and his family from the middle school he attended before entering the high school. It surprises Mr. Ross that he is getting a referral on Roberto because he remembers him as a good student who never got into trouble with staff at the middle school. Mr. Ross arranges to meet with Roberto to discuss the problem.

When prompted to discuss the presenting problems, Roberto discloses that he is very unhappy with the school, that he just doesn't like it. He can tolerate only one of his teachers this year and finds the rest very unapproachable. When asked about his ninth-grade experience, Roberto stated it was just as bad and maybe even more boring than this year. He had hoped it would improve but it was just as bad or worse. He didn't know why he should continue to come to school since he wasn't learning anything important that would help him acquire more skills to work in his stepfather's auto body shop. (At the urging of the new principal, the school had recently shut down its vocational trade program to embrace a more technology-oriented curriculum.)

After making a thorough assessment, Mr. Ross could not link any other environmental or family events to Roberto's disenfranchisement from school. In fact, Roberto's mother and stepfather reported that he helps them a great deal at home, and that he is working part-time on the weekends in his stepfather's auto body shop. They were both worried about Roberto and desperately wanted him to finish high school. Neither of Roberto's parents had finished high school, and they worried that this would limit the opportunities for Roberto. Given Roberto's history and present level of functioning, Mr. Ross hypothesized that Roberto's lack of school interest was due to several factors including Roberto's lack of motivation in school (micro); the school environment and curriculum not engaging him (mezzo); and that Roberto did not have any adult at school that he felt any personal connection with (micro). The majority of the staff at the high school were Caucasian with even a blonde, blue-eyed Spanish teacher. Roberto reports that her Spanish is very different from what he speaks at home, and that he is failing Spanish class because of a lack of attendance and a poor understanding of the grammar and punctuation exercises taking place in class.

Mr. Ross began seeing Roberto regularly over the course of the next six weeks, checking in with him regarding his progress in school. As part of his initial assessment and treatment planning, Mr. Ross contracted with Roberto to attend all of his classes regularly and to make an effort to complete homework assignments in each class. Mr. Ross visited all of his teachers inquiring about his progress in class and whether the teachers had seen any marked improvement in his attitude and school work completion. The reports were mixed but Roberto seemed to be improving in his attitude toward school, and his attendance had improved remarkably. Roberto continued to report about his discomfort in school and how he really didn't feel like there was anything that he could find interesting there. The school social worker, Mr. Ross, asked about his friendships, and Roberto described his peer group as mostly Hispanic males who didn't like school much either. Most of the students Roberto described as friends were kids he had grown up with in his neighborhood. They dressed in clothes that faculty and administrative staff dubbed as "gang related" but only 2 of 12 kids named by Roberto had any significant discipline or judicial infractions. Mr. Ross had recently been silently annoyed at a teacher and assistant principal who made disparaging remarks about this group, referring to them as "gang wannabe's." He asked his colleagues whether they would also designate as gang members a group of students who happened to be Caucasian dressed in similar clothing. They laughed off the remark but the point had been made. The students Roberto was hanging with were not necessarily discipline problems but their grades and attitudes toward school were poor. Mr. Ross considered that the problem he was encountering with Roberto was, in reality, larger than Roberto himself.

Mr. Ross asked if Roberto would be willing to bring some of his friends by to see him since he was interested in hearing their opinions and thoughts about school. Roberto hesitated but stated that he might bring them by some time. Over the next few weeks, Mr. Ross did a little investigating of his own regarding the dropout rates for this high school. After consulting with the dropout counselor of the district and with the coordinator for discipline in the district for suspensions and expulsions, it became quite apparent that there was a disproportionate percentage of Hispanic males dropping out or being "pushed out" of this high school. In fact, 57% of all the Hispanic males had dropped out of high school over the past 5 years, and there had been a dramatic increase in that number over the last 3 years. This coincided with the new technology initiative and the loss of a much-loved Hispanic Spanish teacher who had moved out of state. That Spanish teacher had sponsored several events honoring the Mexican culture and several student class trips to Mexico.

Roberto kept his word and introduced Mr. Ross to several of his friends. Mr. Ross had begun making his presence visible in the areas that Roberto and his peer group "occupied." This allowed Roberto to introduce Mr. Ross without having to commit to coming to the counseling office. After two or three weeks of informal conversation, Mr. Ross asked if they would be interested in participating in a focus group composed of Hispanic males to get a better understanding of their thoughts about school. They agreed to participate, even though they were a bit suspicious of the motives of Mr. Ross.

Later that week, five Hispanic students showed up for the focus group. Mr. Ross stated the focus group was an opportunity for them to tell him what they liked and didn't like about school. The information was to be kept confidential. The group of adolescent boys was quite open with their thoughts regarding school. They didn't care whether it was confidential or not, they stated they didn't feel like they were treated fairly at school. In fact, they felt targeted by teachers and administrators at school. The majority of the group stated that often they were seen as troublemakers and that when they were with each other, some teachers viewed them as "gang involved." They all rallied around one young man who stated that when a group of white boys hang out together, no one thinks anything about it but when Hispanic males group together, they are thought of as being in a gang. Each of them had a story of being frisked for weapons or contraband during their stay at school. When the social worker inquired about whether there had ever been any justifiable cause for this, they stated that one kid in their group had been busted for marijuana possession but he was the only one, and that he had been expelled from school for the incident. They related that after a similar offense by a Caucasian student there had been a five-day suspension and that he was back in school.

Mr. Ross carefully took in the information, noting themes and phrases the boys used to describe their experiences and frustrations in school. At the end of several sessions with the boys, the social worker summarized his assessment of the situation with them to be sure he had accurately depicted their thoughts and feelings. In short, the young men felt alienated from school based on numerous experiences with teachers and administrators. They were able to name only five teachers in their experience who had reached out to them as individuals and whom they saw as being fair. They didn't feel welcomed at the school, and on several occasions the other students who were bused from across town made racist remarks to them. This had polarized the groups, causing many of the Hispanic students to group together for protection and camaraderie.

Mr. Ross had been meeting with Roberto for more than three months now, and there seemed to be a remarkable improvement in his attendance and some improvement in his academic work. Mr. Ross had called Roberto's mother several times to keep her informed of her son's progress. She recently called Mr. Ross to ask for a meeting regarding Roberto. Mr. Ross met with her and Roberto's stepfather after school. They were both pleased with the progress they had noticed in their son, but were concerned about some of the incidents he was communicating to them about his experiences in school. Roberto had told his parents that Mr. Ross had talked with several of his friends and they were curious as to why so many other kids were involved. Mr. Ross explained that he was concerned about the welfare of all the students in the school and especially when the problem might be affecting more than one student. Roberto's parents had indicated they were upset with the school and wanted their son to be treated fairly. Mr. Ross explained that there were several avenues of input for parent participation in the school that included the Parent-Teacher Organization and the principal's advisory group. Mr. Ross asked if they would like him to set up a meeting with the principal, Mrs. C. They indicated they would like it very much.

During the course of his work with Roberto, Mr. Ross (with Roberto's permission) had kept the assistant principal, Mr. E (who had made the initial referral), informed of Roberto's progress. In addition, Mr. Ross regularly attended the weekly administrative staff meetings to keep updated on student referrals and school activities. With permission from group members, Mr. Ross had shared the concerns of the Hispanic students with the administrative team. The principal had been kept apprised of the situation from the outset. When Mr. Ross went to Mrs. C about an appointment for Roberto's parents, she indicated that maybe it would be a good idea to have a Hispanic parent advisory group and that Mr. Ross would be the perfect person to organize it.

Despite the thought of taking on one more role in the school, Mr. Ross saw this as an opportunity to change the culture and environment of the school utilizing parents and school personnel. After several meetings with Roberto's parents and members of the Hispanic community, several recommendations emerged that were included interventions at several levels of the school. These included instigating a dropout prevention program targeted at students exhibiting high-risk profiles that included pregnancy, school failure, family problems, poor educational achievement, etc. It also included a proactive search for more Hispanic representation among the administrative and teacher staff.

Fortunately, a new Spanish teacher and Latino Club sponsor was hired to create a place where Hispanic heritage was valued and promoted. Teachers and counselors established focus groups that followed identified high-risk students throughout the year. Mentors and personal connections for students were emphasized and encouraged. This resulted in a 25% reduction in the dropout rate for Hispanic males over the course of the year.

Development and training for staff in diversity and tolerance took on a priority for the principal and her leadership team.

At the micro level, Mr. Ross had done some preliminary testing and suspected Roberto had a learning disability. His subsequent referral for special education testing resulted in an identified disability, and appropriate accommodations and supports were given to Roberto. Because of his leadership capabilities, Roberto had been encouraged by his mentor to run for student government and was elected class representative. His connection to school was enhanced by this experience and Roberto graduated from high school.

Mr. Ross reports that this case illustration is typical advanced generalist practice and demonstrates that multiple interventions at the micro, mezzo, and macro levels can effect change for both the individual student and the school environment. If Mr. Ross had just focused on the individual student, Roberto, it is likely that he would have dropped out of school. By operating at multiple levels, the impact of the interventions helped numerous students and improved the school environment.

CASE DISCUSSION

Throughout the Roberto case, there are implied examples of advanced generalist skills. These include the use of individual, group, and organization assessment and several methods of intervention. Although assessment is only one stage of the intervention process, a discussion of how it was utilized in this case enhances the reader's perspective of applied advanced generalist practice.

Mr. Ross had to have the ability to view the case of Roberto from various perspectives that included Roberto's psychological and social functioning; his interactions with groups of students; his interaction with school personnel; and his interactions with his family. Thus, the ability to apply the concept of assessment at different levels enabled Mr. Ross to implement problem-solving strategies and change efforts.

ADVANCED GENERALIST ASSESSMENT SKILLS IN SCHOOL SOCIAL WORK

Assessment in school social work is a systemic way of understanding and communicating what is happening in the classroom, within the family, and between family and school, as well as a way of looking for the places where interventions will be most effective (Constable, McDonald, & Flynn, 2002, Ch. 11). Because the school social worker has access to various influential sectors of the child's life, such as parents, teachers, and peer group, comprehensive assessment skills are essential to the practitioner. At the broadest level, the school social worker might utilize a needs assessment to determine the needs of certain populations of students, community perceptions of the school, and attitudes of teachers and other school personnel about the delivery of school social work services. In turn, these assessments can be utilized to change school policies, develop programmatic priorities and service delivery, influence the culture and climate of schools, create a prevention strategy, and intervene in student and school problems.

The credibility and dependability of assessments are enhanced when multiple methodologies are used to gather information. The use of multiple respondents (parents, students, teachers, administrators, community workers, etc.) assists the school social worker in bringing attention and advocacy to broader problems. By using multiple assessment tools to gather the information, an effective comprehensive assessment can be obtained. As in the case example of Roberto, interviews with individual students, parents, and teachers helped formulate a hypothesis of the problem. The practitioner also used the methodologies of *focus groups* with students and parents, *observations* of interaction among staff toward students and student groups with each other, and *school records* such as disciplinary referrals, dropout rate statistics, and individual school files.

At the mezzo level, assessment of groups is an essential skill for the advanced generalist practitioner. Groups come in many forms in the public schools. School social workers are required to work in multidisciplinary teams. These teams are often brought together for the purpose of sharing their particular expertise regarding a student or problem in the school. For most school social workers, the special education multidisciplinary team is a prime example. Collaborative decision-making with representative school personnel, parents, and involved agency staff for the purpose of conducting a thorough assessment and possible intervention plan for a student can create a challenge to those lacking group work skills. In Roberto's case, this group came together and determined that he did indeed have a learning disability. They compiled an IEP (individual education plan) to address his needs in the classroom setting.

In addition to participating in the multidisciplinary team group, school social workers are often asked to conduct or participate in task groups with school personnel whose purpose is to work toward alleviating a particular problem within the school. Both of these assignments require high levels of organization and knowledge of groups. This is especially true with the recent school reform policies that require schools to organize and conduct groups with community and parent participation in the problem-solving process. This type of activity was demonstrated in the Hispanic parent group that the high school principal had asked the social worker to organize and facilitate.

Another example of assessment skills at the mezzo level involves the complex dynamics of learning environments. Assessment of the classroom has great implications on how students are learning. According to Thomas, Tiefenthal, Charak, and Constable (2002, p. 181), "School social workers need to develop an understanding of group dynamics within a classroom, and of the impact of teaching styles and classroom group composition on pupil behavior and the learning process." Assessment of the classroom takes skill in determining the multiple factors that may influence a particular student. These may include seating arrangement, discipline plan, number of children in the classroom, visual and auditory distractions, chemistry and composition of the class, teaching philosophy, available resources, curriculum materials, and numerous other factors of the classroom environment. For Roberto, the observations and consultations with teachers and staff done by Mr. Ross regarding his interactions in school highlight this type of assessment.

Assessment at the micro level includes a variety of formal and informal assessment instruments aimed at individuals. In the case of Roberto, Mr. Ross used his clinical skills to gain rapport and trust to better understand Roberto's difficulties in school. Additionally, he used his assessment skills by identifying Roberto's learning disability, which had impeded his ability to get the most out of school. Thus, assessment of possible cognitive problems along with an ecological assessment of Roberto's behavioral and social functioning assisted the school social worker in planning for meaningful change. Had Mr. Ross focused only on Roberto's performance in school and not taken into account his family and peer group influences, Roberto would have likely followed many of his counterparts and dropped out of school, becoming another statistic.

CURRICULAR IMPLICATIONS FOR GRADUATE SOCIAL WORK EDUCATION AND PREPARATION FOR SCHOOL SOCIAL WORK PRACTICE

An advanced generalist perspective for school social workers is essential. Because school social workers practice in a "host setting" in which the primary emphasis is on education and achievement and not on mental health, the ecological perspective of an advanced generalist is especially crucial. School personnel value the multidimensional philosophy social workers offer. The most effective school social workers are those who are as adept at diagnosing organizational obstacles to educating students as they are at diagnosing client problems. Just as skillful clinical diagnosis involves identifying client strengths and potential for positive change, organizational diagnosis involves seeing the positive features of the organization and building on those. Teaching school social workers to recognize the necessity of maintaining a balance among various constituencies is important. For example, school systems need to demonstrate academic student achievement; administrators need the school to run smoothly; teachers need students to be ready and willing to learn; parents have expectations of how schools should perform; students need to have basic needs met; and each constituency is in potential conflict with another. School social workers must learn to balance their interventions so as to be effective with each of these groups. Thus it is essential to educate and expose school social work students in the use of various theoretical frameworks discussed earlier. Additionally, case examples and field discussions in seminars should emphasize the importance of an advanced generalist framework. It is through this pedagogy that the integration between practice and theory is introduced to students. The use of the examples for interventions made at the macro (community, organizational), mezzo (family, peer group), and micro (direct practice) levels is imperative for students to understand the interplay among the systems being discussed.

Challenges are apparent in implementing an advanced generalist curriculum. First, there are many school social workers who do not practice from the perspective of an advanced generalist. It is not unusual to have school social workers with a more clinical (micro) orientation working in the school system. Although they may be effective in providing therapeutic interventions with individuals and groups, they may not necessarily be familiar with macro-level practice. Thus use of clinically focused practitioners as field instructors in advanced generalist programs may be counterproductive when their orientation conflicts with students' macro-level assignments.

Another challenge to implementing an advanced generalist curriculum, as reported in the literature (Bakalinsky, 1982), is the lack of time to cover the depth of theoretical knowledge required to be an effective school social worker. As seen in the case example above and in the theoretical discussion, it is evident that there are many theories and practice skills to acquire in order to become competent in school social work. The challenge for training potential advanced generalist practitioners is to develop a curriculum that is both broad enough to encompass the practice skills necessary and in-depth enough to be meaningful. As in school social work, finding the right balance among competing constituencies is the key to success.

FUTURE IMPLICATIONS FOR SCHOOL SOCIAL WORK

The practice of school social work is growing and ever changing. Public schools would benefit from employing competent advanced generalist social workers. The changing demographic trends and the recent upsurge in mental health issues for school-aged children calls for a comprehensive view of families, students, and the schools they attend. School social workers can be the conscience for schools pressed to produce students with high levels of academic achievement without regard for the whole child, whose home or community environment does not provide essential basic needs. School social workers must strive to meet the challenges that will result in a safe home and neighborhood and, along with a family, assure that basic needs for survival love, nurturance, and encouragement are met for all children. An advanced generalist social work education is important to achieving this goal.

REFERENCES

Allen-Meares, P. (1977). An analysis of tasks in school social work. *Journal of Social Work, 22*, 196-201.

Allen-Meares, P. (1994). Social work services in schools: A national study of entry-level tasks. *Journal of Social Work, 39*(5).

Allen-Meares, P. (1996). Social work services in schools: A look at yesteryear and the future. *Social Work in Education, 18*, 560-565.

Allen-Meares, P., Washington, R., & Welsh, B. (2000). *Social work services in schools* (3rd ed.). Boston: Allyn & Bacon.

Ashford, J., LeCroy, C., & Lortie, K. (2001). *Human behavior in the social environment.* Belmont, CA: Wadsworth/Thomson Learning.

Bakalinsky, R. (1982). Generic practice in graduate social work curricula: A study of educators' experiences and attitudes. Journal of Education for Social Work, *18*(3), 46-54.

Carter, B., & McGoldrick, M. (1988). *The changing family lifecycle: A framework for family therapy* (2nd ed.) New York: Gardner.

Chavkin, N. (1985). School social work practice: A reappraisal. Social Work in Education, *1*, 3-13.

Constable, R., McDonald, S., & Flynn, J. (2002). School social work: Practice policy and research perspectives (5th ed.). Chicago: Lyceum Books.

Costin, L. (1969). An analysis of the tasks in school social work. Social Service Review, *43*, 274-285.

Germain, C. (1991). An ecological perspective on social work in schools. In R. Constable, S. McDonald, & J. Flynn (Eds.), School social work: Practice, policy, and research perspectives (5th ed.). Chicago: Lyceum Books.

Germain, C., & Gitterman, A. (1995). Ecological perspective. In R. Edwards (Ed.), *Encyclopedia of social work* (19th ed., pp. 817-825). Washington, DC: National Association of Social Workers.

Gutkin, T. B., & Curtis, M. (1982). School-based consultation: Theory and techniques. In C. R. Reynolds & T. B. Gutkin (Eds.), *The handbook of school psychology* (pp. 796-828). New York: Wiley.

Hardcastle, D., Wenocur, S., & Powers, P. (1997). *Community practice: Theories and skills for social workers.* New York: Oxford University Press.

Heller, K. (1990). Social and community intervention. *Annual Review of Psychology, 41*, 141-168.

Jozefowicz-Simbeni, D., & Allen-Meares, P. (2002). Poverty and schools: Intervention and resource building through school-linked services. *Children & Schools, 24*(2), 67-136.

Kapp, S. (2000). Defining, promoting, and improving a model of school social work: The development of a tool for collaboration. *School Social Work Journal, 24*(2), 20-41.

Kirst-Ashman, K., & Hull, G. (2002). *Generalist practice with organizations and communities.* Chicago: Nelson Hall.

Ornstein, E., & Moses, H. (2000). In search of a secure base: Attachment theory and school social work. *School Social Work Journal, 26*(2), 1-13.

Program Review (2001). Unpublished report, F. J. Vecchiolla & A. W. Roy, School of Social Work, Springfield College.

Thomas, G., Tiefenthal, M., Charak, R., & Constable, R. (2002). *Assessment tools of the school social worker*. In R. Constable, S. McDonald, & J. Flynn (Eds.), School social work: Practice policy and research perspectives (5th ed.). Chicago: Lyceum Books.

White, J., & Mullis, F. (1998). A systems approach to school counselor consultation. *Education, 119* (2), 242-261.

Chapter 12

HUMAN RIGHTS AND
ADVANCED GENERALIST PRACTICE

Joseph Wronka
Springfield College

HUMAN RIGHTS AND THE SOCIAL WORK PROFESSION

The profession of social work has on varying occasions emphasized the importance of human rights as integral to the profession. The National Association of Social Work (NASW) in March 1999 stated, for instance, that it "supports the concept that human rights be adopted as a foundation[al] principle upon which all of social work theory and applied knowledge rests...[and] endorses the fundamental principles set forth in the human rights documents of the United Nations" (Falk, p. 17). Previously, in 1988, the International Federation of Social Work (IFSW) asserted:

> Social work has, from its conception, been a human rights profession, having as its basic tenet the intrinsic value of every human being and as one of its main aims the promotion of equitable social structures, which can offer people security and development while upholding their dignity (cited in United Nations, 1994, p. 3).

Human Rights and Social Work: A Manual for Schools of Social Work and the Social Work Profession (United Nations, 1994, p. 3) goes on to say, "Schools of social work are strongly encouraged to develop creative ways of incorporating human rights content into their curricula." Finally, *Social Work Speaks* has referred to human rights as "the bedrock of the social work profession" (G. Waller, personal communication, June 19, 2002).

Whereas the importance of human rights to the profession of social work has been acknowledged, it is noteworthy that the recent Educational Policy and Accreditation Standards of the Council on Social Work Education (CSWE), the official accrediting body of social work programs in the United States, mentions human rights only once in the preamble: "Social work practice promotes human well-being by strengthening opportunities, resources, and capacities of people in their environments and by creating policies and services to correct conditions that limit *human rights* [italics added] and the quality of life" (p. 1).

It is this author's argument that human rights, which is a legal mandate to fulfill human need and "most amenable" to advanced generalist practice (Wronka, 1995a, 1412) ought to be more fully included in social work theory and praxis, particularly in the United States. Home pages of international social work organizations, such as the European Association of Schools of Social Work and Social Work Educators (EASSW) and the International Association of Schools of Social Work (IASSW), in contradistinction to the home page of NASW, assert, for instance: "In fulfilling its mission the EASSW adheres to all United Nations' Declarations and Conventions on human rights, recognizing that respect for the inalienable rights of the individual is the foundation of freedom, justice and peace" (2002, p. 1). That is not to say that social work in the United States has neglected human rights concerns per se. The Code of Ethics of NASW, for instance, speaks of the "respect for the inherent dignity and worth of the person," an integral notion to the idea of human rights. However, the body of knowledge in the international arena that has evolved pertaining to human rights may have been neglected and ought to serve as effective "guiding principles" (Gil, 1992, p. 24) for social work theory, praxis, and policy development in general. Social work, in fact, given its "value base...is in a unique and powerful position to help make the vision of human rights a reality" (Ife, 2001, p. 203) and, we believe, the advanced generalist curriculum is well-suited to this purpose.

The Origins of Human Rights

The United Nations, upon its founding in 1945, officially coined this idea, largely in response to the German Third Reich's atrocities against its own citizens. Governments, during the events that led to the Holocaust and wanton slaughter of 10 million innocents, failed to stop the advances of Hitler fearing to bring attention to their own violations, such as the Soviet Union's Gulag, Europe's vast colonial empire, or the United States' sprawling urban ghettos and de jure and de facto racism (Buergenthal, 1998). Today in 2003, however, no government would dare say that it is against human rights. In this new millennium human rights has become a powerful idea and social construct to move people to action to create a socially just world. Just as social workers are often passionate advocates for social change in general, human rights can provide even further impetus to enhance the human condition.

The Universal Declaration of Human Rights

The issue becomes, however, what exactly are human rights? The United Nations has referred to the Universal Declaration of Human Rights as the "authoritative definition of human rights standards." Referred to as a "Magna Carta for humanity" by Eleanor Roosevelt, chair of the drafting committee for the Universal Declaration, the General Assembly endorsed it with no dissent on December 10, 1948. In brief, the Universal Declaration—which asserts rights people have only because they are human, irrespective of "race, color, sex, language, religion, political or other opinion, national or social origin, property, birth or other status"—is composed of 30 articles, consisting of 4 crucial notions mirroring values of major religions and historical epochs (Wronka, 1995a).

The first crucial notion is human dignity in Article 1, a legacy of some of the fundamental tenets of almost every world religion, in this case, the Judaic-Christian-Islamic tradition, which was the largest representation at the drafting of the Universal Declaration. The second notion, in articles 2-21, is primarily civil and political rights, also called negative freedoms and first-generation rights. They emphasize the duty of government not to interfere with basic human rights to free speech, a free press, assembly, and worship, a legacy largely stemming from the Age of Enlightenment and mirrored primarily in the U.S. Bill of Rights. The third crucial notion, in articles 22-27, is primarily economic, social, and cultural rights, or positive freedoms and second-generation rights. They emphasize the duty of government to provide for basic human rights, such as food, shelter, security in old age, and health care. A legacy of the Age of Industrialization, they are found largely in the Soviet Constitution of 1936. The fourth crucial notion is solidarity rights, still in the process of conceptualization, but primarily the legacy of the failure of domestic sovereignty in the latter half of the last century to solve global problems. Drawing sustenance from the final three articles of the Universal Declaration, which emphasize the right to a just "social and international order," limitations upon rights, and the idea that every right has a corresponding duty, such rights would include the right to peace, a clean environment, self-determination, humanitarian disaster relief, international distributive justice, and the right to development. Where the right to a clean environment, for example, means the duty for each of us not to litter, it also means international cooperation to resolve such global problems as the greenhouse effect and, as in 2002, officially International Year of the Mountains, our "common heritage of humanity," other problems such as plant and animal species extinction, which are interrelated (Wronka, 1998a).

Finally, these rights are interdependent and indivisible. It makes no sense to guarantee only first-generation rights without also guaranteeing second and third generations of rights (Wronka, 1998a). After all, what is freedom of speech to a person who is homeless and lives in a world at war? Thus, it may be more correct to say what "is," rather than what are human rights. It can easily be seen, therefore, how guaranteeing a "just social and international order" to provide for the "entitlement of rights" (Article 28, Universal Declaration) is entirely compatible with social work's notion of human behavior in the social environment.

The Universal Declaration as Customary International Law

The Universal Declaration of Human Rights, furthermore, has become especially pertinent as it has been increasingly referred to as *customary international law*, i.e., a document binding on all governments, especially since the precedent-setting case *Filartiga v. Pena* (1980) wherein the U.S. Federal Second Circuit District Court ruled:

> Official torture is now prohibited by the law of nations. The prohibition is clear and unambiguous and admits no distinction between treatment of aliens and citizens....This prohibition has become part of customary international law, as evidenced and defined by the Universal Declaration of Human Rights. (630 F.2d 884-885, 2nd Cir.)

Briefly, in that case, a federal court in the United States ruled against Pena, a police officer, for torturing and murdering a high school student, Joelita Filartiga, while both lived in Paraguay! What has become known as the "Filartiga principle" has led to the conviction of torturers from other countries, such as Gramajo from

Guatamela in 1991, and Karadzic from the former Yugoslavia in 1995. More important, perhaps, marginalized groups such as the Inupiat Community of the Arctic, have used the Filartiga principle (in effect, the Universal Declaration of Human Rights) in an effort to sue the U.S. government for oil development off the North Slope of Alaska (*Inupiat Community of the Arctic Slope v. United States*, 1984).

The point of the above discussion is that, whereas the Universal Declaration was meant originally merely to be a hortatory document urging governments to abide by human rights standards, today it can be considered legally binding. Furthermore, what may have been considered utopian ideals are now considered legal mandates to fulfill human need. Therein lies the importance of human rights to the social work profession, whose primary mission according to the NASW Code of Ethics is "to enhance human well-being and *help meet the basic human needs* [italics added] of all people, with particular attention to the needs and empowerment of people who are vulnerable, oppressed, and living in poverty" (NASW, 1999, preamble).

Other Human Rights Documents

Before discussing more specifically the implications of human rights to advanced generalist practice, it is necessary to examine the "long train of declarations and covenants following the Universal Declaration" as Pope John Paul II called them (Daughters of St. Paul, 1979), which define even further the rights described in the Universal Declaration. There are six basic covenants or conventions: the International Covenant on Civil and Political Rights (ICCPR); the International Covenant on Economic, Social and Cultural Rights (ICESCR); the International Convention on the Elimination of All Forms of Discrimination against Women (CEDAW); the International Convention on the Elimination of All Forms of Racial Discrimination (ICEAFRD); the Convention on the Rights of the Child (ROC); and the Convention against Torture and Other Cruel, Inhuman or Degrading Treatment or Punishment (CAT).

These documents, furthermore (like UN Charter Article 55, which advocates the promotion of "higher standards of living, full employment, and conditions of economic and social progress and development") have the status of treaty (Weissbrodt, Fitzpatrick, & Newman, 2001). As such, when ratified, as was the UN Charter in 1945, they become "law of the land," as asserted by the Supremacy Clause of the U.S. Constitution:

> This Constitution, and the Laws of the United States which shall be made in Pursuance thereof; and all Treaties made, or which shall be made, under the Authority of the United States, shall be the supreme Law of the Land; and the Judges in every State shall be bound thereby, any Thing in the Constitution or Laws of any State to the Contrary notwithstanding. (U.S. Constitution, Art. VI, Clause 2)

As of the writing of this chapter, the U.S. has signed all six conventions/covenants, i.e., it has agreed to consider them for ratification in its legislative bodies. However, the U.S. has ratified only three: the ICCPR (1992), the ICEAFRD (1994), and the CAT (1994). Once ratified, the documents, therefore, if one takes seriously the Supremacy Clause, then become law, thereby "trumping" the U.S. Constitution. It is unfortunate, however, that the U.S. has ratified them with the stipulation that they be "non-self-executing," that is, nonenforceable in U.S. courts (Buergenthal, 1998) and also with various declarations, reservations, and understandings (Weissbrodt, Fitzpatrick, & Newman, 2001).

Thus, in regard, for example, to the right to family protections, the Universal Declaration asserts in Article 16(3): "The family is the natural and fundamental group unit of society and is entitled to protection by society and the State." Article 10 of the ICESCR further elaborates that "Special protection should be accorded to mothers during a reasonable period before and after childbirth. During such period working mothers should be accorded paid leave or leave with adequate social security benefits." And Article 11 of CEDAW states that:

> States shall take appropriate measures to encourage the provision of the necessary supporting social services to enable parents to combine family obligations with work responsibilities and participation in public life, in particular through promoting the establishment and development of a network of childcare facilities.

Select reservations to CEDAW by the United States are that "the U.S. federal government would not be required to provide paid maternity leave or ensure the continuation of other benefits" and that "equal pay for equal worth would not be understood as requiring a right to comparable worth" (Weissbrodt, Fitzpatrick, & Newman, 2001, p. 128).

In addition to these major documents, the United Nations has developed numerous others, all of which have implications for advanced generalist practice with its emphasis upon macro, mezzo, and micro levels of practice. This multilevel, integrative aspect of advanced generalist practice is consonant with a human rights perspective. Let us illustrate using women and children as our focal population. Whereas, ROC and CEDAW, for instance, address issues of women and children at the macro level, the human rights documents on the Declaration on Social and Legal Principles relating to the Protection and Welfare of Children, with Special Reference to Foster Placement and Adoption Nationally and Internationally, and the Declaration on the Protection of Women and Children in Emergency and Armed Conflict, address issues at the mezzo or administrative level. On the other hand, declarations (such as Principles of Medical Ethics relevant to the Role of Health Personnel, particularly Physicians, in the Protection of Prisoners and Detainees against Torture and Other Cruel, Inhuman or Degrading Treatment or Punishment; Principles of the Protection of Persons with Mental Illness and the improvement of mental health care; and Basic Principles of Justice for Victims of Crime and Abuse of Power) specifically address issues on women and children (and others) at the micro, or direct practice level. To be sure, other documents are still in the process of development and conceptual elaboration, as in, for example, a Declaration on Security in Old Age; Declaration on the Rights, Duties, and Protection of those Addicted to Substances; the Declaration on the Rights and Duties of Men and the Eradication of Violence; and the Declaration on the Eradication of Extreme Poverty.

In addition to United Nations documents, there are regional developments, such as in the Western Hemisphere, the American Convention of Human Rights (1969), which the U.S. still has not ratified; the African Charter on Human and People's Rights (1981); and the European Convention for the Protection of Human Rights and Fundamental Freedoms (1950). In other regions of the world, such as Asia and the Middle East, human rights documents are just beginning to develop, their lateness in part owing to the numerous languages spoken and religious traditions in Asia, and centuries of conflict between Israel and the Arab world in the Middle East.

SKILLS AND THEORIES

Implications for Advanced Generalist Practice

The above discussion may have given the unfortunate impression that a social worker, advanced generalist or otherwise, merely needs to "know" human rights documents to be an effective practitioner. However, human rights principles must be "felt" and the real issue, it appears, on all levels of practice, is to create what has been called a "Human Rights Culture," which is a "lived awareness" of human rights principles (Wronka, 1998a, 2002). Eleanor Roosevelt expressed it well when she said:

> Where after all, do universal human rights begin? In small places, close to home—so close and so small that they cannot be seen on any maps of the world. Yet, they are the world of the individual person; the neighborhood he lives in; the school or college he attends; the factory, farm or office where he works. Such are the places where every man, woman and child seeks equal justice, equal opportunity, equal dignity without discrimination. Unless these rights have meaning there, they have little meaning anywhere. (cited in Department of State, 1994, p. xix)

Eleanor Roosevelt's words clearly capture the idea that human rights are important at all levels of society and, by implication, at all levels of intervention (micro, mezzo, and macro). One *must* not address one without the other. An advanced generalist practice philosophy would concur.

The journey from the mind to the heart, however, is a difficult one. In essence, human rights principles must be in our "gut." Yet that is the challenge that social work practitioners face: to give life to human rights principles so that they are not merely words on paper.

These documents, furthermore, are not perfect. They also are human creations and, as such, must be subject to critical analysis, an essential component of educational pedagogy (Freire, 1970). The practitioner must always be aware of the "structures, dynamics and values" (Gil, 1992, p. 24) and the historical and philosophical underpinnings of human rights discussions (Wronka, 1998a), as they cannot take place within a philosophical vacuum. Eleanor Roosevelt, in fact, referred to the Universal Declaration as "not a perfect document...on the whole, however, it is a good document. We could never hope for perfection no matter how many times we revised the Declaration, for one could always see something a little better than one might do" (cited in Wronka, 1998a, p. 198). Yet, this author would argue that whereas there is no substitute for common human decency in our dealings with others, overall, international human rights instruments represent the collective wisdom of the global community and tend to expand our consciousness and rise above the more parochial visions of domestic principles, and thus expand the knowledge base of social work theory and praxis.

Whereas the demarcation among the levels of intervention (micro, mezzo, and macro) are perceived as having "equal weight" in some advanced generalist curriculums (Vecchiolla et al., 2001, p. 96), and whereas this notion of *levels of intervention* may be a somewhat simplistic conceptualization of a complex reality, it may nevertheless serve as a workable contour to further understand the implications of human rights for the advanced generalist practitioner, and thereby a means to frame select examples.

Before discussing each level, it is necessary to acknowledge that only nonviolence, also integral to the social work profession (Ife, 2001; Van Soest, 1997); the "happiness of reflecting together" (Merleau-Ponty, 1967); and a little humility (Wronka, 1998b) can advance the cause of human rights. Such notions to be sure are inconsistent with a generally accepted notion that military intervention is necessary to curb human rights violations, as evidenced by President Bush's call for military action against Iraq, which NASW opposes, urging the "non-violent resolution of international conflicts" (Mizrahi, 2002). Furthermore, countries may lambaste other countries for human rights violations while ignoring their own, as done during the Cold War. At that time, the United States expressed concern over the Soviet Union's imprisonment of political prisoners, while ignoring human rights violations in the U.S., such as lack of access to health care, homelessness, and poverty among children. However, whereas human rights is not the "silver bullet" to kill the ugliness of an unjust social order, it is, nevertheless, a plowshare that could assist to ground us in a collective understanding of ways to cultivate a just world.

Implications at the Macro Level

Human rights is most amenable to a macro approach (Wronka, 1995a), as the notion of human rights is for all persons: "everyperson, everywhere" (Gil, 1998). Thus at this level the primary issue is to adopt ways that the fundamental principles of human rights documents can adequately affect the entire global population. Consequently, it would be understood that an advanced generalist social work program taking human rights seriously would devote a good portion of the curriculum to international social work including "international professional action...internationally related domestic practice and advocacy, professional exchange, international practice, and international policy development and advocacy" (Healy, 2001, p. 7). With the emphasis upon globalization today, it would appear imperative, therefore, to include human rights concerns with major international players, such as the World Trade Organization (Danaher, 2001; Dommen, 2002).

Nonetheless, whereas most advanced generalist programs do not, in fact, devote great attention to an international perspective, at least one MSW program with advanced generalist tendencies *is* strongly international, and many programs have course offerings in international social work practice. The Springfield College School of Social Work offers an elective on Human Rights and International Social Work. We expect that other social work programs may soon offer more international content as the world shrinks and the realities of terrorism, war, and corporate globalization (direct repercussions of human rights violations) impinge further upon the U.S. (United Nations, 2001; Zinn, 2002). At any rate, even without extensive international involvement, the advanced generalist practice modality, with its integrative, multilevel approach, is consonant with human rights practice in the 21st century. Following are selected human rights interventions compatible with advanced generalist philosophy.

Advanced generalist social workers at domestic and international levels can advocate for the inclusion, for instance, of human rights principles in primary and secondary education. Given that policies actually represent "choices," which, in turn, are dependent upon one's socialization (Gil, 1992; 1998), it is important that children learn at an early age the importance of human rights principles (Reardon, 1995; International Human Rights Internship Program, 2000; Jacob Blaustein Institute, 1998; Amnesty International, 2001). Thus, young persons need to understand the Universal Declaration as much as they do the principles of the Bill of Rights. In the United States, for example, many citizens do not know that shelter is a human right (Article 25 of the Universal Declaration). One possible consequence of incorporating human rights principles in primary and secondary education is that as young children develop they might begin to question why homelessness, a human rights violation, is allowed to go unimpeded in this country. This, in turn, may result in choices made as adults that eventuate in socially just policies that do *not* allow homelessness to exist.

Advanced generalists can also use the media in ways that can play an important role in creating awareness of human rights principles. In Europe, for instance, there are advertisements on television in which actors and actresses dance to music while they read Article 1 of the Universal Declaration, which states poignantly: "All human beings are born free and equal in dignity and rights. They are endowed with reason and conscience and should act towards one another in a spirit of brotherhood." They conclude: "Think about it."

Advanced generalist social workers can do whatever is necessary, therefore, to create awareness of human rights principles. For instance, awareness can be created by having readings of the Universal Declaration of Human Rights on December 10th, Human Rights Day, when the Universal Declaration was signed; or by reading an international convention such as the Convention on the Elimination of All Forms of Racial Discrimination on March 21st, recently declared the International Day to Eradicate Racism by the Secretary General of the United Nations, Kofi Annan. Social workers also can hold conferences pertaining to human rights, as was recently demonstrated at the First International Conference on the Right to Self-Determination and the United Nations (Kly and Kly, 2001), called in large measure by social workers around the world. The conference was a vehicle to raise awareness of the rights of minority groups, such as the Dalits, Kurds, Native Americans, African Americans, Gullah/Geechees, Sami, Basques, Puerto Ricans, and others. A case in point was the colonial situation of Puerto Rico and the struggle of the people of Vieques against the U.S. Navy (Nenadich, 2001). Social workers also can advocate for a Human Rights Cabinet in the United States, as an alternative, or perhaps supplement to, the Department of Homeland Security to coordinate United Nations initiatives with domestic policy concerns.

One action-research project this author initiated with Dr. David Gil of Brandeis University is The Universal Declaration of Human Rights Project, which aims in part to: "monitor executive, judicial, legislative, and public discourse movements towards compliance with the Universal Declaration" with particular emphasis upon economic, social, cultural, and solidarity rights. Thus, given that a highly effective policy instrument is one in which individuals determine a policy based upon a thorough understanding of the facts (Stone, 1997), it would appear to move people to develop socially just policies if they notice that a particular country is remiss in adhering to international human rights standards. One study compared the Universal Declaration with U.S. federal and state constitutions, noting major gaps in federal adherence to economic, social, and cultural guarantees: "Apart from authors' protection for their scientific or literary productions there is no mention of any positive freedoms" (Wronka, 1998a, p. 186). Concerning state constitutions,

> Almost all...guarantee the right to education. Two states speak of the need
> to eliminate poverty and to work for economic justice. Five states guaran-
> tee the right to join trade unions...two states assert that the people of their
> state shall promote health. Four states guarantee the right to participate in
> the cultural life of the community. (Wronka, 1998a, p. 186)

Knowing these gaps may move people to action.

Social workers with advanced generalist training can confidently sponsor bills
and declarations. In Massachusetts there was Human Rights House Bill 850 (Wronka,
2001) entitled: "An Act Pertaining to the Establishment of a Human Rights Commission to Examine How to Integrate International Human Rights Into Massachusetts Laws and Policies." It is one means to create awareness of human rights principles and also to move toward a closing of the gap between the domestic and international arenas (Wronka, 2001). The aim of the commission is to develop a public
forum on these issues, because only chosen values endure. Most recently, the Pennsylvania House passed a somewhat similar bill to "explore its human rights standards" in light of the Universal Declaration (Stoesen, 2002, p. 3). This was the
result of a statewide organizing strategy, in part a collaborative effort of the Pennsylvania Chapter of NASW, the Kensington Welfare Rights Union, and the Poor
People's Economic Human Rights Campaign.

No one can force a human rights culture on anyone. It must be chosen. In Massachusetts, the City of Cambridge's City Council on September 28, 1999 adopted
the Universal Declaration of Human Rights as "law of the land." Whereas it has not
yet has been implemented, symbolic gestures, nevertheless, move people. Eventually knowledge of human needs as human rights concerns may change a person's
"symbolic consciousness" (Gil 1992, 1998) to realize that what may have been
considered "utopian ideals," are now legitimately mandated rights (Tomaseveski,
1993). Also in Massachusetts, the Town of Amherst's Select Board, on December 9,
2002, acknowledging the Universal Declaration as customary international law and
the legal mandate to fulfill human needs, declared December 10th as Human Rights
Day.

Advanced generalist social workers can work toward having their country ratify
important human rights documents, and provide input to and study human rights
reports their country must file periodically to submit to the appropriate human rights
monitoring committee if it has ratified international human rights treaties. Merely a
knowledge of these reports (available at the United Nations web site, www.un.org)

should provide readers with enough information to adequately engage in dialogue with their country in ways that advance a "creative dialogue" (Wronka, 1995b, p. 14) as a means of conflict resolution between international and domestic bodies. One example pertaining to the CAT (Convention against Torture) is the UN Human Rights Committee's concern in the U.S. "about the use of stun belts and restraint chairs as methods of restraining those in custody; the excessively harsh regime in U.S. supermax prisons; [and] allegations of sexual assault on female prisoners by corrections officers" (Tizon, 2002, p. 5). Social workers then can assist governments in improving their human rights records so as to have reports more consistent with the principles of the respective human rights convention.

To be sure, to effect social change it may be necessary to work with groups that have a long history of involvement with human rights concerns, such as the International Fourth World Movement, which dedicates itself to the Eradication of Extreme Poverty (www.atd-quartmonde.org) *and* was instrumental in the United Nations declaration of 1996 as the Year for the Eradication of Extreme Poverty; and the International Human Rights Association of American Minorities (www.ihraam.org),instrumental in the Conference on Self-Determination mentioned earlier. A list of other human rights organizations can be found in Blaustein (1998), *In Your Hands: A Community Action Guide for Human Rights Year and Beyond.*

Implications at the Mezzo and Micro Levels

Human rights principles also can serve as guides to understanding situations of populations considered "at-risk" and consequent appropriate interventions. In the situation of married African women's vulnerability to HIV, for example, the women have access to condoms, but no control over their husband's sexual behavior and often cannot refuse unprotected or unwanted sexual activity. Condom promotion thus would be limited without broad societal and legal changes that would promote and protect women's rights (Mann, Gruskin, Grodin, & Annas, 1999), giving them access to education and work at reasonable wages so they could negotiate sexual practices and protect themselves from HIV infection. Needless to say, such rights are embodied in CEDAW, but have yet to be ratified by the United States.

Furthermore, as mentioned, some human rights documents deal more specifically with at-risk populations, such as juveniles, people with disabilities, and migrants. In addition to the documents already noted, others include the UN Guidelines for the Prevention of Juvenile Delinquency; the UN Standard Minimum Rules for the Administration of Juvenile Justice; the Declaration on the Rights of Disabled Persons; and the International Convention on the Protection of the Rights of

All Migrant Workers and Members of Their Families. Administrative and management skills developed in an advanced generalist program are readily translated in terms of human rights concepts embedded in these declarative documents. For example, advanced generalists can develop training modules and conduct workshops to inform relevant parties of the documents' contents, to examine domestic adherence to them, and to suggest ways to implement them.

Two such training modules for law enforcement personnel in particular are *Human Rights and Law Enforcement* (United Nations, 1997) and *Police and Human Rights* (Crawshaw, 1999). The goal is to develop other training modules that emphasize internationally accepted principles for supervisory personnel in a variety of situations. This is indeed a challenging way to view the often considered mundane notion of administration and training, but clearly contributes a much needed, creative, and mission-driven approach that has widespread implications for the humane treatment of vulnerable persons.

Irrespective of the blurred division among levels of intervention, documents such as the UN's Principles for the Protection of Persons with Mental Illness and the Improvement of Mental Health Care do speak to issues at the micro, or clinical level. They state, for instance (United Nations, 1991), that: "determination of mental illness shall never be made on the basis of political, economic or social status, or membership of a cultural, racial or religious group... or non-conformity with moral, social, cultural or political values or religious beliefs prevailing in a person's community" (Principle 4); "every patient shall have the right to treatment suited to his or her cultural background" (Principle 7); and "the treatment of every patient shall be directed towards preserving and enhancing personal autonomy," "based on an individually prescribed plan, discussed with the patient, reviewed regularly, revised as necessary," and be given "in the least restrictive environment" (Principle 9). Principle 11 asserts: "No treatment shall be given to a patient without his or her informed consent...obtained freely, without threats or improper inducements, after appropriate disclosure to the patient of adequate and understandable information," concerning, among other things "(b) The purpose, method, likely duration and expected benefit of the proposed treatment; [and] (c) Alternative modes of treatment, including those less intrusive." It would be a tremendous challenge to compare these documents with federal, state, and in these days of managed care, with private, for-profit entities, to determine their similarities and/or dissimilarities to these international documents.

To be sure, at both the mezzo and micro levels, human rights documents with their emphasis on dialogue, diversity, and rights for all, would serve as effective guides for managers of programs and clinicians to treat clients humanely and with the utmost regard for their human dignity.

Research Implications

Human rights principles also can serve as standards for conducting research. Thus, given that these documents emphasize, for instance, a culture of informed consent (Mann et al., 1999) and the inclusion of the marginalized into the policy debates (Chapman, 1993), such principles supply a theoretical foundation for the importance of qualitative research to social work praxis. It would be important, therefore, for advanced generalist practitioners serious about infusing human rights into their work to develop interviewing skills that would enable them to understand the voices of those whose input is most necessary for the development of socially just policies.

Quantitative research is also important, as human rights principles can serve as bases, for instance, to develop data sets that visually and convincingly demonstrate among other things, discrimination based upon race. One case in point is a histogram demonstrating the handing out of death sentences to be 600% greater if the race of the victim were black, instead of white (Spirer & Spirer, 1993, p. 58). Such measures also can serve as means to conduct human rights impact assessments before or after the introduction of a specific policy or program, or as a standard of evaluation. For example, the effectiveness of Temporary Aid to Needy Families (TANF) could be evaluated in regards to Article 25(2) of the Universal Declaration: "All children, whether born in or out of wedlock shall enjoy the same social protection" to determine if indeed all children were treated equally.

Curriculum Development

In terms of curriculum development, in the Springfield College School of Social Work students are not introduced to the Universal Declaration of Human Rights until after they have a thorough understanding of a history of the social work profession and policies and programs in the United States (Policy I). In Policy II, after obtaining an understanding that these policies and programs reflect an unjust social order and structural violence in general, students are introduced to the Universal Declaration and the idea of the creation of a human rights culture as a way out of a generally intolerable situation.

With this information, they are able to understand more fully the theoretical basis of qualitative research, as well as, enhance their knowledge of quantitative research. A human rights culture, after all, calls for among other things, the inclusion of the voices of the oppressed into the policy debates. This knowledge of human rights also should enhance students' skills learned in other advanced generalist courses, as well as add to their knowledge base while they engage in their practicums. Needless to say, the challenge of infusing human rights into social work theory and praxis will consistently remain a lifelong process given the ever-evolving nature of human rights principles.

Social Work and the Rights of the Child: A Professional Training Manual on the UN Convention, published in 2002 by the International Federation of Social Workers (IFSW) can perhaps illustrate in summative form many of the issues previously discussed. Noting that "social workers seeking to uphold the principles of the Convention require particular skills" (p. 9) it proceeds to acknowledge "general principles" of the Rights of the Child, such as "non-discrimination," "best interest of the child," and "respect for the views of the child." The manual groups children's rights into general areas, such as "basic health and welfare," "family environment and alternative care," "education and cultural activities," and "special protection measures" in regard to economic exploitation, drug abuse, sexual exploitation, sale, trafficking, and abduction, and those children belonging to a minority or indigenous groups.

The manual continues to say that on the micro level the "social worker has the duty to make sure that work undertaken in a particular situation is within the requirements of the Convention" (IFSW, 2002, p. 12); and, also on the micro level, that "mechanisms should be in place for objective appraisal...[and] in working with the young person...it is important that the views of the young person are elicited and given due weight alongside the often more articulate and powerful parents" (p. 13). On the mezzo level, "resolutions to community problems may be found through communication and negotiation at a municipal level. Such action may involve working with groups of children, young people and adults or all age groups" (p. 13). And on the macro level, wherein

> [social workers are]...in a unique position to comment on the human consequences of social policies...[and] have the duty to work towards informing national and international policy makers about the ways in which people are excluded from their society or culture. Reports from non-governmental organizations and examples of current situations are vital to the monitoring and implementation of international treaties such as the Convention on the Rights of the Child. (p. 14)

In conclusion, an understanding of human rights principles, an analysis of policies, programs, and other practices in comparison with these principles, the development of research-action initiatives and practice skills to implement these rights would fulfill the mandate of the Council on Social Work Education, add to the richness of an advanced generalist curriculum, but more importantly move us toward the development of a socially just world, to which we all aspire.

REFERENCES

Amnesty International (2001). *Crisis response guide: September 11 for junior high and high schools.* New York: Author.

Buergenthal, T. (1998). *International human rights law in a nutshell* (2nd ed.). St. Paul, MN: West.

Chapman, A. (1993). *Securing health care as a human right.* Washington, DC: Association for the Advancement of Science.

Crawshaw, R. (1999). *Police and human rights: A manual for teachers, resource persons and participants in human rights programmes.* Boston: Kluwer.

Danaher, K. (2001). *10 reasons to abolish the IMF and the World Bank.* New York: Seven Stories.

Department of State (1994). *Country reports on human rights practices for 1993.* Washington, DC: U.S. Government Printing Office.

Dommen, C. (2002). Raising human rights concerns in the World Trade Organization: Actors, processes and possible strategies. *Human Rights Quarterly, 24*(1), 1-50.

European Association of Schools of Social Work and Social Work Educators (EASSW). Retrieved June 19, 2002 from www.eassw.org/english.htm.

Falk, D. (1999, March). International policy on human rights. *NASW News, 44*(3), 17.

Filartiga v. Pena-Irala, 630 F.2d 876 (2nd Cir. 1980)

Freire, P. (1970). *Pedagogy of the oppressed.* New York: Continuum.

Gil, D. (1992). *Unraveling social policy* (5th ed.). Rochester, VT: Schenkman.

Gil, D. (1998). *Confronting social injustice and oppression.* New York: Columbia University Press.

Healy, L. (2001). *International social work: Professional action in an interdependent world.* New York: Oxford University Press.

Ife, J. (2001). *Human rights and social work: Towards rights- based practice*. New York: Cambridge University Press.

International Federation of Social Workers (2002). *Social work and the rights of the child: A professional manual on the UN Convention*. Berne, Switzerland: Author.

International Human Rights Internship Program (2000). *Circle of rights—Economic, social and cultural rights activism: A training resource*. Washington, DC: Author.

Inupiat Community of the Arctic Slope and Ukpeagvik Inupiat Corporation, et al. v. United States of America, et al., 746 F.2d 570 (9th Cir. 1984). Retrieved June 6, 2001 from www.msaj.com/cases/746F2d570.htm.

Jacob Blaustein Institute for the Advancement of Human Rights (1998). *In your hands: A community action guide honoring the 50th anniversary of the Universal Declaration of Human Rights*. New York: Author.

Kly, Y., & Kly, D. (2001). *In pursuit of the right to self-determination*. Atlanta: Clarity

Mann, J., Gruskin, S., Grodin, M., & Annas, G. (1999). *Health and human rights*. New York: Routledge.

Merleau-Ponty, M. (1967). *Signs*. Chicago: Northwest University Press.

Mizrahi, T. (2002, October 7). Letter to President Bush opposing military action against Iraq. Washington, DC: National Association of Social Workers.

National Association of Social Workers (1999). Code of Ethics of the National Association of Social Workers. Washington, DC: Author.

Nenadich, R. (2001). The colonial situation of Puerto Rico and the struggle of the people of Vieques against the U.S. Navy. In Y. Kly & D. Kly (Eds.), *In pursuit of the right to self-determination* (pp. 186-190). Atlanta: Clarity.

Pope John Paul II. (1979). *The message of justice, peace, and love*. Boston: Daughters of St. Paul.

Reardon, B. (1995). *Educating for human dignity*. Philadelphia: University of Pennsylvania Press.

Spirer, H., & Spirer, L. (1993). *Data analysis for monitoring human rights*. Washington, DC: American Association for the Advancement of Science.

Stoesen, L. (2002, October). Human rights measure passes in Pennsylvania house: A state is asked to explore its human rights standards in light of a UN declaration. *NASW News, 47*(10), 3.

Stone, D. (1997). *Policy paradox: The art of political decision making*. New York: W. W. Norton.

Tizon, O. (2002). Torture: State terrorism vs. democracy. *Covert Action Quarterly, 73,* 5-10.

Tomasevski, K. (1993). *Women and human rights.* Atlantic Highland, NJ: Zed Books.

United Nations (1991). *Principles for the protection of persons with mental illness and the improvement of mental health care.* New York: Author

United Nations (1994). *Human rights and social work: A manual for schools of social work and the social work profession.* New York: Author.

United Nations (1997). *Human rights and law enforcement: A manual on human rights training for police.* New York: Author.

United Nations (2001). *Terrorism and human rights.* (E/CN.4/Sub.2/2001/1/31). New York: Author.

Van Soest, D. (1997). *The global crisis of violence: Common problems, universal causes, shared solutions.* Washington, DC: NASW Press.

Vecchiolla, F., Roy A., Lesser, J., Wronka, J., Walsh-Burke, K., Gianesin, J., Foster, D., & Negroni, L. (2001). Advanced generalist practice: A framework for social work practice in the twenty-first century. *Journal of Teaching in Social Work, 21*(3/4), 91-104.

Weissbrodt, D., Fitzpatrick, J., & Newman, F. (2001). *International human rights: Law, policy, and process* (3rd ed.). Cincinnati: Anderson.

Wronka, J. (1995a) Human rights. In R. Edwards (Ed.), *Encyclopedia of Social Work* (pp. 1404-1418). Washington, DC: NASW Press.

Wronka, J. (1995b). On the U.N. Human Rights Committee's consideration of the initial report of the U.S.A on the International Covenant on Civil and Political Rights. *Human rights interest group newsletter of the American Society of International Law, 5*(3), 14-16.

Wronka, J. (1998a). *Human rights and social policy in the 21st century: A history of the idea of human rights and comparison of the United Nations Universal Declaration of Human Rights with United States federal and state constitutions* (Rev. ed.). Lanham, MD: University Press of America.

Wronka, J. (1998b, Summer). A little humility, please: Human rights and social policy in the United States. *Harvard International Review, 20*(3), 72-75.

Wronka, J. (2001, July). Human Rights House Bill No. 850: A request for support. *NASW News 46*(7), 4.

Wronka, J. (2002). *Creating a human rights culture: The Dr. Ambedkar memorial lectures.* Bhubaneswar, India: National Institute of Social Work and Social Sciences Press.

Zinn, H. (2002). *Terrorism and war.* New York: Seven Stories.

Chapter 13

WINNING AN HMO APPEAL:
A CASE STUDY OF ADVANCED GENERALIST
WORK IN ACTION

Steven M. Bogatz
Central Connecticut Dialysis Center, Meriden, CT

These are difficult times for health care in the United States. According to a recent study, 1 in 7 have trouble obtaining health care (Center for Studying Health System Change, 2002). Technologically superior, U.S. health care is paradoxically the least accessible among the industrialized democracies of the world. Soaring costs, non-uniform rules, a dwindling employment-based insurance system, and the failure of government to recognize a human right to health care have contributed to the current predicament. The glaring inequities were dramatized in a 2002 Hollywood film *John Q* in which a father, having exhausted all possible avenues, resorts to hostage-taking to obtain life-saving surgery for his son.

In this challenging environment, there are many opportunities to practice advanced generalist social work. At the micro level, the advanced generalist practitioner observes that the type of insurance patients hold often limits their care; the advanced generalist practitioner then seeks to advocate for additional resources. At the mezzo level, one looks for ways to make a particular health care delivery system more accessible to all clients, balancing it against the need of the employer to remain in business. And, finally, at the macro level, one labors for the necessary change that will best serve social justice, as in, for example, a universal health care system. In my social work practice serving patients with chronic kidney failure, I recently used advanced generalist skills to assist a patient in the successful resolution of a managed care conflict. While the ultimate goal was to obtain insurance coverage for a critical kidney transplant, reaching that end entailed employment of a multilevel, complex set of skills. Direct practice with my client, for example, resulted in a supportive relationship emphasizing empathy and acceptance in a Rogerian approach, and extensive advocacy work resulted in justice being served. It was, indeed, one of the most rewarding professional experiences I have yet had.

ADVANCED GENERALIST FRAMEWORK

The advanced generalist education received at the Springfield College School of Social Work provided the foundation to conceptualize and practice effectively in this HMO case. Once I recognized the injustice of the client not having insurance coverage for a life-saving medical procedure, kidney transplant surgery, I felt prepared to act on the situation through an effective advanced generalist intervention. At each stage, I endeavored to assess the people or system(s), apply relevant theory, and then intervene. Throughout, I practiced on multiple levels, moving often among direct service with my vulnerable patient, oral advocacy within my own agency, and written and oral advocacy with a much larger outside institution. The details of the case are presented below, followed by an analysis using an advanced generalist framework.

HMO CASE

I performed a psychosocial assessment of Mr. Trotter (not his real name) in November 1998 when he began hemodialysis on my unit. He was a pleasant, 44-year-old first-generation Greek immigrant who had been happily married for 17 years. Medically, Mr. Trotter had high blood pressure and permanent kidney failure. He had enjoyed an 18-year history of employment as one of the chief cooks at a local diner.

Mr. Trotter came to us with employer group health coverage through his wife, Mrs. Trotter. She worked as a manager for a department store owned by the May Company. Fatefully, in September 1998 the May Company changed health insurance companies from a Blue Cross Blue Shield product to Oxford Health Plans, a regional managed care company.

Unlike many patients, Mr. Trotter did poorly on hemodialysis. Accustomed to working 50 hours a week at the diner, he began dialyzing with the hope he could continue his employment with reduced hours. Though our patient put forth considerable effort, the rigorous four-hour treatments, three times per week, left him too tired and nauseated to work. Despite our best efforts to help Mr. Trotter feel better, five months after starting dialysis he qualified for full Social Security disability benefits.

To their credit, Mr. and Mrs. Trotter had begun working with Hartford Hospital months before his need for dialysis. The wife was found to be a suitable donor and a date was set for the end of September 1998. However, the scheduled transplant never happened because Oxford Health Plans, having assumed coverage at the beginning of the month, lacked a contract with Hartford Hospital and refused to approve the location. Oxford instead referred the patient to Yale, where it had a contract.

Mr. Trotter found the Yale professionals caring and excellent, but his continuity of care suffered, and his case was delayed. By this time, he had commenced dialysis with unfortunate physical consequences. Yale's subsequent work-up of Mrs. Trotter revealed that she had high blood pressure, a new condition perhaps related to anxiety about her husband's experience. Yale eventually ruled her out as a suitable candidate. Mr. Trotter was then placed on a three- to four-year waiting list, a quite common experience for patients awaiting a cadaveric kidney in Connecticut.

At this point, Mr. Trotter's extended family in Greece became interested in the medical challenges he faced. An older sister consented to get worked up in Cyprus, and fortuitously was found to be a perfect, six-antigen match. The Greek doctor, based on what he had seen, wished to proceed with the transplant. A year after he started dialysis, Mr. Trotter called to inform us of his intentions to fly to Cyprus to receive a transplant. Through my monthly interactions with Mr. Trotter, I was keenly aware of how poorly he felt on hemodialysis, and how disappointed he had been with the series of events at Yale. But his call was the first I knew about his intentions to obtain a kidney transplant outside of the United States.

My knowledge of insurance companies and their limitations caused me to fear for Mr. Trotter. Unable to believe that Oxford would ever provide coverage for a kidney transplant in Cyprus when it had refused to do so in Hartford, my first question to my patient was, "Who is paying for the surgery?" Mr. Trotter replied that the procedure cost much less in Cyprus, and that he and his extended family had managed to raise the money. I found myself impressed by the logistical planning Mr. Trotter and his family had undertaken and the sincerity with which he spoke. Nevertheless, I reiterated my concern that the Oxford health care plan would never cover the transplant expenses in Cyprus. Mr. Trotter simply noted that he and his wife had already contacted Yale, his U.S. doctors, and Oxford health plan in their attempt to seek preapproval.

The dialysis team was skeptical that Mr. Trotter would actualize his plan. That is, of course, until he failed to show up for an appointment on Friday, September 10, at which time I confirmed that he had boarded the evening flight to Greece on the previous Wednesday.

About two months after his transplant, Mr. Trotter returned to the U. S. looking healthy and fit. He informed me that he had just submitted his bills to Oxford, and had used my name as the contact for our dialysis center. Upon further discussion, I was amazed to learn that he had paid only 9,000 Cyprus pounds, or $17,500; about one quarter to one third of what the procedure would have cost him in New England. Mr. Trotter informed me that he planned to return to work in a few months.

One week after Mr. Trotter's visit, I received a call from a nurse case manager from Oxford. She wanted to verify that Mr. Trotter had, indeed, been a dialysis patient. She expressed anger at the fact that Mr. Trotter had sought a kidney transplant outside the United States and her perception that her division of Oxford had been made aware of the transplant only after the fact. Mr. Trotter's first denial letter came December 15, signed by the nurse case manager. In part, the letter read: "You did not seek pre-certification of these services, instead, you submitted bills to Oxford after the fact." Mr. Trotter returned to my office shortly thereafter seeking my formal assistance in resolving the HMO denial.

Through involvement with my local professional social work organization, as well as my dialysis clinic work, I had acquired a good understanding of a health plan's member rights in Connecticut. I realized that I first needed to determine if the Oxford Freedom Plan was part of the Employee Retirement Income Security Act of 1974 (ERISA). These types of plans are self-insured by the employers who provide them and are typically exempt from many of the newer state and federal laws giving enrollees needed rights in disputes. Consumer advocates have been complaining about ERISA for years, citing the lack of remedies available to disempowered enrollees. Humorously, ERISA has been parodied as "Every Rejected Idea Since Adam" (Crystal, 2000).

I contacted the May Company corporate headquarters to determine if the plan was under ERISA. I learned that the company was not under such restrictions and felt encouraged that the new Connecticut legislation regulating HMOs would apply in Mr. Trotter's case. Under Connecticut law, a discontented enrollee was entitled to a two-step internal appeal process run by the HMO. The last step could be face-to-face if the enrollee desired, and the State Insurance Commission could review the results if the dispute remained unresolved.

It is unclear to me how much influence, if any, a corporation has over the actions of a health plan designed to protect its employees and their dependents. To the extent that an employer has a vested interest in the health and welfare of its employees and their dependents, I was determined to keep the manager of group benefits for the May Company fully informed of the appeal's progress. When I reached the manager by telephone, she expressed an interest in hearing about the dispute, indicated that corporate policy precluded her from becoming directly involved, and asked me to keep her apprised of progress. In this way, I hoped to subtly increase pressure on Oxford, since the May Company was, for Oxford, "a paying customer."

As a first-generation Greek immigrant, Mr. Trotter spoke with a thick accent and had a limited ability to write in English. We strategized that we would work together to write the necessary letters. We also sent copies to all the medical professionals, since we wished Oxford to know that some of its contractees were watching its decision. Again, I hoped that by shining light on the issue we might increase the pressure on the health care plan.

The two-page letter we composed for the first level of the internal appeal process served six purposes. First, it rebutted the nurse case-manager's incorrect assertion that Mr. Trotter did not seek pre-authorization, by specifically giving the date, approximate time, and exact phone number that Mrs. Trotter had called for just that purpose: seeking prior authorization. Second, the letter apologized for the Trotters' omission in not working harder to persuade Oxford about the benefits of their strategy prior to the surgery. Third, it detailed how Mr. Trotter's cause had been delayed because the employer had switched health plans. Fourth, the letter conveyed how Mr. Trotter's kidney failure had negatively impacted his livelihood, how poorly he was doing on dialysis, and the great urgency he felt to regain his health. Fifth, it illustrated the savvy economic sense that Mr. Trotter's actions made. And sixth, the letter emphasized the improvement in the quality of the outcome that could be expected by the patient receiving a perfect match from a living related donor as compared with a less-than-perfect cadaveric match.

Regarding the economic cost, I had worked with our dialysis billing manager to document the following: while on dialysis for 10 months, Mr. Trotter incurred expenses of $100,203 that Oxford ultimately paid in full. That cost averaged about $10,000 a month. When Mr. Trotter flew to Greece for his kidney, Oxford had 19 months remaining as the primary payer and was therefore legally obligated to pay approximately $190,000 had Mr. Trotter remained on dialysis. When one considers the relatively "small" amount for transplant maintenance medications (approximately $1,000 per month) and the near 75% discounted cost of the operation because of the out-of-country location, the economic benefits of his strategy become inarguable.

I was disappointed, but not surprised, when we received the second denial letter from Oxford. Signed by an Oxford employee with the title of Appeals Analyst, it tersely stated "elective medical care outside of the United States is not a covered benefit under your plan." Yet amazingly, when I read the terms-of-coverage book for his health care plan, nowhere in the contract was there a definition for "elective" medical care. Intuitively to me, it seemed naive at best, or mean-spirited at worst, to refer to the replacement of a life-sustaining organ as elective. Since Oxford had no operational definition of elective surgery, we decided to define it in a patient-friendly manner: "surgery not necessary to sustain life or prevent disability." After conferring with a doctor, we made our next letter succinct with just two sentences: "My doctors and I do not consider my transplant to be elective anymore than we would consider repairing an aneurysm or replacing a hip to be elective. Please schedule a meeting with the [Grievance] Committee...when I and a family member and/or representative can personally appear before the Committee."

Our second letter was sent in mid-January. The earliest appointment we could obtain was for March 22. I used the intervening time to prepare well for our appearance before a review board consisting of a medical director, attorney, and outside consultant. I decided to present our three most important points. First, Mr. Trotter would apologize for not working harder to convince Oxford of the merits of his plan prior to actualizing it. Second, we would demonstrate the probability of improved medical outcome for Mr. Trotter because of his course of action. Third, we would highlight the large sum of money Mr. Trotter saved Oxford.

It was while contemplating this third point that I decided to purchase some common shares of Oxford stock. Having limited confidence in the company's ability to create value in the long term, I wished to bolster my role as a social worker advocate by being perceived as having a stake in the financial decisions the company made. With this move, I felt I could more successfully articulate how a decision against Mr. Trotter would also be a decision against Oxford and against the investors who had entrusted their money to its management.

We engaged in additional preparations as well. I showed Mr. Trotter's contract to an attorney, the wife of a close friend, and sought advice. Appreciating the rewards a better relationship could bring, I cautioned Mr. Trotter about the danger of seeming angry and the need to present himself as likable. I endeavored to take this advice myself. I tried to anticipate arguments Oxford would make and pre-scripted effective responses. A few follow:

"The course of treatment that Mr. Trotter and his doctors followed assuredly served this company and himself much better than complacency would have."

"I am wondering if we can consider today's meeting as retrospective case management. I would like to believe if your case management team had been given more notice and taken time to examine the details, it would have reached the same conclusion that Mr. Trotter and his doctors did."

"You gave no definition for 'elective.' Does anyone here have a problem using that word for an operation to replace an organ necessary to sustain life?"

"How can you willingly spend more to knowingly achieve less? World class companies distinguish themselves by thinking out of the box."

"We of course presume and are confident that Oxford puts the welfare of its insured on no less than an equal footing with its need to make money for its shareholders."

"Short of dying, Mr. Trotter handed your company the best financial outcome it could have possibly hoped for. Instead of refusing to pay, you should be giving him a medal."

Finally, the big day of our meeting arrived. I steeled my nerves by taking comfort in how well we had prepared. We arrived early for our 10:00 a.m. appointment. Upon being shown in we were introduced to the committee members. I was mistaken for an attorney and corrected their misperception by informing them of my role as a social worker advocate. On their side, two lawyers were present. The "outside" consultant divulged that he had been retained by Oxford for advice on improving public perception of the company and that he served on Oxford's board of directors.

What immediately became clear to us was that this committee was sympathetic. Committee members described our previous letters as "compelling" and "persuasive." Without prompting from me, they acknowledged that Mr. Trotter had effectively done his own case management with a positive outcome for all parties concerned. Understanding that important decisions are made within the context of relationships, I strategically decided to do my utmost not to antagonize the review board. Regarding the three points I was prepared to make, I strove to be articulate yet humble, learned yet not pedantic. For visual effect, I produced a stack of Mr. Trotter's dialysis bills that equaled the thickness of a small city's Yellow Pages. I informed the committee that Oxford had been paying about six times the published Medicare rate for dialysis. As the members of the committee shook their heads from left to right with smiles, I finally felt like we were getting somewhere.

Five days after the meeting, we were notified that Oxford had overturned its previous decision and would now agree to reimburse the Trotters $17,500 for the kidney transplant in Cyprus. Justice had been served.

APPLICATION OF ADVANCED GENERALIST PRACTICE PRINCIPLES

Mr. Trotter's conflict with his insurance company is by no means unique. As most health care professionals know, insurance or wealth is often the crucial determinant of care. In the language of metaphor (often useful to appreciate the disparate effects of injustice), insurance is a vehicle: the quality of one's ride depends upon whether one owns a Lexus or a "rent-a-wreck."

An advanced generalist perspective often entails the use of systems theory. Clearly, one needs to understand multisystems to comprehend how U.S. health insurance operates. Advanced generalist practice with a systems theory base is an appropriate way to frame our practice intervention. In the case of Mr. Trotter, we had four interdependent systems that greatly influenced the level of health care to which Mr. Trotter had access: (a) ERISA, (b) the state appeal process, (c) the Oxford insurance company, and (d) the relationship between employer (the May Company) and the insurance provider (Oxford). My knowledge of federal law (ERISA, system 1) and Connecticut statutes (state appeal process, system 2) determined my actions with my patient's insurance carrier (Oxford, system 3.) And because of my appreciation of the relationship between Oxford and its May Company contractor (wife's employer, system 4) I communicated with the May Company to encourage any feedback loop that may have existed. Understanding the interconnections among the systems and their relevance, as illustrated in the case above, helped me effectively navigate the landscape of rules and win the HMO case.

Still further systems thinking was called for in my advanced generalist intervention. From an intra-system or intra-agency perspective, I felt encouraged that I was able to discern the "sentinel effect" (Mark, 1993) and not let it diminish our morale or resolve. The sentinel effect is the impact of any type of barrier (e.g., impersonal phone menu system, long delays on hold, or a requirement to send a letter) on one's ability to gain access to a resource. This effect always serves to dissuade some people from accessing that resource and, at least in the short run, saves the system money. I was steadfastly determined to write our first letter, our second letter, and appear before the committee so as not to lose our case because of this pervasive bureaucratic tactic.

Ecological theory is also important to the advanced generalist perspective. My understanding of ecological theory gave me valuable insights into this case. It enabled me to see how loved ones, concentric to my patient's center circle, played a pivotal role, in spite of the great distance that separated them. From a different perspective, ecological theory helped me to view interdisciplinary co-workers and myself as a workplace family of connected professionals. Transactions between us affected our mutual opinions. For example, while I was initially more startled than upset by Mr. Trotter's nerve in obtaining a kidney transplant in Cyprus, many nurses were clearly angry. It troubled them that he had managed to bend the rules and find a way to circumvent a subpar system, which normally demanded a much longer wait before surgery. Even our skillful physician, the leader of our team, had expressed dismay about Mr. Trotter's goal-focused urgency. She preferred to extol his good his lab values rather than address his reports of intolerable symptoms. Initially, I too had doubts about offering my social work services, as the negative opinions expressed by other health care professionals (nurses and doctors) held some sway. But I recalled my embarrassment upon learning, at Springfield College, of the U.S. government's refusal to ratify the United Nation's Declaration of Human Rights, and my belief that good health care is a human right and therefore worthy of sustained effort. Ultimately, my enthusiasm and determined work on the case encouraged my colleagues to become more sympathetic to Mr. Trotter's plight. Indeed, they too enjoyed our success.

As in all social work programs, the importance of the Social Work Code of Ethics (National Association of Social Workers, 1999) as an essential guide to practice is equally vital to the practicing advanced generalist. Apprehension about taking on Mr. Trotter's case also came from a concern that a different type of professional may have been more appropriate. I was explicitly thinking of the competence portion of the Code of Ethics when I explained to Mr. Trotter that an attorney, rather than a social worker, would perhaps have more suitable training to help him with his appeal. His inability to afford an attorney and a colleague's suggestion led me to search for pro bono legal assistance on his behalf. The three leads I explored were all affiliated with state universities. Unfortunately, one had been shut down for lack of funding, and none of the law students at the other two universities felt comfortable pursuing a case related to the health care system. These results gave me additional confidence and solidified the responsibility I felt to assist in this important social justice case.

Advocacy has been defined in the following way: "In social work, championing the rights of individuals...is a basic obligation of the profession and its members" (National Association of Social Workers, 1995). The policy sequence in my

MSW program prepared me well to influence opinion for causes I believe in. In Policy 2 we learned how to craft persuasive arguments framed by the values of equity, liberty, efficiency and security. The reader will notice that each of my pre-scripted responses prepared for the HMO review meeting touched either an efficiency or equity argument. Our oral presentation before the Oxford committee concentrated on economic efficiency, that is, substantial cost savings with better results. Speaking before the insurance group that I knew had a vested interest in cost containment, I understood that outcome data and numbers could resonate with more influence than appealing to emotion. Assuredly, I felt passionate about correcting an injustice but I channeled that passion into careful preparation and attention to detail in building our case.

As advanced generalist social workers can successfully do, I practiced in different roles and on different levels as this case illustrates. When Mr. Trotter first became a dialysis patient, on the micro level my counseling work contributed to the development of our therapeutic relationship. It was strong enough so that on his own volition he came back to me for assistance, even after he was no longer a patient at my clinic. The fact that he was technically not our patient caused me some concern. I realized that on a mezzo level, my obligation was to assist my employer's current patients. Wishing to be forthright to the company who paid my salary, I spoke to my supervisor. She appreciated my desire to help and we verbally contracted that I would do much of the work on my own time.

As an advanced generalist social worker, I felt comfortable using my clinical skills with Mr. Trotter to establish a high level of trust so that presenting problems could be adequately addressed. Clinically, I prefer to practice in a Rogerian fashion, striving to convey acceptance, warmth, and a strong degree of empathy. The therapeutic model I employ with my patients is based on the five-level method of empathic responding described by Hepworth and Larson (1993). Throughout the four-course practice sequence at Springfield College, as well as my two-year preclinical license period under supervision, I strove to use process recordings to hone my skills at practicing on levels 4 and 5 (moderately high and high levels of empathic responding). At these levels, the clinician convincingly conveys with voice and appearance that she understands exactly what the client is saying and feeling. She draws useful connections and adds insights in a way to facilitate client growth and development. Whether the goal is intra-psychic modification or more concrete action, I have found successful practice on Levels 4 and 5 to be a highly valuable intervention.

Practicing on levels 4 and 5 is seldom simple and necessitates a thorough understanding of the client, their family environment, and culture. Springfield College emphasized the importance of cultural competence; assuredly, a healthy respect and understanding of the client's culture is critical to establishing rapport and trust. Before meeting Mr. Trotter, I had spent four years helping other kidney disease patients trying to get back on their feet. I understood the culture of their vulnerability: the values, expectations, and typical set of beliefs that come with this form of chronic illness and chronic treatment. When Mr. Trotter initially spoke of his frustrations and pain related to kidney disease, I successfully empathized and then offered assistance by providing educational information, filling out insurance forms, and advocating to get him on his preferable dialysis shift.

The culture I was less familiar with was his Greek heritage. Aside from some general impressions formed mostly from the popular media, my knowledge was limited. So I endeavored to educate myself. I spoke to my own relatives and co-workers with close Greek friends and obtained information in this fashion. I also respectfully acknowledged my shortcomings to the Trotters and found that they were mostly happy to explain. No doubt, the cultural information about Greece and its people that I obtained informed my practice. I better understood Mr. Trotter's greater-than-usual initial reluctance to reveal personal and financial information during my intake when he knew me less well. Generally soft-spoken and respectful, Mr. Trotter on one or two occasions displayed ferocious anger when his female physician expressed orders that were medically indicated but made him feel worse. This phenomenon surprised me less and his single-minded pursuit to regain his male role as breadwinner moved me more when I better understood his culture.

Though I had seen Mr. Trotter's anger infrequently, its magnitude worried me for its potential damage were he to display it before the review committee. Manifest anger would negate our strategy to appear contrite and almost certainly harm key relationships. I knew that he understood this point, but I also knew that people could sometimes lose control of their emotions. To better prepare us for the stress we might face before the review committee, I employed the time-tested social work intervention of role-play, or behavior rehearsal as it is sometimes called, a technique I had worked with frequently while obtaining my MSW. Again, anticipating what Oxford might argue, I played the Oxford review board member and let Mr. Trotter play himself. Our goal was to build the confidence level in Mr. Trotter (and myself) in his ability to remain calm and respectful in the face of adversity. This clinical work on the micro level, in essence a form of social skills training, did in fact help us better prepare.

I was again practicing on two levels and in different roles when I informed the Oxford committee that it had been paying my company about six times the Medicare rate for Mr. Trotter's dialysis. On a micro level, this information improved my relationship with the Oxford review committee, since the company was grateful to learn that its contract negotiators had substantial room to save money in the future. On the mezzo level, I was mindful that the disclosure probably served the interest of my employer least well, since it had profited from Oxford's lack of due diligence in obtaining the publicly available Medicare dialysis reimbursement rates. Prior to resolving my role conflict (informant to HMO versus loyal employee of the company billing the HMO) I weighed the harm (potential small reduction in employer's future profits) against the good (appreciative HMO in position to help my client) and again consulted my Social Work Code of Ethics. As a result, I was careful never to reveal my employer's proprietary information. At our meeting's end, I did mention in a modest fashion to the committee my investor role in Oxford. The disclosure of my investor role may have enhanced the committee's perception of the sincerity with which I practiced my patient advocate role.

Related to working successfully on different levels and in different roles, a proficient advanced generalist social worker will display competencies within different skill sets. Within the administrative skill set, I believe I demonstrated leadership and organization. Six months of my professional and personal time could have been less hectic (albeit less rewarding) had I taken the standard route that Mr. Trotter, post-transplant, was no longer my responsibility. I could simply have ended my contact with a referral. The fact that I did not, but engaged myself completely and led previously unconvinced stakeholders to the conclusion that we were right, is a source of pride. It took organizational ability to abide by the system's rules in the resolution process, effectively compose our written arguments, and execute our oral arguments.

Within the research skill set, I needed to review my knowledge (of ERISA and Connecticut statues) as well as learn the details unique to Oxford's appeal process. I read and reread an employer handbook, the newspaper, items on the Internet, and a legalistic terms-of-coverage insurance handbook. In my own agency, I researched and computed figures to uncover the actual past cost and projected future cost of Mr. Trotter's treatment. From a medical perspective, I endeavored to find the probability of a better outcome from his sister's kidney that my patient could reasonably expect and present it in a straightforward fashion to the review committee. For this task I used *UptoDate*, our physician's medical CD-ROM database. Finally, wishing to more fully understand Oxford, I found myself again researching newspaper reports on the Internet. The information I uncovered (Julien, 1999, Leavic, 1999) was sobering and helpful in understanding its for-profit corporate culture.

Pursuing this case, I had no illusions that it would significantly change our larger health care system. Nevertheless, to me, the predicament my patient found himself in and the challenges we faced in winning became a microcosm for much of what is wrong with access to U.S. health care. When my patient should have been concentrating his efforts on getting well, he was instead exposed to impersonal bureaucratic systems, complex rules, and real concerns about money. Practicing in this sort of system every day and witnessing the man-made obstacles that sick people must contend with, one becomes motivated to work as a social change agent. To that end, it energized me to contemplate how my own social actions and advocacy with Oxford managers might perhaps plant a few tiny seeds necessary to grow larger positive change, even if only at one health insurer. The reforms identified with great pioneers such as Jane Adams, Gandhi, and Mandela happened, after all, when the suffering members of their constituencies and their advocates planted enough seeds.

My advanced generalist training at Springfield College makes me extremely aware of the importance of human rights and social justice. Oxford marketers called its insurance product the "Freedom Plan," yet the amount and complexity of its rules severely limited patients' freedom. A reward of working on this case, and to a larger extent advocating for U.S. health care patients, is the multitude of opportunities to make a positive difference in a health care system with vast inequities. Trying to assist senior citizens who cannot afford medications or ill people denied useful procedures because of bureaucratic obstacles, one feels the importance of the work on a visceral level. The advanced generalist social worker sees historical parallels. As the "separate but equal" doctrine was once used to oppress people of color during the era of Jim Crow, language today such as "not medically necessary" and constructs such as the "approved" drug formulary are used to deprive U.S. citizens of basic human needs. In the 1800s, people of color traveled north for freedom; today many U.S. citizens without prescription coverage go hundreds of miles to Canada or Mexico to afford life-sustaining medicines. With Jim Crow, the majority feared losing status and power. With U.S. health care, the richest stakeholders fear reduced financial profits. These affronts to human rights and the lack of social justice demand remedy.

CONCLUSION

The above description of my successful employment of advanced generalist practice principles, working on different levels in various roles with a mixture of skill sets, illustrates the eclecticism and breadth of this powerful professional training. While it would be incorrect to say that I was equally comfortable in all aspects of the above interventions, I did feel capable of taking on each task, sometimes more so after talking to a mentor or rereading theory. My MSW training helped me develop insight to know when that was necessary. From a problem-solving perspective, advanced generalist social work is an exceptional toolbelt: it contains everything necessary to get the job done right, no matter how large or small the challenge.

Understanding the advanced generalist framework also allows me to view access to U.S. health care from a macro perspective. How many of us who try to obtain health care services experience aggravation or intimidation and give up in frustration or suffer in silence? Unfortunately, our current health care quagmire has evolved in the absence of an articulate government policy and the presence of greed that has propelled costs upward. Greed has become more palpable than ever with massive accounting scandals, corporate collapses, and congressional attempts at business reform. In health care, greed drives many providers, manufacturers (especially pharmaceuticals), some employees, and consumers to expect levels of compensation that are clearly out of synch with the rest of society. Mr. Trotter and I prevailed, in large part, because I was able to present a persuasive efficiency argument, demonstrating the significant amount of money Oxford would save.

What we all should find especially troubling in this HMO case is that, left alone, the bureaucracy would have been content to expend an additional $190,000 before considering $17,500 for a superior remedy. It causes one to speculate how many valuable resources our health care system squanders in this inefficient fashion. As a country, we need to find a way to harness our natural tendencies toward greed and promote efficient and universal health care. Until then, perhaps this essay can serve two purposes by providing readers with (a) a small addition to the ever-growing body of evidence that points to a failing health care system, and (b) a parable of hope to motivate those who are now engaged in learning, and will soon undertake, the rewarding practice of advanced generalist social work.

Reprinted, with changes and permission, from "Winning an HMO Appeal: A Case Study in Social Work Advocacy," published in *The Journal of Nephrology Social Work*, Vol. 20, 2000, © National Kidney Foundation, Inc.

REFERENCES

Cecka, J. M., & Terasaki, P. I. (1994). The UNOS renal registry. *Clinical Transplants, 1*. Los Angeles: UCLA.

Center for Studying Health System Change (2002). One in seven Americans face problems getting needed medical care. News Release. Retrieved May 18, 2002 from http://www.hschange.com/content/423.

Crystal, G. (2000, May 20). Pension Perk: Some CEO's tenure counted in dog years. *The Hartford Courant*, p. E2.

Hepworth, D., & Larson, J. A. (1993). *Direct Social Work Practice, Theory and Skills* (4th ed.). Pacific Grove, CA: Brooks/Cole.

Julien, A. (1999, August 11). Insurance complaints rise slightly. *The Hartford Courant*, p. A3. Retrieved January 8, 2000 from http://www.newslibrary.com.

Leavic, D. (1999, November 3). Oxford's profits exceed expectations. *The Hartford Courant*, p. E2. Retrieved January 8, 2000 from http://www.newslibrary.com.

Mark, H. (1993). Health Services Research. Lecture in the course *Health Administration*, University of Connecticut Medical School, Public Health Program, spring semester.

National Association of Social Workers (1995). *The Social Work Reference Library (CD-ROM)*, NASW Press: Washington, DC.

National Association of Social Workers (1999). *NASW Code of Ethics, 1.04*. Retrieved May 27, 2000 from http://www.naswdc.org/Code/ethics.htm.